Bereft

Bereft

A Sister's Story

Jane Bernstein

North Point Press

Farrar, Straus and Giroux

New York

North Point Press
A division of Farrar, Straus and Giroux
19 Union Square West, New York 10003

Copyright © 2000 by Jane Bernstein
All rights reserved
Distributed in Canada by Douglas & McIntyre Ltd.
Printed in the United States of America
Designed by Abby Kagan
First edition, 2000

Library of Congress Cataloging-in-Publication Data
Bernstein, Jane, 1949–
Bereft / Jane Bernstein. — 1st ed.
p.   cm.
ISBN 0-86547-586-5 (alk. paper)
1. Murder—Arizona—Case studies. 2. Bernstein, Laura Ellen, 1945–1966.
I. Title.

HV6533.A6 B47   2000
362.88—dc21
[B]   99-048798

The names of some individuals, along with identifying details, have been changed to protect their privacy.

"Intrusion" by Denise Levertov, from Poems 1968–1972, copyright © 1971 by Denise Levertov. Reprinted by permission of New Directions Publishing Corp.

To my mother and my father

After I had cut off my hands
and grown new ones

something my former hands had longed for
came and asked to be rocked.

After my plucked out eyes
had withered, and new ones grown,

something my former eyes had wept for
came asking to be pitied.

Denise Levertov, "Intrusion"

i think it would be very nice if you'd at least
mail me a postcard, don't you? i mean i am
your sister.

—*Laura*

Bereft

H ER NAME WAS LAURA ELLEN BERNSTEIN, and she was born on October 31, 1945, a green-eyed first-born child of our blue-eyed family. Green eyes, born on Halloween. You must be a witch! people said. So the year she turned eight, our mother, who made all our costumes, and made them roomy enough for our jackets to fit beneath, sewed her a witch costume out of yards and yards of polished cotton. For her birthday Laura posed for the camera with her broomstick and pointed hat, her shiny black dress as full as the wedding gown she would choose but never get to wear.

We had moved by then from Brooklyn, where our parents had been born and raised, to Kew Gardens Hills, in a part of Queens that was so rural there was a pond across the street from our garden apartment, with real cattails and swaying grasses kids set on fire in the fall. The dads in our neighborhood pushed the children in sleds across the pond in the winter. If you closed your ears to the hum of traffic from Utopia Parkway, you could almost imagine that it was the country.

Many years later, when the swamps had long been filled and huge apartment buildings erected everywhere, I had a recurring dream set in our dining room there. It is Halloween 1953. The pond is still across from our building, and the ducks still fly in formation overhead. Night after night in these dreams, Laura is checking the candy apples our mother has set on waxed paper, and peeking at the home-baked birthday cake with brown icing and orange letters.

I am looking down on the party and at myself as well. I'm four years old, and dressed as a hobo, with smudges on my face, patches sewn onto old clothes, and a bundle on a stick, a costume I did not pick myself, though a popular one, perhaps because Depression hoboes are distant enough to be forgotten and street people no gleam in anyone's eye. The war is over! We are all prosperous! A hobo is as much a creature of myth as a witch. Even my father, unemployable during the Depression, his grandest dream, his only dream, to work for the post office, is prospering. He's in sales—barbecue grills and picnic baskets. It's a good firm, owned by German Jews who think highly of him—and why not? He is handsome, wavy-haired, genial, steady: everyone loves him. Son of a *bigler*, a presser in the garment industry, doing better than he has ever dreamed: here he is in a new apartment in Queens, taking home movies at a birthday party for his firstborn daughter.

I am at the door, letting in the guests: my sister has given me this honor. *My sister.* I adore my sister. That we sometimes bite and scratch each other, fierce as animals, is irrelevant. I adore her slavishly, and do everything she asks. She says, "Eat fish food." I do, without question. I eat fish food; I run outside naked; I stand in the center of our living room at a family gathering and call, "Fat lady, fat lady!" to a sullen, obese aunt because *Laura says.* What rifts this causes I do not care: I am a happy slave. "And you do everything she says?" my mother asks.

"Yes!" I say proudly.

"If she told you to jump in the lake, you'd jump in the lake?"

"Yes!" I say, as eager to please my mother as I am my sister.

Laura says, let in the guests; I let in the guests. The timing is perfect. Within me, and bursting to get out, is a joke, the first I've ever told. The day before, I stopped men on their way home from work and mothers hanging wash on the line. And now, as Laura's guests walk in, the princess, the pirate, the ghost, the clown, I ask:

"Guess what?"

"What?" The princess hands my mother Laura's gift and shucks the coat into her hands. Her name is Suzi. Her parents and mine are friends.

"That's what!" I shriek.

She watches me blankly as I fold up with laughter, then files into the dining room to join the others.

There's food to hurry through and birthday cake and then games to play. In a bag on an extra chair are the prizes. After Pin the Tail on the Donkey, it's time for Musical Chairs. My mother chooses a Burl Ives record and stands poised over the record player, while Burl Ives sings in his husky voice, *"Today is Monday, today is Monday!"*

The children scurry nervously around the chairs: princess, fairy, hobo, clown, scary witch with pointed hat. They look anxious and jittery, their rear ends jutting in anticipation of the moment when the music will stop. How serious they are, as if they are jostling for space on a lifeboat.

The music stops.

The princess is left without a seat. She looks stunned, then bursts into tears.

While all around the children are starting to moan, "Sore loser!" and my mother tries to start the record again, my adult self watches, unseen in the room. "Give her a seat!" I think. "Don't you know that she, too, will die young?" The record goes on. *"Today is Friday, today is Friday . . ."* Suzi, the princess, stands against the wall, chest heaving: she wipes her face with her sleeve, tries to compose herself, can't.

What an odd thing, to be a spectral figure wafting near the ceiling of this apartment, to look down on this story I cannot change. The children are so small and lovely, with their painted faces and Halloween costumes. Nothing matters, I think. So what that Laura will only make colored dots in art class and Suzi is clumsy at ballet—it makes no difference. Stop! I think, as the music starts up again. I want to change the ending. It makes no sense! Why must the witch be murdered? And the princess, must she die, too? I want symmetry, a happy ending, a story where all the clues will add up.

Let me forget again, I think, when I awake.

But Laura's voice stays with me: Tell the story, she says. It's the least you can do. *i mean i am your sister.*

Detective Work

1

EVEN BEFORE MY SISTER WAS MURDERED I was a detective, a watcher, a child who stood in doorways, heart beating hard, listening. I was always listening. On the nights when my parents' friends came over, the "boys" to play poker or the "girls" for mah-jongg, I sat at the top of the steps, listening between the clack of tiles—*Four bam, two crack*—or the jangle of coins. You could say it was sheer nosiness, but really it was more. I listened to figure things out. I listened because what wasn't said scared me, even then.

You must understand: my life was ordinary in the days before Laura's murder. If I was haunted by anything in the waking world, it was how pathetically, sadly, embarrassingly ordinary my whole family was, in our split-level house, on our patch of velvety grass, in our suburban town in New Jersey, where we had moved from Kew Gardens Hills when I was six years old. If I grieved then, it was over how ordinary I was, not a scholar, no great beauty, no one special. And still, at night it was different. That was when I lay in bed, trying to piece together the fragments of conversations and quarrels

I overheard, to make sense of the adult world. Did my parents hate each other or were they just mad? Would my mother really sell the house? I watched the shadows on my wall, listening hard.

Is it possible that I never fell into deep sleep, that from childhood I was always half awake and listening? There is no reason I should have heard the phone when it rang that night in September 1966, since the only phone upstairs was in my parents' room, behind their closed door. But I did hear it, and I sat up in bed, in the pretty room my sister and I had asked to share, where we had slept side by side every night until she had left for college three years before. It was as if I had been in training my whole lifetime for this moment. I heard the harsh metallic ring of the phone, looked at the time on the radium dial of the bedside clock Laura had bought me for my seventeenth birthday that summer, and got out of bed. I walked into the hall, and then, like a voyeur, pressed my ear against my parents' door. Already I knew everything, and nothing at all. I heard my mother say, "Are you sure?" and "Are you positive?" I heard her hang up the phone and say, "Our baby is dead." And then I heard nothing.

If angry words and pieces of sentences had been the source of fear before, now silence brought me terror, what was not said, what could never be spoken. The only thing I remember my mother saying to me about Laura's murder was, "I'm sorry." Her apology confused and upset me, since she had done nothing wrong. I do not remember anyone telling me that my sister had been stabbed to death while chaining her bicycle to the window grate at the back of the Casa Loma Hotel in Tempe, Arizona. I did not, in fact, know many details of her murder until nearly a year later. But I was a listener and absorbed things, because that was when the refrain—*four times in the body and twice in the head* —began to play in my head.

For years I was convinced that I did not miss my sister after she was murdered or feel what all the condolence cards so delicately referred to as our "loss." When I remembered this time, it seemed that after Laura died, I moved on with little fuss, just as I had been advised. I got "right back into the swing of things," and behaved in what my mother called "a normal way." Within days after Laura's murder I started an art scholarship in her name, and spent my evenings at my desk, tallying checks and writing charming thank-you notes to all the donors. When that was done, I worked on my college applications, drafting essays in which I wrote that the most significant event in my life was the week I spent as part of a domestic exchange program in Plymouth, Wisconsin, suburb of Sheboygan.

My parents were practical people who passed on their distrust of the intangible, their firm belief that it was nonsense— worse, self-indulgence—to ponder things that could not be seen or touched. Years later, when I doubted that I could have been so buoyant after my sister's murder, I sorted through photos of myself from this period and found solid evidence of the vibrant, chatty girl who recognized and sought pleasure and anticipated the future with such eagerness, the kind of all-American girl you'd see from afar and think: Life has treated her kindly.

Yet in this house where nothing was said, I knew soon after the murder that someone, "a boy" about my own age, had confessed to Laura's murder. Somehow I knew that my mother had gotten a subpoena for an arraignment and refused to appear. I learned, though I don't know how, that someone, maybe a customer of my father's, had collected the headline stories about Laura's murder and mailed them to us. "Did you ever hear anything so stupid in all your life?" I heard my mother say in rage. I was standing motionless, breath held, listening. That's how I knew that we had those newspaper articles, tangible, undeniable evidence of what had happened to my sister.

Perhaps, then, this story begins on an evening in the spring of 1967, six months after the murder, when I came home from a date with a boy, so drunk the house was like a boat in rough seas. I navigated slowly, holding on to walls and banisters, listing toward my parents' room to tell them I was home. I knocked lightly, then opened their door an inch. We exchanged the usual words. How was your night? they asked, and I said, Great. I had a lot of fun.

Sleep tight, they said.

And I blew them kisses and murmured: You, too. Sweet dreams, I said, and backed into the hall.

Their lights went out and I worked my way into the den, shutting the door slowly behind me. I did not lock it before I opened my father's desk drawer, did not worry that someone would wake and tiptoe in after me to ask why I was rifling through the drawer that was deep enough for large envelopes. I could not have said what I understand now, that my parents would not catch me because, since the murder, they fell into a deep sleep as soon as I came home at night. They had not noticed that I had dyed my hair black the week before, or that, when I paused at their door to say good night, I was sometimes so drunk that I could barely stand. That I was alive was enough.

I cannot recall how I knew where to find the newspaper clippings. I had not planned to look, did not know I needed to read them, never considered where they might be. But I found the envelope without searching, slid out the file and sat at my father's desk.

It is not necessarily true that shocking things blur with time. Sometimes the details stay vivid and blindingly hot. Thus I recall not only how seeing those articles split me in two, as if by an ax, but the rust-colored shag carpet, the plaid sleeper-sofa across from the TV, the large, carved desk with family photos beneath the glass top, where in those days I often found my father sitting.

It was here that Laura and I had modeled our new clothes for him after our mother took us shopping, had spun in slow, awkward circles and waited for him to turn his full attention to us and say, "Not bad," or "Adequate," his highest compliment, or, once in a while, against all logic, "Very adequate."

In those days, I did not understand my parents' reluctance to praise, did not know why, no matter how funny my jokes, my mother would only say, "Har-de-har-har," in a dry voice, and my father, "Adequate." I did not yet realize that what seemed to me an indictment, proof of my failures, was a kind of superstition, two generations old. My grandmother, after all, had been called Baba, or "Grandmother," at birth. The other baby girls in her family had died and her parents hoped to thwart the evil spirit of Lilith, the baby snatcher, by calling the new baby "old woman." My mother was a modern woman, in no way superstitious, but when she was feeling affectionate, she said, "I hate you!" and when I was dressed up to go out for a prom she said, "Uch—*Ugly!*" Not that it mattered, since the evil spirits would not be fooled again.

I pulled the clippings from the envelope. They were stiff and yellowish, already decomposing. A banner headline, the size used when President Kennedy had been shot. ASU COED STABBED TO DEATH ON TEMPE STREET.

Her body curled on its side.

Slim coed, petite coed, Brooklyn-born coed, she was called. Murdered, knifed, slain, stabbed to death. The words and pictures were unbearable, but I went on, clipping after clipping, absorbing each word the way a punchy boxer takes the blows, just stands and takes them. *Four times in the body and twice in the head.* There was no question of turning away. I needed to take the punishment.

I sat and read these articles. I looked at the photos of my sister crumpled on the pavement, and at the photos of "the boy," the murderer with the benign face and mild expression. I did not cry. Nor did I put pieces back in my father's desk when I was done. I took the whole envelope. I needed to have it. Such fuss had been made when I took scissors or tape from this drawer, yet no one ever mentioned the envelope. No one seemed to need it, as I did.

A long time would pass before I looked at those clippings again. But they followed me, as if of their own volition, from New Jersey to dorm rooms and walk-up apartments in New York, to flats in London, and back again to the States, always with me, whenever I moved. I don't remember unpacking them or putting them in a special place. But they were with me. I know this, because years after the murder, when I needed to learn what had happened, I knew exactly where to find them.

2

LATE ONE NIGHT in March 1989, when my sister had been dead for twenty-three years, I walked upstairs to the office I had in the attic of my house, opened my file cabinet, and took out a folder marked "nonfiction" in orange crayon. I was living in New Jersey then, with my husband, Will, and two young daughters, as many years apart as my sister and I had been.

I rarely thought of Laura. I kept no photos of her on my walls, told no stories about our life together, spoke her name so infrequently that when I did, the sound of it jarred me. My parents never mentioned Laura, at least not to me. But they still lived in the house where we had been raised, and when I brought my daughters to stay the night, Charlotte, my ten-year-old, slept in what my mother referred to as "Laura's bed." "Your aunt Laura," she said one night, as if in explanation.

A look of confusion crossed Charlotte's face. I saw it, thought no, I will not darken her childhood, and turned away.

That moment stayed with me—the oddness of that impossible appellation, "Aunt Laura," the expression on Charlotte's face. I was surprised to find that my instinct to protect her from my history was stronger than all the promises I had made to tell her the truth no matter what. The thought of her asleep in the bed of my murdered sister, knowing and not knowing, troubled me so deeply that toward dawn I slipped into my old room and stood in the darkness until I could see her curled beneath the blanket, breathing softly. I remembered how quickly I had wakened the night of the phone call all those years before, as if I had been expecting disaster to strike. Of course I would tell Charlotte about my sister. If I didn't, she would spend her nights half awake, listening, stitching together fragments of overheard conversations, vigilant and scared, just as I had been.

Before I had figured out exactly what I might say, Charlotte asked me, and it was not, "What was your sister like?" the question I expected first, but "Why was Laura murdered?"

"For no reason," I said. It was what I had overheard and what the newspapers had reported. A motiveless crime, it was called. That I had nothing else to say suddenly seemed unbearable. To my daughter, the sister I had deeply loved was nothing more than a girl who had been stabbed to death for no reason. In a way, it was who Laura had become to me.

Several days later, Will, a biologist who worked at a research lab several miles from our house, told me he was going back to work after dinner to check on an experiment. I decided then to go up to the attic as soon as the kids were in bed. I helped Charlotte with her homework and ran a bath for Rachel. While the tub filled, I imagined meeting my sister again. In an image borrowed from a reunion scene that had made the news—the vast, messy customs area at Kennedy Airport; two sisters separated for nearly a quarter of a century—I imagined catching sight of Laura across the room, the two of us stumbling over suitcases and gifts to get to each other, weeping and embracing in each other's arms. And then what? How could I explain why I had made myself forget her? What would I say if she knew that the only time her name came up was when Charlotte slept in her bed?

I imagined her linking her arm through mine in the parking lot, saying, "Tell me about yourself, baby." I could say that I was married to a man much older than I, a scientist; that we lived in the suburbs, less than an hour away from where we'd grown up. What words could I choose to describe someone as complicated as Will? Smart, funny, volatile. And my marriage?

"When it's good, it's good, and when it's bad, it's *really* bad." That was what I'd said to a friend I hadn't seen for years, and she had laughed and rolled her eyes and said, "Don't I know." It made me feel that a lot of what Will and I struggled with was the ordinary kind of stuff couples face—a new baby, a move from city to suburbs, day after day filled with twice the number of commitments as time allowed. We'd been hit by some unexpected things too, like the news, shortly after Rachel's birth in 1983, that she had a rare disorder that left her at "considerable risk" for any or all of a long, devastating list of deficits. The initial diagnosis was wrenching; the long wait to learn the extent of her impairments was even worse. Still, enough time had passed for me to think of Rachel's birth as a storm that blew our house apart, and to feel that the best we could do was wait for the winds to die down before we could start the necessary repair work.

That March night it seemed as if we had gotten our household back in order. Will had finally finished his Ph.D. I had a new book out at last. We were enjoying the kids. Rachel was not completely blind, as we had feared, and though she was retarded, we had by then accepted it. Her problems had made me even more determined that our life be a success and our family a happy one, not just for me, but for Charlotte, because I had seen how my sister's murder had forever damaged my relationship with my parents. I would not let my house be a sad place. And I believed that, against the odds, it wasn't. I knew that sometimes I was like a bouncer at a nightclub, standing in the doorway with my fists clenched, guarding against anything that threatened to get in the way of our happiness. There were pieces of my marriage I told no one about, just as there had been pieces of my childhood life that I had no wish to share. Still, I was proud of my tenacity and the effort I had expended to keep us together.

"Ordinary" was the word that came to mind when I thought about my family. At seventeen that characterization had filled me with anguish, but in 1989 it brought me a mixture of relief and pride. How conventional we were in our old house, in this gracious New Jersey town. We took our kids out for pizza on Elm Street once a week. We bought them shoes a few doors down the block, looping the ribbons from their helium balloons around their wrists to keep them from flying away. On sunny days, we brought our stale bread to the duck pond and crouched on its muddy banks to feed the ducks. This scene—the pond, in a small park with cherry trees and a grand white Presbyterian church—was so lovely it was reproduced as a jigsaw puzzle. Charlotte once saw it in a toy store on Cape Cod—"Duck Pond in Spring," stacked beside "Grist Mill in Autumn." I liked to think of us as part of that scene.

When our friend Joseph, a scientist like Will, followed me around the house one day, eager to understand the mind of a writer, I was happy to tell him what went through my head when I was alone, pleased to describe my deepest thoughts.

Need milk, I said. Gee, the bananas are pricey. Brown shoes or black?

Sometimes I looked at our lives and thought, pleasure welling within me: How perfectly mundane.

In the attic that night, I cleared the manuscripts from my desk and spread out the yellowed newspaper clippings. I saw my sister's curled-up body, read the lurid headlines and the text. This time I was completely unmoved, no pounding heart, no trembling hands. I spent the next few hours studying the clippings, putting them back in the folder only when I heard Will's car pull up outside the house. Twenty-three years had passed. I was over it. I could say that I had a sister and could speak of her with ease. That I rarely did so had nothing to do with my own pain—I felt no pain!—but with other people's discomfort, it seemed to me. If I said I had a sister, people invariably asked how she died. If I told the truth, I had to figure out how to comfort them.

It's okay, I always ended up saying. It was a long time ago. I'm over it.

I was over it. I was unscathed by the past, "disgustingly normal," a friend told me, "the least neurotic person I know."

When I decided to write about Laura, I had nothing more than a vague notion of bringing something of her back to life so she would be more than a murdered girl. If asked, I might have explained that I was trying to sketch something for Charlotte, a modest piece of writing that said: This is my sister. That I remembered so little of Laura did not trouble me at first. I believed that once I evoked a single detail of our life together, other memories would return.

I searched through cartons and found certificates for trees planted in Israel in her name, a wallet card saying she had been a Polio Pioneer, a self-portrait she had drawn, a prom photo in which she stands beside a big-eared boy, condolence letters from her friends. But Laura herself remained elusive, as if who she had been was obscured by the murder itself. It loomed over her, insistent, so big and dark that one day I gave in to it and began to draft a scene that took place on the night she was stabbed to death.

I worked in a feverish way on this scene, so detached from the rest of my life that I never knew when the day had come to an end until the dog, alerted by the sound of buses and kids on the street, pushed open my office door. Then I went downstairs and entered a world with kids and homework and household chores, a place my sister had never known, and where no one knew her.

Though I did not speak of Laura still, I began to have visions of looking for her. I might be in the swimming pool with Rachel when the airport scene would replay in my head, Laura and I stumbling across suitcases and gifts to find each other—a scene in which she was always faceless, for although I recognized her, I could never see what she looked like. I might be at dinner with friends when I would picture myself, as if in a dream, walking down the streets of Tempe, looking for someone who knew her.

In the morning, I would climb the stairs to my attic office and set to work drafting and redrafting that single scene, unable to get it right, and unable to move on. Then one day I realized that months had passed.

. . .

It wasn't that I had trouble remembering the night I heard about Laura's murder: to the contrary, it was chiseled in my brain as deep as engravings on a tombstone. The problem was that I could not seem to put myself back into the night. In every draft, it is a stranger who sees my childhood house, from the outside first—*a split level in a development of similar houses, on plots that are lush with the shrubs and trees planted twelve years before in the rich soil of former truck farms.* A stranger stands on the sidewalk, feels the mugginess, thinks: *The chirping of crickets and cicadas is like the heartbeat of the sleeping town, steady and comforting.*

In some drafts, the stranger enters the house through the garage, edges past the pine crate that holds Laura's red motorcycle, an engagement present from her fiancé. The stranger passes through the recreation room, with its brown-and-beige tiled floor, the old TV, the shelves of paperback books no one really wants, through the kitchen, and upstairs to watch the sleeping girl. I knew that I was the girl sleeping in the bedroom Laura and I had asked to share when our parents bought the house. But I could not connect with her, could only bring her into focus when the stranger's eyes adjusted enough to see the maple bureau, the chest of drawers, the matching beds. "The bed against the wall is empty," I wrote. "But the girl in the second bed is fast asleep."

I believed the problems I was having with the scene were writer's problems, the issues I faced technical ones. I looked at the versions in which I referred to myself as "she" and thought that to write of myself in the third person felt like a tired convention. I did not want to write it that way. It felt contrived to be the stranger sitting on the edge of the girl's bed, and not the girl herself.

And so I kept rewriting the scene. At night, I vowed to move on and write something else, and in the morning, I woke, full of resolve. I will scrap it, I told myself, as I climbed the steps to my office. But as soon as I sat down to work I knew that it was impossible to go forward until I got the opening scene right. And so I kept re-creating the evening, unearthing every minute detail—the football buttons, the woolen beanie perched on the lamp finial. And each time, just as the stranger sits on the bed, I wrote, "Her name is Martha."

I could say that Martha was my given name, and that until I was eighteen it was what everyone called me. I could identify the girl in the bed as myself. But she stubbornly remained "the girl asleep in bed," while the best I could do was narrate from a distance.

She is seventeen years old and just beginning her senior year in high school. For the first time in her life, her considerable energy is focused on something: going away, leaving this room and house and sleeping town. It is as if she is riding a bike down a steep hill: down is where momentum takes her, down and away. Everything is about leaving: the catalogues on her maple desk, the dreams she has in class and at night. Her boyfriend is so sweet and conventional that when she kisses him, a great restlessness wells up. She frets too much about the curse of being ordinary to know that she is happy, that her life has been filled with pleasure and ease, that she deeply loves what she yearns to leave. Her mother has a historian's bias of being more interested in the sweep of events, their causes and origins, than in the psyches of individuals. People she sees as part of a group and nothing more. Her daughter's preoccupation with leaving she sees as "only natural," and the daughter herself, a "typical teenager," words that precipitate a quarrel, since the daughter's greatest struggle, the burden that makes her ache most, is this sense of how typical, how pathetically ordinary she really is. Leaving will change all that. When she leaves she can fall in love, the way her sister has. If leaving means breaking free of what binds her, love she sees as the thing that can change and transform her, strip away all that is ordinary.

The bed against the wall is empty.

I could take this scene up to the moment the girl in the bed hears the phone ring and feels her heart hammering in her chest. I could write—could remember—the pennants on her walls, the shelves she painted to display small glass animals and favors from Sweet Sixteen parties. I could write—could see—her senior beanie perched on the lamp finial, with buttons pinned to the felt that say, "Beat Ridgewood," and "Beat Hackensack." I knew that when she heard the phone's harsh metallic ring she sat rigidly, as if wakened by a nightmare, too frightened to move, then, without warning, too frightened to stay in bed. But I could not make myself the girl or move beyond that evening. Worse still, I was unable to write anything else. I was stuck.

3

I FLEW TO PHOENIX on October 31, 1989, with a small
reporter's notebook bound at the top. Beside me was a
woman in a lavender pants suit with creases sewn into the
legs. She was reading a religious tract and slyly attempting to
decipher my impossible handwriting.

To explain my trip, I had stories that nested in stories, like
Russian dolls.

When the woman beside me asked, "What brings you to
Phoenix?" I closed the notebook and talked about hiking down
the Grand Canyon with my husband. I would, in fact, do this at
the end of the trip.

To my parents, and to the caregiver at home with my children, I had simply said that Will was going to Phoenix for the
annual neuroscience conference and that I had decided to join
him for a much-needed vacation. It was true that I was desperate for a break.

Will knew that I was flying to Phoenix to find out more
about what had happened to my sister, but not how badly I was
stuck. Even I didn't like to think much about that.

I had the names of people who had been involved in the case, culled from the newspaper articles. And though I had not made my phone calls or set up my appointments ahead of time, I had contacted an investigative reporter from the *Arizona Republic*, who found phone numbers of attorneys from the bar-association directory and gave me suggestions on how to get the transcripts from the trial.

That I had imagined this journey countless times did not make a difference. Now that I was so close to where my sister had been murdered, I had the strange ambivalence one feels in making a fantasy come true, and realizing, suddenly, how much scarier reality is, and how different. I wanted only one thing of this trip: to be a good detective, to get the facts I needed, and then to go home. I wanted to finish "the scene" and move on to something else. On the first page of my new notebook I had written, "I don't think about Laura much." My thoughts were not on my sister but on her murder, as if the murder were a separate thing, and her connection to it tenuous and unimportant. I was ashamed of how little I thought about my sister. It made me feel cold and self-serving, an exploiter.

"Batman and the Devil," I wrote next, for when I saw the costumed children I realized that it was Halloween. It was true that I did not think much about Laura, but I had booked a flight to Phoenix on her birthday and began to investigate her murder on the day she would have turned forty-four.

By the end of my first full day in Phoenix, I felt that I had failed at my detective work. Although a surprising number of people involved in the case were alive and had local addresses, no one seemed willing to talk to me. One defense attorney, whose office was in Phoenix, had "stepped out." A detective, still with the Tempe police, had also "stepped out." It was as if the two of them were partners in a little dance. The other defense attorney, now a judge at the Arizona Court of Appeals, was away from his desk. Although the former prosecutor was in, his secretary informed me that he was too busy preparing a case to talk to me. But (sighing) she could take my number.

Every avenue took me down a dead end. There was no index in the main library to the microfilms of the *Arizona Republic* or the *Phoenix Gazette*. The *Arizona Republic* reporter had suggested I call the prosecutor's office to get copies of the transcript or the court records, but that office handled only misdemeanors, I was told. It was the county attorney's office that handled felonies.

True, said the clerk at the county attorney's office, they did handle felonies—but not murders. I could try the Crime Victim Foundation.

A woman with the kind of soothing voice I imagined was helpful on suicide hot lines told me that the Crime Victim Foundation was set up to give aid and money to victims of violent crime. But not to get frustrated! The court records were available to me. To see them, I had first to get a court case number and take it to the Records Division of the Clerk of the Superior Court.

I got the court case number and drove to the Superior Court on West Jefferson Street.

The clerk studied the case number and gawked at me. "The murder was committed when?" she asked.

"September 21, 1966," I said.

She set her elbows heavily on the counter between us. "If the transcripts exist at all, they're probably in deep storage.

Why don't you try the Department of Public Safety? They keep a repository of records."

The Department of Public Safety turned out to be yet another wrong turn.

My frustrations and fears escalated as the day went on and the dead ends mounted. I had waited too long, I was absurd. I was like my husband, who had tried to retrieve a shirt he had left at a Chinese laundry for two years. The owner had eyed my husband without for a moment averting his gaze, then ripped up the ticket, and laughed.

But I could not stop. Now that I was here, I was determined to find something. If I couldn't get my hands on documents, then maybe I could find people and places connected with the murder. I drove feverishly through the streets in my red rental car, the map mashed wide open in the passenger seat, fretting over my dreadful sense of direction. I was always losing my way, always late. "Directionally challenged," Charlotte called me.

My sister had transferred to Arizona State University because her fiancé, Howie, had enrolled in a graduate program at a school called the American Institute of Foreign Trade. Friends who had matriculated there the year before told Howie that the school had a national reputation, and that he would be all but guaranteed a good position upon graduation. In 1966, the economy was booming and corporations were going multinational. He and Laura had talked about living in Europe for a while, before they had kids.

Over the years I had thought about Howie so often and with such fondness it was hard to recall that I had barely known him. We had met for the first time in Chicago one afternoon in 1965. Then, in August 1966, he had stayed at our house in New Jersey for a week: the only other time I had seen him had been a month later, at Laura's funeral. Even so, whenever his name came to mind, I thought, I like him *so* much, exactly what I had said to my friends in the summer of 1966, when he flew out to see us.

I loved Howie's love for Laura. My sister had always been argumentative, but Howie's love settled her; it softened her voice. I loved, too, how comfortable he was in our house, how much he liked our family's talk and noise. My parents' bluntness he thought of as candor and warmth. He respected my father, and thought of him as "self-made." My mother was the kind of person he had read about but never met, ardent and political, eager for debate.

In those days, I loved to tiptoe through our house when everyone was asleep. It was the only time when no one called my name. The train tracks were a mile away, but on summer nights when the windows were open, the mournful whistle of passing trains seemed to rush through our kitchen. One night that summer, Howie caught up with me. We sat at the kitchen table, eating peaches and cherries and talking late into the night. He told me about Vietnam, a country I could barely have found on a map. How soft-spoken he was as he explained his opposition to the war, and described the rallies and protests he and Laura had attended. Laura seemed to view the government as a seducer, immoral and cruel, ready to steal away her guy, but Howie was more like a parent struggling to comprehend the bad behavior of a President who had lied to the people and to Congress.

My mother was certainly not shy about expressing her political opinions. "Those bastards!" she said, whenever she discussed the hawks. But her rage spilled over; her lectures always made me feel guilty and stupid, and I closed myself to them completely, cuticle-picking, nail-biting, eye-rolling, shifting in my seat: all attitude, all nothing-you-can-tell-me-that-I don't-already-know to mask my utter ignorance. Howie's respect lifted me high above my adolescent concerns. It was a first step up, a window onto a world outside my own narrow one.

I found the American Institute in the phone book, with an address on North Central Avenue, and late on my first day in Phoenix I decided to drive there. All I saw, block after block, were body shops and car dealerships with flags flapping in the wind. I thought it was an odd location for Howie's supposedly elite school and expected that the neighborhood would change. It didn't. When I reached the street address, I found a long, low warehouse, guarded, it seemed, by a lineup of big-haired women smoking cigarettes.

I drove around the block. Then, in desperation, I pulled into the parking lot.

The receptionist was on the phone, arguing with her boy-friend. When she finally hung up on him and acknowledged my presence, it was with a great deal of displeasure. Yes, she said wearily; this was 1300 North Central Avenue. Yes, it was the American Institute. But it was a school for court reporters—she didn't know anything about any graduate program.

I went back to my car, upset beyond reason. "Everything a U-turn or dead end," I wrote in my notebook.

I drove farther down the dismal avenue until I reached a convenience store with a phone. A trio of bikers wearing shirts with torn-off sleeves stood beside it. I pulled into the parking lot, got out of the car, and awkwardly walked past them. I dialed the number of the crime reporter at the *Arizona Republic.*

While the phone rang, I thought about the lovely hotel where I was staying with Will, and about the pool beneath the palm trees. I wondered why I was standing outside this convenience store, shoving coins into a pay phone, why I didn't just drive back to the hotel, slip on my bathing suit, and drift on my back.

The reporter picked up and I told him of my frustrations—no newspaper index, the transcripts in deep storage, the U-turns and dead ends, the missing graduate school.

"I can get you the clips," he said. "But, Jane. You want some advice? Slow down. You're going like gangbusters. They don't like that around here."

I hung up, somewhat shocked, and got back in my car.

The next morning, I stopped at the newspaper office and found a thick envelope full of photocopied clips and a little card that said, "Good luck!" I went to the bank of phones in the back of the lobby, piled quarters into a neat stack and knocked them down, summoning up the courage to call all the people I had tried the day before. This time around, I tried to slow down and strip from my voice the nervousness that sounded harsh and impatient. I heard myself say, "My name is Jane Bernstein," and the sound of my voice echoing in this public place made me wish I could change my name again. "My sister was murdered outside the Casa Loma Hotel in September 1966," I said, and with the words, my heart literally ached, catching me by surprise.

Everyone was alive. Everyone remembered my sister's murder well. Everyone seemed eager to talk.

Later that morning, I talked to a cop, a judge, a man from the parole board. I spoke Laura's name aloud more often over the next two days than I had in all the twenty-three years before. I bought microfilms of the police records found in deep storage. At the end of the day, I stopped by the law offices of Dushoff and McCall. I watched Jay Dushoff, a defense attorney in 1966, pace slowly around the room and tell me that he remembered the case vividly because it was "entirely possible" that the wrong man was in prison for murdering my sister.

"Case breaks," I wrote that day. I was the consummate hard-boiled gumshoe, straight out of a detective novel, minus the bottle of booze in the file cabinet. When Dushoff suggested that the police, pressured to solve this "sensational murder," might have coerced a confession from a naïve, eager to please, mildly disturbed young man, I listened closely, careful to get down his theory verbatim, so busy and intent that I failed to give myself the chance to register it fully.

The detective assigned to my sister's case who was still with the Tempe police agreed to meet with me at the station house. I drove across the Mill Avenue Bridge into Tempe, late in the afternoon of the third day of my investigations. It was my last interview, I believed, the end of my detective work. Phoenix, ever bright and lovely, had made me uncomfortable in a way I could not define. I felt something lurking in the shadows, something bad. Tempe was worse. The sound of the name made me shiver, the two syllables on my tongue, Tem-pee, left a bitter taste. I'd intended to study this place, but the late-afternoon sun was like a dagger in my eyes, and before I could fully orient myself, the police station was in front of me, a tan box set back from the road.

I walked inside and asked for Lt. Erich Schoenfeld. The receptionist picked up the phone, but before she could speak, a tall man with black, slicked-back hair and leathery skin took a step toward me and said, "I'm Lt. Schoenfeld." He straightened in a military way and scrutinized me frankly. Then he shook my hand. "The Casa Loma is a couple of blocks away," he said. "Why don't we go over there."

Schoenfeld held the door for me and led me out into the blazing sun. I followed behind him, scrambling for my sunglasses.

At the corner of Mill and Fourth Street, he paused. "This place was bad in 1966," Schoenfeld said. "Hippies and motorcycle gangs. There was even a tea house up the block." "Tea"— a slang for marijuana I hadn't heard for years.

I followed Schoenfeld to the rear courtyard area of what had been the Casa Loma Hotel and was now a restaurant called Mill Landing. Schoenfeld showed me the window, covered with grating, where my sister had chained her bike. He brushed his foot across the cement patio where her body had been found, and looked up at me. "You take someone to the crime scene, it usually stirs up emotions," he said.

He waited for me to speak. I found my sunglasses at last. All I could think was how bright the sun was.

"We worked around the clock on this case," Schoenfeld said. "Not like now, with the cops being strictly nine to five. They work late, they get *overtime* pay."

"That's good, isn't it?" I asked dumbly.

"We didn't quit until we found our man," Schoenfeld said, with obvious irritation.

He brushed his foot across the cement and studied me again.

"What do you feel?" he asked.

My throat closed up. Any answer will do, I told myself. But I could not think of a relevant response, could not manage to fake something that would satisfy him, not even expected words like, "We were all so shocked." Schoenfeld stood, squinting, waiting silently, until I began to feel that I was guilty of something, though I didn't know what.

We walked back to Schoenfeld's office. The chief was waiting for us with his arms crossed. He was a compact man, a

Vietnam vet, with a silver tooth and ears of two different sizes. He interrogated me for a few minutes, radiating pure malice. Then he let me go.

I got back into the red rental car and studied the map of metro Phoenix. I had promised to get back to the hotel in time to have dinner with Will and his friends from graduate school. I could not get lost.

I memorized the turns and paid attention to the road. But the image of Schoenfeld brushing his foot against the cement and asking me what I felt kept replaying in my head. "Nothing" was the answer, though I was too ashamed to admit it.

Dinner that night was at a hokey *faux* cowboy place in the hills above the city. The restaurant had antler-and-cattle-skull decor, and waitresses with tight, fringed blouses, plenty of cleavage and spurs on their boots. My husband's friends were a lively group, full of reminiscences and talk of present work and future collaborations. Someone had ordered several portions of fried rattlesnake for us to share. When the plate went around, I dug right in. I'd been a vegetarian for fifteen years, but that night, when my husband asked why I was eating rattlesnake, I argued vehemently that rattlesnake was a vegetable and therefore okay to eat.

I was unshaken by the day's events. I did not think about my sister. I did not recognize my argument as absurd.

At night, in my dark hotel room, I drift toward sleep. I am like the rattlesnake I've eaten. All my skins have split and shed and blown away, the going-like-gangbusters woman in the red rental car, the least neurotic person in the world, the mother of the disabled child, the wife who is losing the talent for pushing back all that is wrong, the writer stuck on a single scene. All these skins are gone, until what's left is the observer.

As if from a distance, I see a girl standing in her parents' doorway. I hear the girl's mother say, "Our baby is dead." I recall this with a kind of omniscience, as if I am the author of the girl. I am not the girl, but I am so close I can feel her long, slow walk back to her room, the way the door rubs against the carpet when she pushes it shut, the way she snaps the lock. I remember her opening the closet, looking at the neatly hung clothes and thinking: If necessity is the mother of invention, who or what is the father? Jay Gould, robber baron or millionaire industrialist? I remember her worrying about the essays she needs to finish for history and about what is "suitable" to wear the night her sister has been stabbed to death.

I remember that while she is wondering—technology, desire?—people begin to fill the house, and someone, not her mother, begins to wail and shriek, *Oy got, oy got!* She knows it is their friend Miriam, because the girl is no longer in her room, hasn't been in her room for hours, but has left the bedroom strewn with discarded clothes and is now walking in circles around the dining-room table, around and around. She listens to the wailing, and, once each revolution catches a kneesock that keeps creeping down. The words, *four times in the body and twice in the head*, seem to come from the air itself.

The wailing makes her furious. She wants to smack Miriam across the face and say, "How *dare* you cry." She wants to shake her and say, "Stop making a racket." You cannot cry—never, no matter what. It is not allowed in this house. It's as bad as being selfish, as bad as "thinking of yourself before others." It's as shameful as "not even reading the newspaper," as "not giving a damn about anything else except your own little world."

Someone helps Miriam to the couch, not the girl's mother, because the mother pulls the girl into the kitchen. She pours a glass of water. Then she holds out her palm and says, "Here, take this."

I continue to drift in and out of sleep. I am aware of my own breathing. I know that I am in Arizona to be in the scene instead of watching it, and when I think that, I remember the words, "Breathe deep . . ." and a dental assistant holding a black mask over my face and saying, "Breathe deep, and you'll forget everything."

I'm eleven years old, and waiting to have three teeth extracted. I've been here once before and know that the "sweet air" in that mask is nitrous oxide, and that, if I allow myself to inhale the seductive sweetness, I will fall asleep. It's what they want. I'm supposed to relax and breathe deeply.

The dental assistant is saying, "Now count backwards to ten, and when you wake, it will be all over."

I don't want to count backwards. I don't want to sleep. The last time I had listened to these instructions and counted backwards, I'd woken up with the metallic taste of blood in my mouth, spaces where I once had teeth, and no memory of what had happened. This blank space, this not knowing, shook me deeply. It is the only fear I have when the black mask covers my nose and mouth. I will not count backwards and fall asleep. No fuss, no fighting. But I will not sleep. I have devised a plan, inspired by a movie I saw about a prisoner of war holding fast during torture. I will not count. Instead, I will tap on the arm of the chair, and concentrate hard on the tapping to keep myself awake.

I do that, tap and tap and do not count, and dream that I am running on a deeply sloping roof, trying to reach the chimney. Villains pursue me, two of them scrambling after me. I am almost to the peak when one of the villains grabs hold of my leg and yanks so hard a current of pain shoots through me. He keeps tugging until he rips my leg out of its socket. And now the second villain joins him and starts pulling, too. I'm hanging on to the chimney with both arms while they yank at my second leg. I can feel the ripping of the flesh and sinews, the crack of bone. The pain is unbearable and still they pull until that leg, too, is gone. My arm is next. They tug on it, the whole time calling to me in dreamy voices. "Mar-tha!" in a soft singsong, as if I am a puppy gallivanting away from them. "Martha!" sweet and melodic, as if it is a game.

When I open my eyes, the mask is gone. Tears are streaming down my face. My finger is still tapping on the arm of the chair.

But it's okay. I had felt what was happening to me. I needed to know what I felt, to be able to name it, own it.

The morning after my sister died, I clenched my jaws—no!—like a toddler in a high chair. My mother's demands had always been impossible to resist. That day, her gaze was enough, a look that said: Don't start, not tonight. I did not want that tranquilizer, did not want it in some deep way I could not understand or explain.

I felt that it would kill me to take it, but I could not trick my mother the way I had tricked the oral surgeon. I took the glass my mother proffered, swallowed the pill with the smallest sip of water, then continued the refrain, *four times in the body, twice in the head*, and the long journey around the table. For a while I concentrated on the furriness of the undissolved pill and the lump it left in my throat. In time, even that was gone.

4

FACTS—YOU COULD BELIEVE IN FACTS. You could
trust what you saw or read. All else was suspect.

When I used to do my little comic routine about my
family, I described my parents as that common breed of Jewish
agnostic. They had no faith in any unseen God. They believed
in tangible things, dry goods, books. They believed that *The
New York Times* was the repository of wisdom and truth. The
worst sin you could commit in my mother's eyes—and "sin"
was the word she used—was failing to read the newspaper.

I could understand this as a legacy inherited from their
immigrant parents, who could not afford to trust in the intangible.

The facts of my maternal grandfather's life are as follows:
mother died, father remarried. Stepmother did not like him.
Left his father's house, changed his name, married the woman
we called Baba. My grandparents lived not far from the Dniester
River, in a land with shifting boundaries and names, Russia,
Romania, Moldava, depending upon the year. One day, while
riding in a horse-drawn cart beside his pregnant wife, my

grandfather was held up by a Cossack. He did the unthinkable—struck the Cossack with his whip, knocked out his teeth, overturned his cart. And so he fled.

The journey across the land and sea to America has been taken by so many millions it's hard to restore to my grandfather the weight and meaning of his particular voyage, to imagine one man and one woman, gambling everything on the possibility of a better life.

My grandfather tried a lot of businesses in America, yard goods, armaments. His family grew. They forgot to fool the baby snatcher: Along the way, a girl died. Later, a boy. After a number of years, they settled in Brooklyn, my grandfather, by then a father of six, with a modestly successful business in suspenders and garters.

I, too, distrusted the intangible and believed in facts, and when Will and I flew home from Arizona in November 1989, I had a lot of them, in trial transcripts, police reports, and a complete set of news articles and editorials. I scrutinized these facts, studying the documents until I could quote whole sections by heart. I thought all the answers were in these papers, and that once I assembled them I would understand what really happened in Arizona, and somehow feel settled.

I did not even trust memory to resurrect an image of Laura, but searched through a pine box of memorabilia until I found a plastic bag full of letters she had mailed me over the years.

Laura and I had written to each other whenever we were apart. Her big, loopy, girlish handwriting told the brief story of how she ended up in Arizona.

First, the boy she met. "Sweet and wonderful," she wrote.

It was 1964. Laura and the boy—Howie—were students at Bradley University in Peoria, Illinois. She was a sophomore.

He was a senior, "six feet tall, with wavy black hair." They studied together almost every night and on weekends swam in a quarry, where the water was "clear and cold and forty feet deep." ("But don't tell Mommy because it's illegal.")

It was love, she wrote me several months later. It was the real thing, the kind that would last forever.

They decided to get engaged. Howie wanted to buy her a diamond ring; he didn't care what size so long as it was perfect. Like their love.

She was "growing her nails and buying *Modern Bride* magazine and everything." She was "the most excited person in the world."

Howie had originally planned to go to law school but that meant three more years of school and no guarantee of a deferment. So in January 1966 he enrolled in the one-year program in international trade his friends had told him about. Laura stayed behind in Peoria.

Being without Howie was pure torture, my sister wrote. She was lonely and scared. "I'm praying that the God-damn US government doesn't drag Howie away from me."

They altered their plans and decided that Laura would finish her sophomore year at Bradley, spend the summer at home in New Jersey, then transfer to ASU for the fall semester. In December they would marry. "You'll be my bridesmaid, naturally," she wrote.

I loved that my sister was in love and that she was transferring to Arizona State University to be "close to her fiancé," and I told everyone I met about this move, sure that they would find it as stunning and exciting as I did. I never questioned the move or thought how young she was. I did not know that marriage was big and complicated. The only thing that gave me pause was Arizona, a place that seemed extraordinarily foreign, in my imagination a land of cowboys and allergy sufferers and a weird square-jawed senator, Barry Goldwater, whose mere name made my parents shudder.

Being "close" meant separate residences until their December wedding. Laura did not know exactly where, only that the dorms were full and the sanctioned off-campus housing was completely rented. And so, instead of a diamond as perfect as their love, Howie bought her a motorcycle, a small red Honda she called "Louie" after a friend, Louie Schwabacher, whose name amused her.

As I worked to put the pieces together in my attic office in New Jersey, I remembered all the balmy nights Laura and I rode on Louie during our last summer. I was frightened at first, but she taught me to hold on to her. "I'm not going anywhere," she would say. "Just hold on and *lean* into the curves."

When Laura flew to Phoenix, she left the motorcycle behind. She encouraged me to ride Louie—it would impress my friends, she said—until she called our parents with her permanent address, and asked that they ship it to Arizona.

Arizona State University was established in 1850 as Tempe Normal, a teachers' college, and for a long time was the kind of state school attended almost exclusively by the sons and daughters of local people. But 1966 was a boom year for many universities and ASU got a record number of applicants, a larger percentage of them out-of-staters than ever before. Even so, it remained a conservative place. ROTC was still compulsory, and most of the students looked as if they had been plucked straight from the Eisenhower fifties. The boys had a short-haired, buttoned-down look. The "coeds" had bouffant hair and wore circle pins on their crisp white blouses. Officially, undergraduate women under twenty-three had to live on campus unless they were "with parents or guardians or close relatives or working in private homes for room and board." In 1966 more than five hundred students were without dorm rooms or official housing, so the school bent the rules and let women live off-campus, provided they had a letter from their parents.

I imagine that my mother wrote a letter on her cream-colored stationery that had "Mrs. David Bernstein" on top. "Dear Dr. Nichols, Kindly give our daughter, Laura Ellen Bernstein, permission to live off-campus."

I imagine the letter coming easily, for my mother, outspoken though she was, and proudly "different" from the "typical suburban mothers," had traditional expectations for us as girls. Of course we would go to college, because nothing was more important than education, but then we would get married and raise our children. And so, of course, it was appropriate for Laura to be near her fiancé for the three months before their wedding.

My sister was edgy in new situations, with none of our father's ease around strangers or his predisposition to think the best of everyone. But she needed a place to live, and so, on her first day of school, Laura went to the housing office, where she met an eighteen-year-old freshman named Jhan Livingston, from Palos Verdes, California. "Jinx" was another "victim of the housing shortage," according to the newspaper.

It took little time for them to decide to live together. On Laura's second day in Tempe, she and Jinx found an apartment to share on East Lemon Street, about a mile from campus.

In ceramics class, Laura met a girl named Ellen Leschen. Like my sister, Ellen was Jewish, Brooklyn-born, an art major, engaged to be married. She was staying at the Casa Loma

Hotel, on the corner of Mill Avenue and Fourth Street. The Casa Loma, built in 1888, was a Tempe landmark, and until the late 1950s it had been the largest, most popular hotel in town. By 1966, though, it was a disreputable residence hotel that housed the roughest bar on the street. Nonetheless, it had been deemed acceptable as official off-campus housing.

On the third day of class, Laura joined the campus chapter of Students for a Democratic Society. She was walking back to her apartment on East Lemon Street after a meeting when a car mounted the sidewalk and came toward her. This scared her enough to ask someone from SDS for a ride home the next night, but not enough to stop her from making a date with the girl from ceramics class. They agreed to meet at Ellen's apartment on the evening of September 21.

But, first, dinner with Jinx. Laura made lamb chops, peas, mashed potatoes. She needed practice cooking, she told Jinx. She was worried about how little she could do in the kitchen and wanted to get more experience before she and Howie got married.

At 6:45 p.m., Laura left for Ellen's apartment. The Honda was still in its shipping crate in New Jersey, so Laura borrowed Jinx's bicycle to ride the mile and a half to the Casa Loma Hotel.

My sister rode down Mill Avenue at twilight. She dismounted from the bike on Third Street and took it around to the back of the Casa Loma. She leaned her bike against the wall of the hotel and was chaining it to the window grate when someone came out of the shadows, stabbed her four times in the body and twice in the head, and left her to die.

I imagined this and knew I should be horrified. I knew it because whenever I spoke of it, I felt the horror in others' eyes.

"How awful," they said, and looked away with discomfort. The leathery-skinned Lt. Schoenfeld who had taken me to the crime scene had not looked away. He studied me, waiting for me to come up with a suitable response.

What did I feel? he asked.

That it was odd for more than an hour to pass before anyone noticed Laura. It was already 8:30 p.m. when a boy burst into the Tempe Police Station, eighteen years old, in a red-and-gray-plaid shirt and chinos, running so hard he had tripped and skinned his knees, and now leaned on the desk and gasped hard for air, barely comprehensible when he told the desk officer what he had seen in the back of the Casa Loma Hotel.

Now hold on, son. Start from the beginning.

A girl he thought was dead. He'd left her with some friends.

The teenager's name was David Mumbaugh, and when he caught his breath he told his story to Officer Williams and Detective Schoenfeld. Mumbaugh was a draftsman trainee for the Arizona Highway Department, a job he'd held since his graduation from Tempe Union High School three months before. He'd stayed late at work that night, and on the way home decided to drive by the Dana Brothers Used Car Lot on Third Street and Mill Avenue to take another look at a used car he liked, a Dodge in great shape.

He had gone past Third Street by mistake, so he parked his car on Fourth Street and was walking the block back to the lot when he saw a beam of light close to the ground—something odd about it made him turn. He saw what he thought was a body.

My sister, lying on the pavement in the breezeway of the hotel, not far from the crowds on Mill Avenue, the bikers and beer drinkers and college kids. Choppers lined up along the sidewalks, cars jamming the streets, crowds belly to belly in the bars. Mumbaugh's first thought was that she was drunk, he told police. He had said, "Lady, are you all right?" and felt her pulse.

She was not all right.

Lights were on in an apartment across the alley. Mumbaugh shouted and ran over to the building. He told the two fellows he had roused about the woman he thought was dead, then left these "two unknown subjects" with the body and ran to the station alone.

That night Detective Schoenfeld, one of three men assigned to the case, wrote in the police record: "Mr. Mumbaugh states that he did not see the two unknown subjects at the scene upon his return and has not seen these two subjects since."

Officer Josh Hall went to the crime scene, "in regards to a woman laying on the sidewalk and possibly dead. A friend of person reporting occurrence to Police" directed Hall to the victim.

He parked the patrol car between a station wagon and the corner on the north side of Fourth Street, just west of Mill Avenue.

A white male standing on the corner took him down the alley next to the hotel. It was very dark, street and sidewalk both.

He observed: "A white female laying next to the hotel wall on the sidewalk, between two bicycles, a boys gold bike and a blue and white girls bike. The victim was dressed in a pair of lt. levis and a dark blue pullover type shirt."

There was "a spot of blood on the south side of the victim which appeared to have been stepped in. A group of small spray type blood spots further out on the sidewalk and the victim."

A bicycle chain lock by her left hand. A striped cloth bag under her head. Her right wrist or hand was through the strap of the bag. A white-and-black plastic flashlight was behind her rear bicycle tire. It was not burning.

He "checked the wrist for pulse with negative results."

Then "checked the victim's neck for pulse with negative results." The victim was "very warm, warmer than normal."

When Detective Dale Douglas arrived at the crime scene, he found "eighteen citizens and five Tempe Police Officers." The crime scene and surrounding area had been secured, and was in the process of being lit and photographed.

A close examination was made of the area immediately around the body. Numerous strands of hair were discovered and gathered into evidence.

Detectives "secured the victim's hands with plastic bags to preserve any evidence which might be found on them."

Identification found in the purse held in the victim's right hand was that of Laura Ellen Bernstein, "white female, 5'3" 110 lbs., brown hair, green eyes."

The body was chalked on the concrete.

It was one foot from the victim's forehead to the wall of the Casa Loma Hotel; 10½ inches from the left knee to the concrete window base of the hotel's basement window; right toe 20 inches from the wall of the Casa Loma Hotel; left toe 29 inches to wall.

The body was lying on the left side.

Twisted to the right at the waist.

The head was turned approximately 45 degrees to the left with arms away from the body in a somewhat hands-up position.

The victim's right hand clutched a blue-and-white striped cloth purse. Touching her left hand was a plastic-covered bicycle-chain lock.

I knew, as I read all this, that I should feel something. But I couldn't. It seemed at first that the language itself was a distraction. Victims and perpetrators—words from cop shows and stand-up routines, made funny from overuse. Descriptions written by cops who should have been charged and sentenced for failure to love the language, if only there were such a crime. "White male, appeared to be the wino type." "Searched the area with negative results." No heart or soul beneath the words: nothing evocative. The reports meant to be omniscient, a camera-eye seeing all, hearing all, because the tiny shifts and changes that in ordinary life might seem irrelevant could not be judged so in a crime search. Nothing was supposed to be judged at all, only gathered and noted, details set down with ultimate precision.

Murder was uncommon in Tempe in 1966, and what murders there were most often were committed by people who knew each other, by spouses or estranged spouses. Murder, said Michael Garvey, executive director of Arizona's Board of Pardons and Paroles, was "historically a concatenation of one singular act of passion."

"You might not know right away who did it, but things kind of lay themselves out," Dale Douglas said. He was the youngest of the three detectives assigned to the case, and, like Schoenfeld, had arrived at the crime scene minutes after Mumbaugh reported her death.

This murder, he remembered, my sister's murder, looked different from the start. She was killed so close to Mill Avenue, where throngs of people congregated, yet more than an hour passed before anyone noticed. The money was still in her wallet. There was no sign of intended rape. Who wanted her dead, and why?

Twenty-year-old white female. Hair long, straight, and parted on the side. Large hoop earrings, blue shirt, white jeans, moccasins. A record in her basket called "I Speak with the Spirits." To Douglas, she dressed like the crowd that went to that new place on Mill Avenue, where the old Elks Club had been, a coffee shop named Euthanasia, where people "set" around on pillows reading poetry, and where they had a big rope hanging from the rafters and people would swing and chant.

Her hair. My sister's brown, shoulder-length hair was mentioned so often in police reports and news accounts it was as if her hair were the key to this case, the center of the investigation. Her hair, so ordinary in my memory, thin and straight, was remembered as the most distinctive thing about her: A woman reported seeing my sister riding her bicycle on Mill Avenue at twilight the night she died: Laura had stopped by putting her feet down instead of using the brakes on the handlebars "such as a person would do if riding a motorcycle," the woman said. But it wasn't Laura's manner of braking that made the woman notice her, but rather "the length of her hair, which was tied at her neck."

This woman seemed to recall that a boy was on a bike, too, pursuing her, perhaps, though she could recall no details of the boy or his bike. Only "the victim's long brown hair which fell across her back."

I read through the newspaper again: STUDENT STABBED TO DEATH IN DARK.

The first head shot the papers used was a painfully unattractive one, Laura looking blankly at the camera, dark brows and intense eyes, her narrow face exaggerated by the tightly pulled-back hair and hoop earrings.

Bereft

She took a "shortcut to death," the afternoon papers said. She had a rendezvous with death.

She was a "beatnik type" who carried "far-out jazz albums" in her basket, an outsider who had been seen distributing literature for a left-wing organization. The presumption of guilt was a strong, thrumming subtext. "You've got to remember where you are," Schoenfeld had told me. "This place was a cotton town. People didn't like outsiders."

And yet in 1966 murder was still a horror, especially the murder of a twenty-year-old middle-class college student. "It wasn't like one Mexican killing another," said one of the detectives. My sister was a young, white college student in a benign town, a college town, where, in attorney Jay Dushoff's words, "the entire business community then derived from the college, where the establishment must have felt: Spare no horses! Solve this crime!"

And so they spared no horses. Twelve cops searched the area around the Casa Loma. City employees pitched in by mowing the lawn next to the hotel so the police could scrutinize it inch by inch, combing through the nearby lots with metal detectors.

By morning, forty people were interviewed: Laura's fiancé, Howie; her roommate, Jinx; the girl she went to visit; residents of the Casa Loma and nearby apartment buildings.

Douglas and Schoenfeld went to Euthanasia, but it yielded nothing: no leads, no motives, no connections to known drug dealers. They interviewed three hundred people over the next two days and learned absolutely nothing. And so they found themselves relying on David Mumbaugh because he had been there so soon after it happened. Mumbaugh checked out okay: His boss at the Arizona Highway Department had

She took a "shortcut to death," the afternoon papers said.
She had a rendezvous with death.

She was a "beatnik type" who carried "far-out jazz albums" in her basket, an outsider who had been seen distributing literature for a left-wing organization. The presumption of guilt was a strong, thrumming subtext. "You've got to remember where you are," Schoenfeld had told me. "This place was a cotton town. People didn't like outsiders."

And yet in 1966 murder was still a horror, especially the murder of a twenty-year-old middle-class college student. "It wasn't like one Mexican killing another," said one of the detectives. My sister was a young, white college student in a benign town, a college town, where, in attorney Jay Dushoff's words, "the entire business community then derived from the college, where the establishment must have felt: Spare no horses! Solve this crime!"

And so they spared no horses. Twelve cops searched the area around the Casa Loma. City employees pitched in by mowing the lawn next to the hotel so the police could scrutinize it inch by inch, combing through the nearby lots with metal detectors.

By morning, forty people were interviewed: Laura's fiancé, Howie; her roommate, Jinx; the girl she went to visit; residents of the Casa Loma and nearby apartment buildings.

Douglas and Schoenfeld went to Euthanasia, but it yielded nothing: no leads, no motives, no connections to known drug dealers. They interviewed three hundred people over the next two days and learned absolutely nothing. And so they found themselves relying on David Mumbaugh because he had been there so soon after it happened. Mumbaugh checked out okay: His boss at the Arizona Highway Department had

Bereft

She took a "shortcut to death," the afternoon papers said. She had a rendezvous with death.

She was a "beatnik type" who carried "far-out jazz albums" in her basket, an outsider who had been seen distributing literature for a left-wing organization. The presumption of guilt was a strong, thrumming subtext. "You've got to remember where you are," Schoenfeld had told me. "This place was a cotton town. People didn't like outsiders."

And yet in 1966 murder was still a horror, especially the murder of a twenty-year-old middle-class college student. "It wasn't like one Mexican killing another," said one of the detectives. My sister was a young, white college student in a benign town, a college town, where, in attorney Jay Dushoff's words, "the entire business community then derived from the college, where the establishment must have felt: Spare no horses! Solve this crime!"

And so they spared no horses. Twelve cops searched the area around the Casa Loma. City employees pitched in by mowing the lawn next to the hotel so the police could scrutinize it inch by inch, combing through the nearby lots with metal detectors.

By morning, forty people were interviewed: Laura's fiancé, Howie; her roommate, Jinx; the girl she went to visit; residents of the Casa Loma and nearby apartment buildings.

Douglas and Schoenfeld went to Euthanasia, but it yielded nothing: no leads, no motives, no connections to known drug dealers. They interviewed three hundred people over the next two days and learned absolutely nothing. And so they found themselves relying on David Mumbaugh because he had been there so soon after it happened. Mumbaugh checked out okay: His boss at the Arizona Highway Department had verified that he had worked late on the night of the twenty-first. The car Mumbaugh said he went to see at Dana Brothers was still in the lot. My sister had only been in Arizona for ten days, and the few people who knew her were steadfast in their descriptions of her. Intelligent, nice, spent her spare time cooking in preparation for her marriage, going to "art" movies, seeing her fiancé. In the words of the girl who lived at the Casa Loma, Laura was "real hep but not a shallow person." Jinx, Laura's roommate of ten days, told police that she never knew Laura to drink intoxicants.

Never saw Laura display a violent temper.

Never knew Laura to be immoral.

The police asked Jinx if Laura had intercourse with her fiancé, as if an affirmative answer would lead them on their way. A girl like that.

What did I feel, sitting in my attic office twenty-three years later? Momentary outrage at the presumption. That kind of girl—has long hair, sleeps with her boyfriend, must have brought it on herself. But they could not even incriminate her this way.

COED HADN'T TIME TO MAKE ENEMIES, the papers said seven days after her murder.

Eight days passed, then nine.

The newspaper coverage had changed by then. It seems no coincidence that after police failed to show any trail to or from Euthanasia, or gather incriminating words about her activities, the awful shot of the beatnik girl was replaced by a high school yearbook photo: Laura with her hair slightly teased and rising in wings by her ears. Now the newspapers reported that she was "associated with Future Teachers, Girls Leaders, and Chorus Club." Now she had worked at Sears, Bambergers, and

Hearst Publications. Now the newspapers reported that, although she liked odd clothes and the arts, "her image as a beatnik is not consistent with her employment record."

There were the jeans and moccasins and the peevish comment from the dean of women, that my sister had not "found the time to come to the dean's office to discuss her housing plans," as was the official rule, but she was all right.

A week after the murder, a memorial service conducted by the Reverend Charles Seller, pastor of the United Campus Christian Fellowship, was held for her on the mall outside the social sciences building on campus. Two hundred students attended. Even the Reverend made reference to Laura's long, straight hair, the way she dressed, and her association with SDS. "Laura's faithfulness to her own convictions sometimes led her to adopt a position of dissent from certain attitudes of our society," he said. "To us, this demonstrates the essence of the character of her own Jewish religious heritage . . ."

I was indignant when I read this. My sister sat for a few hours at a literature table, worked for an organization that would come to represent a dissent so broad it would split the country in two, but at this service she was a Jew and a protester, and the congregation was asked to forgive her.

Still I was no closer to understanding why Laura was murdered, and unable to answer the question Schoenfeld had asked when he took me back to the Casa Loma Hotel. What did I feel?

5

I CONTINUED TO INVESTIGATE Laura's murder for the next five years. I simply could not stop. I spoke at commutation hearings. I met the murderer's father. I drove out to the prison where the murderer had served most of his time. By 1994, 1 had in my possession the complete police reports and court transcripts, as well as the murderer's entire prison file. I had become well-versed in the history of victims' rights and the reason for its opponents in the state of Arizona. I had interviewed cops, lawyers, wardens, parole board members, advocates who worked for the victim/witness program. In all likelihood, I had every word ever written about my sister's case, all these documents divided into folders, arranged in alphabetical order from "attorney general" to "victims' rights," and stored in two file carts I had bought for that purpose.

I knew everything, the whole story. I had written and revised it dozens of time, but it felt flawed to me. I used writers' terms to describe the sense of failure, of incompleteness—defects in its spine, its arc, its voice—that I seemed powerless to fix. Sometimes, miserable that my obsession with this project was ruining my career, I would imagine setting a match to all those facts. What kept me going was an inescapable feeling that only a single piece was missing, and as soon as I found it, everything would fall into place. I kept poring through my files, jotting down the names of people I had not yet interviewed, looking for the elusive piece that always seemed to be just around the next bend. Once I found it, I could write "Case closed," and really believe it.

By this time, home was Pittsburgh, where we had moved in 1991, so I could take a position teaching creative writing at a university. Will told our new neighbors in a jolly way that he was the "trailing spouse," a name he had picked up from the realtor. It wasn't long before he was asked to join a medical research group. Will had a chronic liver condition, and his health had begun slowly to deteriorate. Still, he seemed to thrive at work. Then, in 1994, the principal investigator in the group accepted a position in Boston, and nearly everyone in the lab decided to follow along.

I remember Will telling me that the whole lab was relocating. I remember how muted our discussions were, how quickly we came to the decision that he would also go to Boston. We were oddly vague about how long he would stay—nine months, a year—and agreed loosely that he would return on weekends, though we never decided how often. Will's family was originally from the Boston area. We knew a lot of people there. And he would be so much closer to our beloved cottage in Maine.

There was no question that I supported Will in his decision to join the others. As the move grew closer, it occurred to me that maybe I had done more than support him, that I had pushed him. I could not imagine our family life ending, yet it was as if I were eager for him to leave. It bothered me, being so unclear about something as major as this. I found myself telling people about the upcoming move, just so I could listen to their responses. They looked so troubled. "That will be hard," they said, and, "Boy, will you miss him."

The night my sister was murdered, I had tried on one outfit after the next, looking for something suitable to wear, as if the right clothes would give me comfort. Now I tried on responses to Will's leaving. Nothing fit. Nothing brought me closer to thinking yes, that's exactly what I feel.

I am haunted by the memory of moving day. I recall walking onto the front porch in the middle of the day and watching Will rearranging cartons in the trunk of his gold Toyota. The driveway was so cluttered it looked as if we were having a yard sale—boxes, books, files, tubs of clothing, Will's fat-tired bike. He was alone, though. He had been packing all morning by himself. Rachel was on the next-door neighbors' swing. I could see her when she was high in the air, could hear her joyous laugh, could imagine, from this distance, that she was any child. I didn't know where Charlotte was, though at fifteen she was most often wherever and whatever we were not.

I watched Will put the last of his possessions into the car. We had been married by then for nineteen years. I could page through family albums and recall the depth of my love for him. And it occurred to me that it was ridiculous for a sick man to move far away from his family, and it occurred to me that I wished he were already gone. But I was so devoid of emotion that what reverberated in my head was Erich Schoenfeld's question of five years earlier. What did I feel? Nothing, when Schoenfeld had brushed his foot against the cement in the back of the Casa Loma Hotel. Nothing, when I read the harsh, bald descriptions of my sister's corpse. And now, five years later, the mystery had spread, and I did not know what I felt about anything at all, and I needed to know, because my life was unraveling, and it looked as if I was the one who had begun to pull at the knot and tug at the delicate strings that kept our family together.

Will started the engine an hour later. I grabbed the sandwich and juice box I'd packed for his trip and assembled the kids and the dog on the driveway so we could see him off. I said, "Drive safely," and, "Call when you get in." And then we stood there and waved until the car turned the corner.

I am haunted, too, by the ordinary events of the next few days, how we dressed for school, ate our meals, argued about the length of time the dog had to be walked. Our household was the same as before, only now there was an empty place at the table and in my bed. When people asked how I was managing, I said, "I'm just keepin' on keepin' on," as indeed I was, then and at other times. I realize now that I was a master at this, and that it became my undoing.

I did not want to speak to Will on the phone, though I could not have said as much then. And I did not want to see him, though I could not have articulated that either. I was keeping on, I was okay. And maybe things would have stayed that way, and I would have remained benumbed and confused for the rest of my life. But I began to wake myself up with a start in the middle of the night, my heart pounding. I woke remembering that I had seen my sister floating through our old dining room in Queens in her witch's costume. And I woke leaden with despair, overwhelmed by the conviction that moving forward was futile, that there was no reason to get out of bed, nothing in the distance to strive for.

Of course, I did get out of bed when the alarm went off each morning—I had a job and kids and was good at keepin' on keepin' on. As if nothing were amiss, I hopped in the shower and toweled myself dry. But when I looked in the mirror, instead of my own face, I kept seeing the face of a boy I hardly knew.

Several weeks after Will's departure, I made an appointment with a therapist, and at the scheduled time sank into a wide, soft leather chair and said, "I'll admit I have some issues."

On paper my life looked hard, I said. A spouse who'd just moved, a retarded kid, a teenager, aging parents who had just relocated to Pittsburgh. A sister who was murdered a long time ago. But I'd worked through these things and didn't need to hash them over again. Yes the murder had been terrible, but for my sister, not for me. I didn't die. And anyhow, I was over it. The only reason I mentioned it was because I knew that, with shrinks, anything you left out took on extreme significance, they'd make a giant deal of it. He needed to know that, despite everything, I had always been able to live my life with grace and pleasure. Always. No matter what.

What was different was this business of waking myself up in the middle of the night and feeling that I didn't want to bother going on. I no longer had whatever I once possessed to get through the days.

And there something else, this thing with my face, which was really upsetting me. It had started when Will had set up a video recorder in our dining room shortly before he moved. I was sitting at the table with the kids, talking and eating. I looked like a dead person in the video. It wasn't just the light, the angle, my age, a bad haircut. It was this wooden look. First it was only the video. Later I started to see this look when I caught my reflection unawares. My face reminded me of the tough boy in my eighth-grade class. At the moments of greatest humiliation, he would jerk out his chin and say, "I ain't cryin'." He wasn't a friend. I barely knew him. For some reason, I could never forget his stony face. And maybe even this wouldn't have mattered if I could still hear the sound of my own laughter. I had lost that. I didn't know where or how, only that I did not laugh anymore. I didn't want to look back, but I was spooked to walk down the street and see in the reflection from a store window, not what I thought of as my own face, but the face of that boy I barely knew.

Listen, I said that day in the small room. Don't give me any insights. I've been in therapy several times: I'm bursting with insights. Don't think it's enough for me to cry. These days, all I need to do is get in my car, hit the buttons of the radio, and the right song will set me off. So I don't need to cry. I need to figure out why I feel so emptied out.

I did figure it out. And it wasn't a question of finding a piece that had been missing. I had all the pieces. I couldn't put them together because I was stuck in a story I had created for myself. It took Will's leaving and these sessions for me to take myself out of that story and put myself into the story I had been trying to write about Laura's murder.

For a long time, I marked the night I found the newspaper articles in my father's desk drawer as the start of my search to figure out what happened to my sister. Now, after twenty-eight years, I began to examine what happened to me.

Little Chick

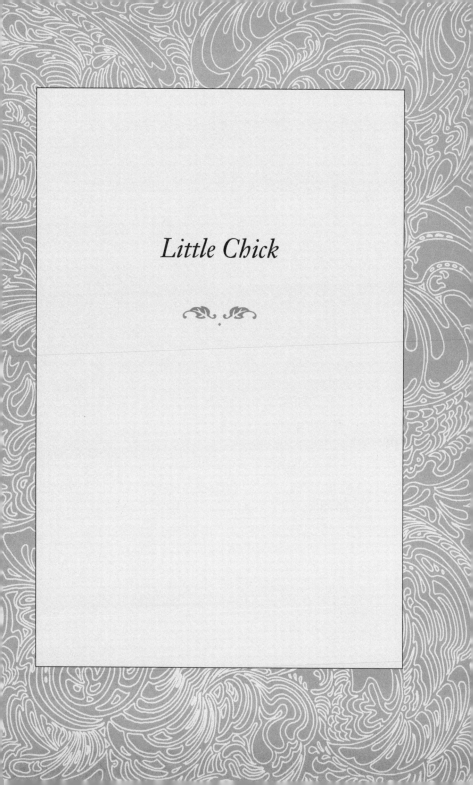

6

WHEN THE SUN CAME UP the morning after my sister's murder, there were so many people in our house that passersby might have assumed we were having a party. Miriam had stopped screaming, and the cousins and neighbors were very well behaved, no wailing or making a racket. Another family named Bernstein stopped by. Someone had phoned them to ask if they were the parents of a girl named Laura who had been murdered in Tempe the night before. And so they rang our doorbell—to tell us, to share their good fortune? Their motives puzzle me still.

I had been walking around the dining-room table for a long time, pulling up my sliding kneesock without breaking stride, and thinking hard about my history essays and the phone calls I needed to make. The tranquilizer had taken effect and I felt very steady. I had decided what to wear and that I would stop my long journey around the table at precisely 7 a.m.

When I went upstairs, I found a skinny, long-necked man— a reporter, it turned out—rifling through the top drawer of my bureau, where I kept my underwear. He turned when he saw me, but his hand kept moving through the pile of panties, as if he were one of those low-order animals that keeps running even after it loses its head.

I let it pass. I had to call my friend to tell her I didn't need a ride to school. This felt more important than telling the stranger to quit rummaging through my drawers. I backed out of my room and ventured into my parents' bedroom to use the phone.

Stabbed. Murdered. I wanted to say the words. I was eager to try them out, to see what would happen. And yet I felt phony. I felt that when I relayed the news I would be putting on an act, looking for attention. I had often been accused of these things.

I dialed my friend's number.

"I'm not going to school," I said when she answered the phone. My heart thumped as if from stage fright. I had not known what a gap there was between thinking words and speaking them. "My sister was murdered," I said.

"What?" said my friend. "You're kidding!"

I could not reassure her: for a moment I could not speak at all.

"Martha!" she said, panic edging into her voice. "Tell me you're kidding!"

I could not fill the void with those words—"sister," "murder." Absolutely could not say them, then or for the next seven years. Not just the words, but everything they stood for. The silence was like a vise and squeezed the breath from me.

"Martha!" said my friend a second time.

The sound of my name filled me with self-loathing. I said, "Stop using my name," and hung up.

I remember how naked and infantile I felt, full of blind, thrashing rage turned inward: my name, my self. I remember the unbearable hatred, and a moment later, the immense relief of seeing my cousin Roz standing in the doorway. I beamed at her, happy again. "Hi," I said. "Hello."

"Honey," said my cousin. I felt her struggle to find words. "Mom and Dad have to fly to Arizona. They're going to bring Laura back." She didn't say that one of my parents—my father, as it happened—had to go to the morgue and identify my sister. But somehow I knew this. "They want you to stay the night with me," she said.

"Okay," I said.

I grabbed a few things—some clothes, my homework—and got into her car.

Stepping out of the house put me in another dimension. Suddenly the morning was any morning. It was so ordinary that my cousin stopped at a grocery store on Paramus Road. When she asked if I minded if she ran in for milk, I thought: Why should I mind? While I sat waiting, a procession of cars filled the lot. Men hurried into the store and returned with coffee and Danish, newspapers folded beneath their elbows. A man slid into the car beside my cousin's, gingerly put his coffee on the dashboard, and then unfolded the paper. I wondered if he was reading the news, four times in the body and twice in the head. *The victim's sister sits in the car beside him.* I thought exactly that, struck by what felt like irony. I felt safe behind the glass, unreachable.

Roz's sons were having breakfast when I got to their house. My twelve-year-old cousin kicked the aluminum chair leg and hummed while he ate. She asked me if I wanted to nap. Sure, I said, though I felt as if I would never sleep.

She took me into her bedroom, showed me her high old-fashioned bed. Framed photos were arranged on her bureau.

The older ones were colorized black-and-whites. Everyone had rosy cheeks and blue eyes. I studied the photos. I thought about the letter Laura had written me before she had been stabbed four times in the body and twice in the head. I had put off answering her. I counted the days since I had mailed my letter to Tempe, counted and recounted, trying to imagine that she had received it. Eventually I fell asleep.

The next evening, four neighbors took me to the airport to meet my parents. Their plane was late, or we were very early—all I recall is that we had a lot of time to pass. They nudged me toward a concession, sat me at a counter seat facing a rotisserie where skewered hot dogs rotated endlessly. One neighbor wiped the sticky counter with a napkin, while another insisted that I order something—a soda, a hot dog—anything I wanted. What I wanted was to be left alone, but to placate everyone, I asked for a 7Up.

One of the men slid into the seat beside me. He was my favorite neighbor, a sweet, slow-moving man who showed up in our kitchen each Saturday morning to tell us a joke.

That night, he said, "This is a terrible time," as if without his words I might never have known it. "You're at the beginning of your life, but your parents are at the end. You can have a child someday, but they never can. They only have you."

"I know," I said.

He nudged the untouched 7Up toward me. "You have to be everything to them," he said.

"I know," I said, though already I was trying not to know anything about what my parents felt.

After what seemed like many hours, a disembodied voice announced the arrival of my parents' flight. We walked to the gate and watched passengers enter the terminal, men in cowboy hats, string ties, fancy belts with silver and turquoise buckles, women with skin as brown and creased as old shoes, flight attendants. I tried to feel nothing, but I was stunned by the sight of my parents. It was as if I had never been separated from them before, never seen them from a distance. They're old, I thought, with alarm. My father had always seemed like a large man, with a powerful chest and muscular arms. But the man who approached me was short and balding and old.

There had been a fad a few years before, in which we fried marbles. We'd set a high flame under a cast-iron pan and let the dry pan heat up for a half hour. Then we put our best cat's-eye marbles into the pan and rolled the marbles until they became veined with cracks. Most of the time the marbles stayed intact but sometimes the cracks went so deep the marbles shattered. That night in the airport I stepped back to avoid my father's embrace. I knew that no one could touch me or meet my eye, or my sadness would come rushing out with such force I would crack into thousands of splinters. I could not crack, no matter what. I had to be everything for them. I had to be good.

Later I would read that four hundred people attended Laura's funeral. All I remember was how badly I wanted to sit with Howie. Instead, I was trapped beside my parents, sweltering and self-conscious in a charcoal-gray pinstripe suit with a sailor-style top that my mother had made me wear. The only time I was jolted from my obsession with this itchy, hated suit was when the coffin was brought out, and I thought: *My sister in there.* Then my body grew rigid and a flush of heat came over me, as if I had been stricken by a blazing fever. My father began to weep openly. It took so much effort to stand straight-shouldered and tall and be as good as was necessary that it made me hate him.

When the service was over, I walked into the startling daylight between my parents, solemn and proud, filled with a bitter, unspeakable feeling. A hearse with open doors was waiting for us. I slid to the far end of the seat, careful not to let my mother's leg touch mine, and watched the mourners stream out of the chapel.

As soon as we reached the cemetery, I edged through the crowd until at last I was beside Howie. I kept my eyes on him as Laura's coffin was lowered into the pit. I watched him twist off the ring she had given him and throw it into her grave. The gesture seemed so beautiful and romantic that I took off my ring and threw it into the pit, too. Immediately I regretted my gesture, which seemed stupid and unoriginal. Laura had nothing to do with my ring: my parents had bought it for me because I had begged for it nonstop, swearing I would not lose it, as I had a legion of shoes and jackets and gold necklaces.

Howie flew home not long after the funeral. I really did not understand that he would no longer be part of our lives. I hugged him goodbye before he stepped into a car. Then I called out, "Hey, *write* me, okay?" It was what I said to guys I knew who were leaving for college. "Promise?"

For a few days there was a reprieve. People crowded the living room, making conversation about inconsequential things. I could visit with my cousins or Laura's friends or drift into the kitchen, where the counters overflowed with trays of food—bagels, casseroles, and Danish. In the evenings, my friends stopped by, not one or two, but six at a time, the bravest holding a bakery box filled with bland, pale, crumbly cookies. How startled they were, all in a cluster, too timid to talk until I talked; too scared to laugh until I laughed. Like a conductor, I knew how to keep things moving. I could work the conversation, lead them away from their awkwardness to a place where we all felt fine and so it was all right.

Then shiva was over, and the house was empty except for my parents. We vacuumed the house and wrapped up the food. The mirrors that had been covered according to Jewish tradition were unveiled. I remember seeing my reflection after so many days, looking at the face of the girl whose sister had been murdered, and it was the same ordinary face, the same blue eyes and round cheeks, but I hated it nonetheless.

The next morning, I woke to the buzz of my father's electric razor, and when I opened my eyes, my mother was standing over me, saying, "Life goes on."

I nodded mutely. I thought that if I opened my mouth my guts would spill out. I got out of bed, picked out something to wear, and made myself leave the house. That day I walked to school alone.

As soon as I entered the building, I saw my friends clustered around the tables and blue chairs in the student lounge, the girls hugging their books to their chests and laughing in high excited voices, the boys in their letter sweaters, books at their sides. Their laughter ebbed when I approached; they rearranged their faces. I walked closer, suddenly weary, as if I had not slept the night before. I knew that I needed to fool them. I knew, too, that I needed to fool myself into thinking that I was exactly as I had been before. And I did that, too. I set my friends at ease with lighthearted conversation, the way I had when they had visited. It was not a façade; it was a sliver, a piece of who I was, though this piece would become the only part I would recognize as myself. This was the girl who set up the scholarship fund in Laura's name, the girl who was "a real survivor," the laughing, vivacious girl in photos, who so soon after the murder clowns with friends, poses in her father's glasses, plays with the new dog, dressed in a T-shirt that says, "I am a Herring Maven."

Sometimes the shell of exuberance cracked, and another girl was revealed, someone boneless, disgustingly soft, afraid of everything. But there are no photos of that hated self. That girl, Martha, was so ghostlike it was as if she had no corporeal self, no body to reside in.

Always afraid, I think, when I recall her. Hiding in my room for long stretches of time. Avoiding my parents. And when I did pass, giving them wide berth, avoiding their eyes, as if we were strangers in a train corridor.

Before the murder, we had been so noisy that I ran around closing windows in all the rooms to keep our tumult from the neighbors.

And now: ticking clocks, murmurs, an occasional car.

I did not dare to leave my room without opening the door a crack and listening. I might hear the mocking sound of canned laughter from a TV sitcom and know my mother was in the den with the door closed. I might creep downstairs then, stealthy as a thief, and discover from a plate in the sink that my father had floated through the kitchen before me.

I could not think of my parents' despair or the way their lives had been shattered, but I could hear a disembodied voice in the house saying,

You are everything to us. You keep us going.

In this dreadful silent house, where no mention of my sister was made and no one cried, I tried my hardest to be good, because I was all that was left. But at every waking moment I knew that no matter what I did, I could never be good enough.

Even before the murder I had been tormented by all that I was not. Even then, my mother's love was easy to lose, for she was *not* a typical Jewish mother, she liked to say, did not love without qualification, did not think her children little geniuses, perfect darlings who could do no wrong. I had to earn her love each day, with every action, or I would lose it completely. Even before the murder, her wrath was fierce and unexpected, and sometimes I did not know what I had done to enrage her, why she was slapping me or threatening to sell our house. But sometimes I knew perfectly well that I was exactly what she called me—bitch on wheels, liar, sneak—and when she hated me, I hated her right back, and hollered at the top of my voice, "I *hate* you!" And it was okay, because at night's end I could curl up on the couch beside her while she sewed and watched TV, and we could talk as if nothing had happened.

Now it would never be okay. There was no place I could hide, no ease or comfort in the house. All I had was the knowledge that I could not fail and was destined to do so.

Even my fluency and comfort with words were buried with Laura. When my father was out of town and my mother and I were alone for dinner, something I had once enjoyed, I became as tongue-tied as I sometimes was with strangers. I called the Mark Twain book we were reading in English *Fuck Hinn*. The Pyrenees were the mountains that separated Spance. Once I phoned my mother from a friend's house and, seeking small talk, asked, "Have the carpet installers come? Did you get laid?"

Such silence on the other end of the line, such a long fall down the dark hole in which everything I said or did not say brought me a measure of shame and discomfort. No one knew of my profound distress. Even I did not know, since I refused to recognize that ghostlike part of myself. But this was when I had begun to cast off things and people, one by one. I did not know why. I was like a feverish person, blindly kicking off covers. My boyfriend, the girls in my crowd—their presence made me restless and testy. The only dream I had was to move. I'd leave forever and never return to this stifling, small-minded town. Thinking that, I would feel a great lightness and joy. I would imagine lifting my arms and ascending high above the roof-tops. But then I would see, from overhead, my empty room. My mother sitting at the edge of the bed. (*Are you sure? Are you positive?*) And I would plummet, lock my door, refuse all calls, immovable now, a rock.

Alone in my room with the door shut tight, I wrote hundreds of letters. I responded to everyone who sent a condolence card, thanked friends and strangers for their donations to the scholarship fund, all this in a lefty's awkward, down-sloping hand. I wrote to friends in college, and to the admissions offices of dozens of schools across the U.S. That I was determined to go to college in New York City did not stop me from applying to places in the Midwest and upstate New York.

I wrote to Howie, too, or perhaps he wrote first, as he had promised. He sent me photos, all of them sunlit, as if the world was literally a brighter place before the murder: Laura swinging from rings in a playground, small and thin, with shiny hair and a smile that is oddly tentative. Howie and my father propped on their sides on our gorgeous lawn, my father shirtless, as he always was on warm days. Howie, gangly and unsure, on a small burro.

He also mailed two silver pins that had been Laura's. Every night I would find the letters, carefully untuck them from the envelopes and reread them. Then I would take the two small boxes from hiding, lift the cotton layer and study my sister's jewelry.

I can't say how I knew that the letters and jewelry should be kept a secret. But I was right to feel this, for one night in November, two months after the murder, my mother came into my room, saw the pins nestled in cotton in the open boxes, and asked me where I'd gotten them.

"Howie gave them to me," I said.

My mother stood over me. I had never known her to be so silent.

"We're writing to each other," I said.

Now the look on her face filled me with intense shame. "Don't," she said. "It isn't healthy to hold on to him. He needs to make a new life for himself."

I suppose I nodded. I know that when she walked from my room l felt as if I had done something unforgivable. I pushed the jewelry into the back of my drawer and tucked his letters in a stack of notes my friends passed to me in class. I never wrote to him again.

I fought with my parents all the time, I think, when I remember the months after Laura's murder. I think this mistakenly, because the habit of saying "my parents" has been with me for so long, the way of merging them into a single being with one voice and one point of view. In reality, it was my mother and I who fought bitterly. I simply avoided my father.

He was different—his whole family was different. While my mother's brothers and sisters were small, sour, and bookish, my father's clan was plump and cheerful, his sisters bosomy, emotional women, leavers of wet waxy lipstick marks on everyone's cheeks. "Your father is so sentimental," my mother always said, with a kind of grudging affection. After the murder, my mother and I set the household rules without ever speaking of them. We ganged up on him. He was not allowed to cry, either.

My father was a predictable man, his moods slow to evolve. When he was sad or upset, he would breathe in a soulful way, taking deep, noisy, whistling breaths, as if he were an old machine in need of oiling. I shunned him at these times, as if he were dangerous. But he had moments of peace. I remember finding him during a rainstorm, sitting on a lawn chair in the open garage, a bowl beneath the gutter pipe to collect the rainwater. And I remember that, within months of the murder, he began to wander through the neighborhood on Saturday mornings, just as he had before, his spirits buoyed by sunshine, jelly doughnuts, the feel of wet grass between his toes, and crab grass rooted out.

Time, instead of healing, seemed to make things worse for my mother. Her isolation increased. She had "no use" for people she had tolerated before, "no patience for their nonsense." And because I loved my mother and saw her deep unhappiness, I knew we should never fight. Never, I would resolve. No matter what.

Then suddenly we would be screaming at each other. And when the hatred curdled within me, filling me with something sour and unfamiliar, it was for Martha. I hated her, hated myself. There was no one else I hated, no matter how much I tried, no person, not even the murderer. A sick boy, I overheard my mother say. I feel sorry for him, she said.

I would swear that all winter I walked around the house with my hands over my ears, blotting out our voices, shrill and angry. I would swear I did this all day, every day. But during this time I raised money for the Ski Club, went out on dates, and visited Miriam's daughter Suzi at her college in upstate New York.

I had dreaded seeing Miriam, but when I slipped into the back of the car beside her for the long drive up to Ithaca, there was no sign that she had ever wept and pulled at her hair and cursed in Yiddish. Instead, she was the woman I had once loved, with her helmet of champagne-blond hair, her hugs and clattering bracelets. The drive was long, and I grew drowsy. Miriam saw me nodding, and in her husky smoker's voice said, "Put your head on my lap, cookie." I did as she asked. She stroked my ordinary brown hair and said, "Just like spun gold." And I fell asleep.

Suzi invited me to the mixer held by her sorority house the following night. It was hard, standing at the punch bowl, in the red wool dress my mother had helped me choose for this occasion, in this room full of "sisters." Still, I remember how full of delight I was when I reported to my mother that I'd had a *fabulous* time and that I had been mistaken for a freshman.

And yet it's as if this journey and the sorority mixer were part of someone else's life, for, in my memory, all I did for months was fight with my mother. In my memory, something in the air ignited these awful battles in which I screamed and covered my ears and tried to silence the refrain inside my head, failing always.

Things began to take on life; things had feelings. My sister's empty, neatly made bed, her wedding dress and engagement gifts, the clothes she had not taken to Arizona. My sister's things carried her scent and our sadness, and my mother and I fought bitterly and repeatedly over them.

One day when I came home, I found that Laura's side of the closet had been emptied. Her clothes were packed away in boxes on my floor. I was kneeling over her beautiful, broken-in boots when my mother came in.

"Take what you want," she said. "Except for the shoes. There's some superstition about not wearing someone else's shoes. The rest I'm giving to charity."

I could not imagine wearing my sister's clothes, yet the thought of them in a box—a box!—was more than I could bear. "Just *leave* everything," I said.

"For what?" asked my mother. "Just to have? To keep in a closet?"

Just to have—yes. I wish I could have said that. Instead my reply degenerated into, "Leave me alone," and, "It's *my* room."

"Listen to you. Like a two-year-old—me, me, me. It's a sin to keep things you don't wear. Poor people can use them."

Did I clap my hands over my ears then? Did I think, Don't fight, don't? Never, no matter what? Maybe I did, though what I remember clearly was howling, "I don't give a damn about your poor people!"

My mother slammed the door, disgusted by the sight of me.

At night, I imagined walking among rows of garment workers in a sweatshop, *Jewish* garment workers who knew of my waste and looked up from their sewing machines when I passed, never a word, but such *hurt* in their eyes. I averted my gaze, but hurt was on their tables, too, as if the fabric had feelings and ached from being unworn.

Laura's things had this power. She was dead and we would never speak her name. We stood over cartons of her clothing instead, shouting, "Leave me alone," and, "Always looking for trouble." When I stormed into my room, locking the door behind me, I was left with a single wish—to rip off my skin and live in some other body.

. . .

I took my sister's boots—the kind Bob Dylan wore on the cover of *Freewheeling*—and looked for trouble in them, as if trouble would give me the comfort that eluded me, now that there was nothing else. Trouble meant drinking and boys.

I didn't like the taste of liquor, which to me was clear stuff or brown stuff, but I swallowed it like bitter medicine and waited for the rush of warmth. Drinking was not about numbing myself or forgetting. I drank to feel alive. At every other waking moment I was restrained, vigilant, wildly, frantically uncomfortable. Drunk, I was bold and provocative, courageous enough to look for trouble.

I might go to a bar with my friends in Washington Heights, just over the George Washington Bridge, some ratty little neighborhood place. I'd wear jeans and Laura's boots. If I saw someone I liked, I would meet his eyes. I liked how it felt to look so directly at someone, and then to look away and wait. I liked the drumming inside my chest. I wasn't as wild as my friends thought; I wasn't really out of control. There was mastery in this business, the way you had to carefully balance waiting with suitable forward moves.

He might start up an ordinary conversation. *You from around here?*

And I would tell the truth, no matter what.

Jersey, huh?

I'd wait for the "accidental'" touch. His hand against my shoulder.

Yeah? You look about twelve.

He might grasp my shoulder. He might put his hands around my waist. We might dance to no music.

It was scary, but I moved forward—always. I did not want physical pain, did not want to be bullied or raped. If I could have articulated what I searched for that year, it would have been this: Shake me so hard that when I look in the mirror I can see someone new. Take me out of this skin. Push me further than I can go alone. Make me do things. Ask me whatever you want. Ask if I have a sister. Make me say the words—*four times, twice.* Make me speak her name.

As soon as I was accepted by NYU, I began to imagine a future for myself, based on some hazy vision ten years gone, with beatniks, bongos, folk music in smoky clubs. Every morning I woke up and thought: Soon I will leave. I began to mark an "X" over each day on my calendar, like a convict in a bad movie.

That summer, I took a job in New York as a typist for a film-distribution company that rented films to summer camps, mental institutions, residential homes for delinquent boys, state penitentiaries, the kinds of places that ordered Bible stories and uplifting movies. It was a dreadful office, on a drab side street not far from Penn Station. I shared an open space with a file clerk and two other typists, who loathed each other in a noisy way. This was not the New York where I had longed to live, and where, in fact, I would move in the fall. I spent a lot of time dreaming about the towns and cities I typed on invoices—Bound Brook, Martinsville, Rahway—wondering who lived in these places, imagining myself walking down strange streets, discovering something new.

The job was so full of small humiliations I was reminded constantly how miserable I was, trapped in my Martha self. One of the typists was an immense woman named Dottie, with dull black hair teased into what looked like a wasps' nest. She wore massive spotted muumuus that matched her name, and bickered endlessly with the other typist, a sour, anorexic little spinster who dyed what was left of her hair bright red and wore huge costumy rings on all her fingers. Dottie liked to pull me aside whenever Hortense was nearby and tell me loud secrets about Hortense's "sickness," how she lived in an apartment where newspapers were stacked to the ceilings. Hortense would catch me in the rest room, weave her arm through mine, parade me back into the office like her beau, sit on the edge of my desk to say how nice it was to work with a girl who had class, unlike *someone* whose name we would not deign to mention. Back in shipping was a nearly blind young man with a limp that made him dip sideways like a dancer when he walked. He was there before anyone in the morning, and never seemed to leave at night. He invited me to watch movies with him, enticing me with newer titles, and once, by offering me bourbon in the kind of tiny fluted paper cup that dentists use. "Boor-bon," he called it, like Humphrey Bogart in *Casablanca*. It was like the dream I had, in which my limbs were torn off, the way I felt tugged by these people, this way and that, too weak to do more than duck and hide.

I started to leave the building during my lunch breaks. I had cream cheese on date-nut bread sandwiches at Chock Full O'Nuts, or floated through Gimbels. Sometimes I merely walked the side streets lined with wholesale notions stores— beads on one street and trim on another. I discovered what a small place Manhattan was, how much ground it was possible to cover in half an hour. Sometimes I meandered all the way down to Union Square before I turned back.

I had vaguely known Union Square as a place where my mother sometimes journeyed when she was struck by a hunger for bargains, and where a legless beggar rolled around on a dolly near the subway entrance. It was as gray and shabby as the West Thirties, but it became the place I rushed toward at noon, as if for an assignation. I went there directly each day without understanding why, drawn by an obscure desire, like a dog to a scent.

SDS had its New York office on Union Square, and that's where my journey ended. Not in the building, but outside in the street. I knew that SDS stood for Students for a Democratic Society, and that the students who belonged were against the war in Vietnam. I knew that Laura had joined the ASU chapter as soon as she arrived in Tempe, and that in her short time there she had sat at literature tables. But I could not have said this to anyone, not even to myself. I had no idea why, when I stood outside this building, my heart beat so hard my chest would ache. I did not know why joining this organization was something I had to do before I arrived at school.

I could not bring myself to walk into the building, but one evening after work, I inked up my fountain pen with fuchsia ink and wrote an airy e.e. cummings–influenced kind of letter that began:

> *hi! i'm jane! I'll be a freshman at nyu in the fall. can you please tell me how I can join sds when I get there?*

It was the first time I had used my middle name instead of my first, and it made official my silent, inchoate struggle to shed the whole little-sister self called Martha. I refrained from making hearts over my "i's," but the rest of the flourishes were there, including my signature spider. I know this because someone in the SDS office responded on the back of my letter, telling me whom I should contact if I wanted to start up a chapter at school.

dear jane, someone wrote in response.

dear jane.

You'd think it was a love letter, the way I carried it everywhere, folding and unfolding it, reading it in secret a dozen times a day, until the paper split into thirds. Jane. I was not Martha, I was Jane.

I remember the morning when I broke the news. It was August 1967. I was eighteen by then. Laura had been dead for eleven months. I had just woken up and was standing in the kitchen, where my parents were eating scrambled eggs, and our new dog—the old dog had died two days after Laura was murdered—was sucking up crumbs beneath the table. Who do I see when I look back? A leggy, round-faced girl in baby-doll pajamas, hair dyed black and dead straight after a night wrapped around orange-juice cans.

I was waiting with nail-biting, eye-rolling impatience for my parents to turn their attention from the nerdy-sounding announcer murmuring the news on WQXR, because I had something *important* to tell them, something they had to hear right then.

I chewed off a broken pinkie nail and tried to spit it into the trash can across the room. At last, my mother looked up. "I'm changing my name," I said. I went on at some length, emphasizing that my parents were never again to use my old name.

"Martha is an elegant name," my mother said. She often said this. "Jane is just *bleh*."

I struggled to respond and ended up saying, "I hate being called Martha." But it was no longer as simple as liking or hating my name.

Now, when I have been Jane for nearly twice as long as I was Martha, I understand how hard it is to call someone you've known for seventeen years by a different name. At the time, I was outraged that my parents could not seem to remember my request.

My friends tried. When they phoned they said, "Martha? I mean, *Jane?*"

I stopped talking to people who would not use "Jane," didn't answer my parents if they used the wrong name, would not help anyone out. I remember my aunt Florence calling and saying, "Hello?" in her shrill voice. "Who's this?"

"Jane," I said.

"*Who?*"

"Jane," I said.

"Is this 797-1540?"

"Yes," I said, between my teeth.

"Who's this?"

"Jane," I said, suppressed rage flattening and softening my voice.

"Hello?" said Aunt Florence. "*Hello?*" And banged away on the receiver.

If I had been in my right mind, I would have said, "Hi, Aunt Florence, it's *me*, Jane, you know, the person who *used* to be Martha?" But I could not do this, not because I was stubborn—my mother's assertion—or lacking in humor—her other assertion—but because I literally was unable to speak the name or to explain why I could not speak it. I did not see how ardently I was struggling to shed the self that was Martha, a self that included much of my past. I certainly did not know that when I did shed the Martha self, I would be left raw and empty, as if my whole history, my having once had a sister, were tangible things that had been scooped out of my body.

To my parents, I was a pain in the ass about it. They were right: I was a pain in the ass.

"On the subject of Martha," my mother wrote in a letter dated October 16, 1967, a month after I had left for college:

You absolutely must develop a sense of humor in regard to your parents. We don't call you Martha to annoy you, but habits are very hard to break . . . If you expect to invite classmates to your home, and we want you to, please explain to them that you were called Martha for many years and that your parents slip once in a while. If you would learn that there is no crime in people knowing that you changed your name—no shame at all—you'd be more relaxed about the whole affair . . .

A reasonable letter—my mother's letters, literate and maternal and filled with lectures on deportment, proper care of one's possessions, and politics, were always reasonable. But what stops me now are two words, "crime" and "shame." There was a crime. I was ashamed. I could not be that Martha or hear about her, not for an instant.

7

WHAT WAS IT LIKE to leave home a year after Laura's murder?

When I was asked this question in 1994, my inclination was still to say what a normal kid I was, a typical college student of that era. And then, as if to justify this claim, I went back to my files one day, skipping past the legal documents and interviews, past the hair, fiber, and fingerprint analysis done by the FBI, past the letters I had written to prison wardens, to defense attorneys, and to a man who had served time in prison with my sister's murderer. I dug further back, until I unearthed letters from high school friends at other schools, and letters from my roommate Leslie that begin, "Dear Chica," "Dear Juana," "Dear Juan."

In a box I found transcripts reminding me that I did well in school. A black pamphlet called "How the United States Became Involved in Vietnam." Ticket stubs from a Country Joe and the Fish concert at the Anderson Theater on Second Avenue and Fourth Street, where, depending on the night, you could catch rock concerts or Jewish theater, and you could see in the lobby posters with psychedelic art and a sign in Yiddish that a friend, fluent in the language, translated as: *Nuh smucking in lobbeh.*

These tangible things would allow me to tell how I had fulfilled my dream of moving to New York City and had arrived there at an astonishing time of change, discord, and possibility. I could tell how I lived in a former residence hotel two blocks from Washington Square, so recently converted into a women's dorm that nine rent-control tenants still lived among the undergraduates, nine ancient, solitary gents who doffed their hats when girls scampered by in bathrobes. I could say that I liked my roommate, went to subtitled films, became active in the antiwar movement. Did well in school but was no genius, had friends, met a boy I liked, smoked some pot, chewed some mushrooms, in winter dressed in old fur coats.

And if Charlotte said in disgust, "You wore *fur?*" I could explain that antique furs were in fashion. My three, a skunk, a silver fox, and a white one, had been engagement presents to friends of my mother. I might tell how I named them after their owners and how the skunk smelled funky when it rained. I might say that when I wrote to tell my mother how much I loved the furs, she informed me, scorn barely disguised, that these "Brownsville bed jackets" were practically a uniform on Pitkin Avenue in Brooklyn. The Brownsville girls who had them were like the Long Island girls who "caused the stereotype," she wrote, sharp dressers who wore the "most extreme" styles, used the most makeup, and dyed their hair.

Those were the days when I looked up from my own narrow concerns, and, seeing a world in need of improvement, tried to exert my force.

This is the story that I might pass on to my grandchildren, if they were curious. Helped start a chapter of SDS. Did a lot of marching and chanting, in Washington, D.C.; in front of the New York Hilton the night Dean Rusk and "Diamond" Charlie Englehart were speaking at a banquet there; at the UN to protest the rise of fascism in Greece. And the mounted cops came toward us on giant steeds, I might say, huge horses with flaring nostrils, tanklike and unstoppable, and I was scared. But we were right, I would say. We were not petulant, ill-mannered kids whose idealism was misplaced. We knew, despite official assertions to the contrary, that the "conflict" was a war, that it was escalating wildly, crossing borders into Cambodia and Laos, that it was doomed and corrupt. Not so many years passed before our staunchest enemies began to agree.

If I told this story, I would show my mother's letters, too.

When I left home I asked my mother to write and not phone. She did not seem to find this odd, though we were all of twenty miles apart. I would not mention that the letters were safe, while seeing my parents or hearing their voices sent me into a spiral of misery. I would show the letters and say: So much for the notion that young radicals were the spoiled sons and daughters of overly materialistic parents. I would say what I failed to understand at the time: that my mother took great pleasure in my activism and pleasure in sharing memories of the time when she had worn cotton stockings—not silk from Japan!—and marched against fascism.

Poring over these documents and letters in 1994, in an attempt to understand my adult life, I found a letter my mother had written in October 1967. Suzi had died the month before and my parents had just come back from dinner with her parents. Miriam was in a bad state, my mother wrote. It was unhealthy, the way she carried on. "Keeping busy is the best thing for her—then she can behave normally and not think at all . . . Right now I feel very glad that you, Daddy, and I are quiet people—our pain and loss is just as great, but somehow I think we made it easier all around . . ."

This is the only letter that mentions my sister's murder, or Suzi's death almost exactly one year later.

Suzi died in a car accident. She and her boyfriend were driving on a winding road in Ithaca, New York. It was late on a September night; they were in a convertible. I don't remember anyone telling me exactly what happened, though I must have overheard, because the gruesome details of her death became part of the refrain in my head. I was supposed to leave for college in a few days. I remember my mother's saying that it was a terrible thing to have to start school so soon after yet another tragedy. "What's this world coming to?" she asked. I shrugged my shoulders and locked myself in my room. That night, I began to strip the posters and pictures off my bedroom wall and fill boxes with things to take to school.

The chapel where the funeral was held was hot and crowded. As the rabbi spoke and people wept, I thought of Miriam stroking my ordinary hair. I knew that after the service I had to go into a room where Suzi's parents and grandparents were receiving people, that I had to approach them and say, "I'm sorry." I could not imagine anything harder than facing them and saying those words. My body filled with that terrible heat. I walked forward, thinking how nothing could make me step into that room.

"I'm sorry," I said. And Miriam said, "I know." Then she said she liked my dress.

The next night, I looked up to see my mother standing in my doorway like an uneasy guest. My walls looked bruised, as if I had hurt them by leaving.

"Miriam wants you to have a few of Suzi's things," my mother said. "There's a watch and some skirts . . ."

"I'm not interested in her stuff," I said petulantly.

"She wants you to have it," said my mother.

I clenched my teeth and tried to shake from my memory Miriam's tenderness, the way she'd said, "like spun gold," and wept, *Oy got, oy got!* as if she had known that almost exactly a year after Laura's murder, her own daughter would be killed.

"You don't have to be ashamed," my mother said. But shame washed over me, a weird acid that softened my bones.

The morning after Laura's murder, I had taken the tranquilizers to numb me, when what I had desperately needed was to feel the wounds thrust deeply into my own heart. Once again, I said no, that I would not take anything of Suzi's. But I was too weak to resist, too eager to be good. The next day, when I climbed into my parents' car for the drive to college, Suzi's skirts were hanging on the hook above the back window.

We got on the highway, and left behind the empty bedroom with the bruised walls, the little girls who had played together in Queens, both of them dead. We were three ordinary people in a large sedan, Mom riding shotgun, but sitting sideways in the seat so we could talk. Surely my mother felt sad that she would return to an empty house, but she did not say and I did not feel an undercurrent of sadness. If anything, her enthusiasm filled the car. All that summer, she had expended her energy, getting me ready for this next step in my life. She'd bought me a new coat, a little black dress, suede pumps, lizard shoes, sweaters and skirts for casual dates. I liked to believe that moving to New York was my private dream, but I knew that she took great pleasure in the fact that I was living not just in New York but on Fifth Avenue—in her eyes, the height of elegance.

Cars were parked all along the curbside outside the dorm, their flashers blinking. Girls in tiny skirts made their way down the sidewalk, their weary, burdened parents trudging behind them. We pulled into a space beneath the awning. My father opened the trunk. Each of us took an armful of my things and squeezed into sections of the revolving door. I was eyeing the other girls, already seeking potential friends. We were so powerful suddenly, our parents, laden with our lamps and clothes and ratty stuffed animals, already hurtling toward irrelevance.

As soon as the cartons were loaded into my room and the skirts were in the closet, my parents began to fret about getting a parking ticket. Ever believers in the short goodbye, they kissed me quickly and left.

I walked into the closet. This was too great, I told myself. My parents were gone. I had no reason to feel so hollow inside. I was dressed in my favorite clothes—bright yellow turtleneck with thin navy stripes, jeans, sandals made of harness leather— and free at last. In my back pocket was the "dear jane" letter from SDS, proof that I was Jane, no questions asked. Everything was fabulous and yet I was unable to free myself of the hollowed-out feeling. Above me was a naked lightbulb. I pulled the cord and stood beneath the hot light, as if I were an egg in an incubator, waiting to hatch.

I don't know how long I stood under that hot light, only that I was still in the closet when the key turned in the lock and I heard my new roommate say, "What a dreary space!" I experienced her words as a revelation. Dreary, yes, with grayish walls and a view of an air shaft. I watched her touch each bed, scrutinize the wing chair, peer into the closet. "What a lot of skirts!"

she said, and a chill passed through me, as if the ghost of my past self had just wafted through the closet. I gave a slow shrug of privilege, passing easily as a girl who got whatever she wanted, a girl who knew comfort and ease.

When I stepped out of the closet, it was all gone, the years I had shared a room with my sister, the two of us talking deep into the night, the games we played, the feel of her arms around me, her scent, her green eyes, the shape of her hands, her bitten nails, her pride in me, the steadiness of her love. Gone were Laura's knife wounds, and the dark winding road where Suzi's body lay. All that was gone. And I had only love and despair, fluttering like moths above the rack of a dead girl's skirts.

My roommate, Leslie, was from the suburbs of Boston. With her pale skin, her sad blue eyes, and shaggy brown hair, she could have passed as my cousin. I would like to believe that our affection for each other would have grown even if I had not been so eager to adore her. But from the start I liked everything about her. Leslie was so much more sophisticated than I, knew what was done and what was not done, what was stunning, and what was "aesthetically unpleasing." She was funny, too, a gifted mimic, who launched into Southie accents, Latin accents, and vague, cartoonish Eastern European ones. She threw around French words, and, at her most serious, had a haughty way of speaking, in which she drew in air sharply and closed her eyes, so that everything she said, even the most trivial statements, seemed fraught with emotion. She was often sad, which shook me and bound me to her. She'd been a troubled child who suffered from night terrors and had tried to set her fingers on fire, and her parents, whom she called by their given names, had been forced to part with their cash, sending her to a succession of marvelous Teutonic men, all for naught, because really, she said, she was crazy as a loon.

I was awed. This was the era of R. D. Laing, *King of Hearts;* the notion that insanity was the sanest response to insane times was a popular one. I was not the only one who had the highest regard for the crazy, who used the term with no disparagement at all, but with envy and respect. If someone had asked me outright, I would have admitted that I wanted badly to be crazy myself, which for me meant eccentric, uninhibited, absolutely free, the opposite of how I saw myself, which was as an ordinary, "boojie" Jewish girl fettered in every imaginable way, raised in the most maligned, most ridiculous state in the Union. As for Leslie, she wasn't *really* crazy: she was witty and smart. From the start, without even knowing it, I began to absorb her mannerisms and inflections, her way of dressing, her habit of giving objects and people funny names, her dismissal of certain things as "not done." I adored whom she adored and shuddered with her at the sight of people she detested.

"Do I *like* her?" I heard her say of me on the phone one night. "She was sent from the heavens. Already we're quite attached."

I found myself saying and feeling exactly the same. My twin, my other half, heaven-sent.

If at first my love found a resting place, so did my despair. The war was raging, and no one seemed to care. It astonishes me to look back to September 1967 and see that, at the start, only four of us attended SDS meetings. We met in a coffee shop on University Place that had in the window a bust of Apollo, covered with a layer of dust as thick as fur. A long-limbed Egyptian-looking beauty from Queens, with heavy hair, bracelets up to her elbows, and rings on all her fingers. An articulate, well-informed, slightly spastic boy, who seemed to have no agenda outside of coffee-shop debate, and who often drooled or sprayed crumbs during a diatribe. His girlfriend reached over and wiped his face, as predictable and unobtrusive as a page turner at a piano recital. It was her sole contribution to our group, as far as I could tell.

Once I persuaded Leslie to join me at a meeting. When I pressed her for comments, she confessed that her views were much like mine. The war was bad. She knew that was the case. But that boy . . . showering her with crumbs . . . was unspeakable. She would not return.

I went without her. I could not stay away.

In a month there were a dozen of us. I never said a word. I listened to the others talk about a military action or a town destroyed, and an odd chemistry occurred. In the heat of my emotion, my language dissolved. Images formed. Skinny children, burned by napalm, ran barefoot down dusty roads, their agony raw and elemental before my eyes. I could taste the salt of their tears. Perhaps it was a deeply self-protective instinct that kept me from speaking, as if I somehow sensed on those evenings that I was like a poorly sewn garment, and so much as opening my mouth would cause me to split all my seams. I told myself that I didn't speak because I was not smart enough, never able to articulate what was closer to the truth: to speak about the war would make me cry, and if I began to cry, I would never stop.

It wasn't just in these meetings that I could not speak. The Jane who had risen from the ashes of Martha was a different being. Gone was the rambunctious girl whose arm shot up first in a classroom, who called, "Ooh, ooh!" waving her arm end-lessly, propping it up with the free one, leaning way over, kneeling on the seat, begging to be heard. The fervent beg-ging—"I have two things to say!"—the childish, "Oooh, *me!*" became "Who, me?" For this new self was raw and uninformed, with no history, no experience to draw on.

I found a place for myself in the movement in those early days. Maybe I was mute—"shy" was the way I thought of myself, though this was not really the case—but I could write, type, sit at tables, hand out leaflets.

I was the girl with the purple hands from all those late nights typing leaflets on mimeograph master sheets.

I was the girl outside Main Building, such a somber face, long hair parted in the middle, "like curtains," was how my mother described it. The girl who tried to tuck leaflets into everyone's hands.

Leslie and I found boyfriends. After a while, we decided we loved our boyfriends. We told them so one weekend. Soon after, we slept with them. It was the first time for both of us.

Sometimes when we were out in our floppy hats and ratty fur jackets, we shared the pleasure we took in our boyfriends. Jon, my boyfriend, was a short green-eyed boy with mutton-chop sideburns, a guitar player, a lover, as I was, of folk music, blues, and rock and roll, who early on in our relationship took to waggling a finger at me when I got vehement or giggly and saying, "Now, Jane, settle down." Because I was still strug-gling to tamp down the tiny edge of Martha that surfaced when I was happy, I secretly thought this bossy, dogmatic guy was good for me.

Leslie's boyfriend, Robert—a dear, she called him; a lamb—was tall and soft, with a bristly mustache and coarse hair that was already thinning in front and gave him a stolid, middle-aged look. His passions were poker, the French horn, and a book called *The Story of O*, about a woman's complete submission to a man. I knew this because Robert demanded that Leslie read it. She did, sadly, then passed it on to me. The book scared me. I wondered about his obsession. But she said he was a darling boy. Exquisitely sensitive.

Her eyes were sad when she sang his praises. Her voice had a catch to it. "Love is such wretched agony," she sometimes said. To please her, I agreed.

Often, when I returned from classes I found her sitting at her desk, looking at her untouched books propped between bookends, her colored pencils with uniform points, the vase of dried flowers. Sometimes I could see that she had rearranged these things. Perhaps the larger books had been moved to the center of the row this time. But I knew that mostly what she had done was sit. Sometimes she sat for hours. The sight of this filled me with panic—no one was home behind her eyes, no one within the shell of this girl I adored. I would drop my dog-eared, doodled-up books, the pages ruffled from highlighter, and try to make her laugh, to jolt her from this state. I danced around her, mocked her, flew into rages. Nothing helped. All I could do was wait for the day when her eyes were lively again, and we would be walking up Fifth Avenue, resplendent in Mimi the silver fox and Dora the skunk, and she would stop to gaze in a shopwindow and, seeing our reflection, say, "Look, Juana. Like two peas in a pod!" Then the world was right. Then there was no sister, no murder, no decapitated friend.

When Leslie was happy, I loved the world. I loved my classes and thought my professors were brilliant. I loved the city, my boyfriend, the mescaline we swallowed, the store on Bleecker Street where we spent hours looking at old records, the docks where we meandered. I loved the gull that wheeled over the greasy patches of the Hudson. An urban gull, like me, I thought. I even loved my aunt Dora, former owner of the skunk, for mocking my love for everything. "Love love love," she wrote to me that year. "Why don't you join my club instead, the *Ich hab zey in drerd* club, and say the hell with it all."

When the semester ended, my parents took Leslie and me out for lunch. We were to meet them at Lüchow's, an old German restaurant on Fourteenth Street; afterwards, they would take me home to New Jersey. I was tense and miserable all morning. If someone had asked me what I feared, I would have said "embarrassment." My parents might quarrel loudly at lunch; they might call me Martha, tell idiotic stories from my childhood, reveal how foolish and ordinary I was.

At noon, Leslie and I walked up Fifth Avenue, a wet wind in our faces. Leslie was miserable, too. She had gone to see Robert the night before, she said. His friends were coming over to play poker. Before they arrived, Robert locked her in the bathroom. He made her swear not to speak or cough or make any noise at all. She linked her arm through mine. At first it was funny, she said. She was sure that eventually one of them would need to pee and she could then pop out, like a girl in a cake. But hours passed. No one walked by the bathroom. Robert was so sensitive—to make a noise would be the ultimate betrayal. So she was stuck in there, with nothing to distract herself, not even reading material.

"By the time he let me out, I was a quivering mass of sheer nothingness," she said.

We were at the restaurant by then. "Please," she said, though I had not spoken. "This is not a topic for further discussion."

She pushed open the door.

The maître d' bowed formally when he saw us, a smile twitching at a corner of his lips. Charmed, perhaps, by our young faces and old furs.

The people I feared so dreadfully were sitting at a round table, my father in a blue shirt and tweed jacket, my mother in a mohair suit and a brilliant silk scarf. Handsome and stylish, both of them. They stood, took Leslie's hand, embraced me warmly. And then, before we could shake our napkins loose, they began to talk. My father named the main drag in Leslie's hometown, ticking off the stores in her area where he did business; my mother discussed the de Kooning exhibit they had recently seen. Happy noise that made the waiter back off, that left me peaceful at the periphery, wondering: What is wrong with me? Why am I so tense?

After lunch my parents and I retrieved the car and stopped at the dorm. I picked up my bags and got back into the car for the short ride back to New Jersey. We drove up West Side streets and then through the dark tunnel, leaving the sunny, glorious city behind.

I remember feeling surprised when we pulled into the driveway. The house looked just the same, inside and out. But it was as if a bomb had exploded. There was no sister, no murder, no history irrevocably changed, only rubble, which we stepped through wordlessly, and rage, like land mines, that made me fearful day and night. "Hate" was the word I gave to everything I felt when I was in my parents' house. "I just hate it here," I whispered to Leslie on the phone the next day. Then, sleepless in my narrow bed next to the empty one: I hate this room. I hated the suburbs and the name they kept calling me. I hated being called down to dinner, hated my mother, hated the silence, the conversations, my old friends, my self.

And yet each night after the dinner dishes were washed and put away, my mother and I played Scrabble, then sat on separate couches in the living room, talking late into the night. My father was always somewhere else. He might surface to have a snack, in which case he would offer to bring us one of his highly resistible concoctions, stewed prunes over ice cream, sandwiches with Russian dressing and cranberry sauce, a chicken carcass stripped of all but a few ribbons of flesh. My father so rarely talked to me that sometimes I imagined that he was an envoy from a remote country and my mother's principal duty to act as his interpreter, "his liaison," as she herself had written in a letter. "Your father says," the messages all begin. My father was thrilled to have me home, she said. My father thought I looked well. Meanwhile, I rarely saw him.

One night my mother and I quarreled about Dow Chemical, makers of napalm. Perhaps I boasted about the way we had disrupted company recruiters who came to school. My mother had read about this demonstration in *The New York Times* and said we were ill-mannered. The recruiters weren't forcing students to be interviewed; they had a right to be on campus.

This made me snort. She was *such* a liberal, I said, believing the radical line that liberals were worse than apolitical types, less tractable, more set in their ways. She could not possibly expect me to believe that manners counted when we were dealing with a corporation that made a chemical meant to burn the skin off children.

"The students had a choice of whether or not to go to the interviews," she said. "You're depriving them of that choice. You seem to forget that we live in a democracy."

"If Hitler came to your door, you'd ask him in for tea? You'd say, Pass the sugar, please? You'd politely discuss the issues?"

My mother was a far more skilled debater than I and knew better than to get waylaid by the Hitler reference. Immigrant daughter that she was, she brought up the Bill of Rights and the importance of free speech. She paraphrased Winston Churchill, and trumpeted the glories of democracy. But what she called freedom seemed to me a world of compromises, lies, imperialism, immorality, and it was ridiculous to think you could fight it by sane, liberal means.

When I spoke, though, all I could actually say was, "What a crock of bullshit!"

The lamps on their automatic timers switched off and left us in the dark. "So!" My mother laughed. "The best defense is offense?"

I was up from my seat, beyond words. I stomped up the stairs and locked myself in the bathroom, where, for the next half hour, I scrutinized my ridiculous, imperfect face in the mirror, as if I might learn something from my reflection.

If only I could drift down from the present and show my teenage self how much pleasure my mother took from these quarrels. Politics was her sport; debate the game she loved best. Even arguing was a connection, it seems now, a way to bring me out of hiding. If only I had understood how connected she felt to me, now that I was no longer so selfish and self-centered. If only I could have seen that we were on the same side, that my activism gave my mother an opportunity to remember her own.

How lively her letters were, full of cautions and instructions. She hoped I had an edifying experience when I demonstrated in Washington, D.C. I should be careful not to "sign anything or join anything" until I knew damn well I was "not being used." I should respect the other guy's point of view, make sure the subtractions were correct in my checkbook, congratulate my cousins on the birth of their baby boy. I should pay more attention to my spelling and be wary of extremists, because extremists at both ends were "terrific rabble-rousers."

What irked my mother was the despair I sank into after these visits. "I prefer happy letters," she wrote.

What worried her was my affection for my roommate.

"A lovely girl," she said of Leslie. "Absolutely delightful."

But when I said, "Yes, we're quite attached," her face froze.

"Is she your only friend?"

"I have other friends," I said, wary now.

"Don't get so dependent on her," she said. "It's not healthy to expect her to be your sister."

"I don't *expect* her to be anything," I said.

Leslie was sitting at her desk when I returned to school for spring semester. Day after day she sat listlessly.

I tried hard to bring her out of her funk. I hung weird ads on the wall, hoping she would be amused by the headlines: DOG NEARLY ITCHES TO DEATH! and I LOST HALF OF MYSELF WITHOUT TAKING DIET PILLS! I bought her a pet mouse, demanded conversation, tried to ignore her. I wrote her letters, hectoring her and praising her.

She proclaimed the weird ads "aesthetically unpleasing." I ripped them off the walls. She confessed that she loathed rodents. I put a notice on the board, and in forty-eight hours the rodent was gone. But still I could not make her smile.

If not for the war, I would have spent all my spare time trying to please her.

SDS had grown huge by then. The university had given us space to meet, rooms big enough to accommodate fifty or more people, and now strangers stood up front, young, articulate guys who claimed to promote the organization of leaderless, nonhierarchical groups while never for an instant ceding their power. Men with thinning hair, in red-and-black-plaid lumber jackets and shiny black shoes, attended the meetings, as did students from other schools, bent on radicalizing the elevator operators.

We broke up into study groups and ad hoc groups. I joined a guerrilla theater troupe that had just formed, swayed by a discussion about the weakened impact of peaceful protest, which was becoming as banal and annoying as a jackhammer. We would promote activism by dramatizing the horror of the war, making people respond viscerally. And we would force them to attend by performing without notice in a public place. But first, since we were nonprofessionals, we had to do some body work, to learn how to move and how to act with conviction.

The theater group met in a room that had gym mats on the floor. The leader talked to us about our bodies and went on at length about control and letting go. To gain control, we had to relax and clear our minds completely—these two things together—until our bodies melted into the mats and we became as loose as babies sleeping in the sand.

I was sitting on the mat, trying to figure out this contradiction, when the leader clamped his hands on my shoulders. "Wow," he said. "Are you ever uptight."

It was the worst insult in an era in which the world was made up of us and them: *They* were uptight, *we* were relaxed. We were free spirits. We could be boneless and sink to our knees.

But I couldn't.

It became a skill I had to master, a job as crucial as learning to avoid the police horses used for crowd control at demonstrations. Nights I stayed late and practiced dropping to my knees on a mat and rolling onto my side. Eventually I got good enough to choose, for our upcoming performance, to be an innocent Vietnamese peasant, killed in the rice paddies by GIs. I began to collapse in the hall of my dorm. I could fold from the waist and end up sprawled in bed. Going boneless became an obsession, my sport, the proof that I could be everything I was not.

While I was busy learning to be boneless, Leslie was getting quieter and more removed. When she wasn't with her boyfriend, she slept a lot, cut most of her classes, floated around our room with a vague, anesthetized-looking smile on her sweet, pale face.

If I could relax and be boneless, everything would fall into place. I would not be upset when she would not talk to me. I would go with the flow. I would be cool when she sat in the room looking at the wall. My heart would not thump.

One day, she disappeared. We were supposed to meet in the room at six, but a half hour passed and then an hour. I thought about what I would say when finally she did show up, how I would use the words "tardy" and "cross" in my mocking reprimand, those being the most uptight, schoolteacher words I could unearth.

I listened to the voices of girls walking down our corridor, waiting for the elevator to take them down to the Crystal Room before the cafeteria closed. Lots of them I liked. All I had to do was write Leslie a note and join them. But I was afraid to leave the room. It was as if I believed that Leslie was in danger and her safety depended on my staying behind the locked door.

She did not show up that night or the next day. The world outside my room was treacherous. I could not leave. I could not talk to anyone. I cut my classes and stood sentry by the door. At the end of the day, when hunger overtook me, I planned my exit with utmost care, listening at the door until I was sure the corridor was silent.

Then I walked downstairs with my head high, a parody of a girl absorbed by higher things. It was early, and the only diner was an old man in a blue shirt, alone at a table for two. He doffed his imaginary hat at the girl who pretended to be lost in her thoughts. I brought the tray back to my room, locked the door, and stored the food on the windowsill.

On the third day, I was walking into our room with a tray when I saw Leslie sitting at her desk.

"Where were you?" I said.

She listlessly arranged her pencils, light to dark.

"You just leave? You just one day disappear?" I was like a woman betrayed, my hands flying, rage making my voice quavery and shrill. "And now you don't even have the courtesy to look at me?"

She turned. Her face was utterly blank, as if she were dead inside. It was the look I would see on my sister's face, when later I would dream of her. Unreachable. No matter what I said or did, nothing would change. I ranted on, aware of how ugly and ridiculous I was in my useless rage, how meaningless my accusations, for even as I was shouting, "I had no idea where you were! I thought you were hurt!" I knew where she had been, and that she could not talk.

. . .

We drifted back into our life together. We were friends again. We braved the cold in floppy hats and black boots, Leslie in Dora and me in Mimi. "Adorable," she would say, linking arms with me to steady herself on the ice.

The world was glorious again, my classes fascinating, even math, where I had no idea what was going on. The man in my freshman comp class, with thighs so powerful the little hinged desktop did not fit flat across his lap, revealed himself to be a major league baseball player; the guy on the bongos outside our dorm played with Richie Havens and was happy to demonstrate bongo basics to any girl who asked.

Life was so great that the next time Leslie disappeared I was as stunned and unprepared as the first time. I had no memory of the past event. I could not comfort myself, could not stop the floodwaters of panic that rose inside me. I knew that she was with her boyfriend, somehow held captive by him, but I imagined her like a stray dog, wandering in the streets, easy prey. I stood by the door for hours. I went over to her desk, contemplated leaving bite marks on her beautiful, unused pencils. In her desk drawer were pretzels in an unopened bag. Her belongings puzzled and saddened me, everything lovely and untouched. Notebooks with empty pages, unopened books. Shirts in cellophane. A still life.

I listened to the flow of laughter in the hall, voices moving closer until I heard a knock on my door. My body was a leaden thing, all pulsating misery. "Jane?" I could not look through the peephole or answer the door. "Someone is there," I heard a girl say. A note slid under the door—not Leslie's handwriting. I left it there.

She did not come home.

My windowsill was crowded with uneaten food—green Jell-O speckled with soot, apples, cottage cheese gone pink, bitter cups of icy coffee. Back in the room I tried on my coolie hat and peasant's dress, socks beneath the straw sandals I had bought on Eighth Street. I looked at myself in the mirror. It was winter in New York, but not in Southeast Asia, where I worked in the rice fields. I was going to die the next day. I was going to be laboring quietly, a peaceful soul, and an American, someone I had never met, a stranger with war in his heart, was going to kill me.

I slid into my bed and waited to be overtaken by sleep.

I suppose I did sleep, because that night I dreamed that the world was coming to an end, the whole world, and not just me. Everyone would be dead. In the logic of the dream, this was cause for, if not exactly celebration, then great relief. I wasn't going to die alone. In the dream world it was spring, and the trees, like the huge maples on my parents' street, were pale green, and the pug noses, the seed pods, rustled in the wind. Everything was lush and beautiful; the air fragrant from blossoms and vanilla from the cookie factory upwind of our house. My childhood was sweet in the dream, and I was stripped of all cynicism and restlessness and loved my street and town. The thought that all this beauty would vanish seemed a tragedy. Everything would die—a leaf, the striated tree trunks, the squirrels. How could I not have seen this?

I began to weep in a way I never did in life. I cried so violently that I woke myself from the dream. I sat up. My olive bedspread was folded in thirds at the foot of my bed. My face was sticky with tears and snot, and my shoulders and chest felt bruised. But the weeping continued, disembodied, as if it had left my body and taken a place somewhere else in the room.

Which it had, because when my eyes adjusted I realized that Leslie was sitting in her own bed, crying in the dark.

. . .

The next morning I woke ready to die. I got out of bed and dressed in my peasant garb—straw hat, black dress, and sandals. I shoved my books into my canvas sack and shuffled down Fifth Avenue. The cold was bitter and my inner knees were chafed. No one's gaze lingered on me. I was unremarkable to passersby, just a peasant.

I had Spanish class first and was a minute or so late. My beautiful teacher circled my chair. She put her hands on her slender hips and looked me over—the hat, the dress, my reddened feet in sandals. In her sweet, melodic voice, she said, "¿Qué pasa, Juanita?"

I looked up. How could I tell her en español when I could not even find the words in English?

After class, I walked across Washington Square to the Student Center. It was an unfamiliar place to me, the domain of commuter students. I was surprised how crowded it was. The couches and chairs were all taken, the tables cluttered with notebooks and sandwiches in waxed paper. The air smelled of burnt coffee and hard-boiled eggs. Through speakers mounted high, the Hollies sang "Bus Stop."

I passed a love seat where four girls were squeezed together, peeling wrappers from candy bars. The GIs closed in then, hefting their plastic rifles. I knelt in the rice paddies, afraid of everything. I was thinking how much I loathed the song, when they shot me.

My knees buckled. I collapsed in front of the four girls and writhed slowly at their feet. They ate their candy, completely unmoved.

8

WHEN I LOOK DOWN on the girl who feigned death on the Student Center floor, who do I see?

A girl who rises, dusts off her peasant dress, and walks with her chin held high, proudly, willfully meeting no one's gaze.

She has forgotten her sister and everything she overheard about her sister's death. But the murder will stay with her as a feeling, a refrain, a nightmare. She will struggle to feel worthy of being alive and not know why. She will feel unworthy of tenderness, skeptical of attention. Fear is what she trusts and so she courts it unknowingly. Fear pierces her armor, wakens her. When she is afraid, her heart pounds; she calls it love.

Years later, she will seek out murderers, as if they can teach her what she most needs to learn. She will contact a man released from prison after seventeen years and arrange to meet him for breakfast. She will sit across the table from him, fascinated and repelled by his powerful hands and burly forearms. When he tells her that in prison he dreamed his crime over and over, and woke each morning haunted by the absolute irrevocability of his deed, she will feel that the two of them are alike beneath the skin. She, too, dreams a crime over and over. She, too, is haunted by its absolute irrevocability. Her dreams are veiled, the knowledge of the murder reduced to an odd refrain, *four times, twice.*

But the girl who walks up Fifth Avenue has no sister. She has no reason to be sad.

She walks into the revolving door, waits for the elevator.

No one is in her room. She locks herself inside. Later someone will knock on her door. The sound is like gunfire; the voices, the sound of her name, even her new name, fill her with terror.

But she is okay. Look, she is fine. She has an exam coming up. She opens her book and loses herself in the pleasure of small details. *Ma, Ma, where's my Pa? Going to the White House, ha ha ha.* She meets a friend for soup at Zum-Zum. Catches a flick at the Eighth Street Playhouse. She does not starve herself, cut herself with razors, flunk out of school. She does not sit around with a long face. She will not look for sympathy.

Time passes. It's the winter of 1970 now. I am walking up Second Avenue, dreamy and cheerful, when I see my friend Brad. How is this possible? Brad has dropped out of school—like Leslie and Jon—and moved to Santa Cruz.

What good friends we had been, part of a larger group but always seeking each other out. *Really* close, and at the same time careful to keep our distance by defining ourselves somewhat too often. Friends, good friends. Friends from school, and from the Fillmore, the rock theater where both of us had jobs. Brad was the head usher. I was a "candy chick" at first and worked in front of a huge ornate mirror at the downstairs concession.

Stoned customers would slap down their money for Milk Duds, then lose blocks of time staring at their own reflections.

Brad left New York after our sophomore year; Jon and I split up. I moved from the dorm into an apartment, and at the Fillmore, graduated from being a candy chick to being a "box-office crazy." Never again would I feign death. Never would I be so raw and needy with a friend, the way I was with Leslie. I was over that, a healthy girl, "very together." I worked hard, made dean's list, began dreaming of a future after graduation. The day I saw Brad, I had just come from the narrow, flea-ridden, graffitied little box office and was walking up Second Avenue to a little dairy restaurant called B & H, where I could get soup and bread for fifty cents.

It's like this: a gray day, the passersby somber and woebegone. Ukrainian women in babushkas, and hippies with matted hair, everyone in black and white. And then Brad, a flash of color, everything about him—the way he bounces when he walks, joy his natural state, so that we do not simply meet, but fall in step together, Brad's arm around my shoulder. He brushes his cheek against my fur. "Meet Dora," I say. And he says, "Dora, baby."

We keep walking as if we had planned to meet like this. Walking, deep in conversation that feels as if it has no start and never needs to end. Maybe we have soup, and maybe we stop and look at books. Time seems not to exist, and yet I know it passes because the sky darkens. We smoke a joint on Astor Place and take the IRT downtown. Brad and I are alone in the car until the next stop, when a man steps on, rumpled, dressed in a loose-fitting coat, from which he extracts an onion, and then another. I hang loosely from the strap, stoned, digging the motion of the train, the way my limbs loosen and my body weaves to sway with it. The man lines up the onions on the floor, but perfectly. Brad throws his head back in laughter. The city is a circus: I am such a happy spectator.

We move to the door. Brad is right behind me. When our station approaches, I lean back against his chest. He wraps his arms around me, and I intone like the narrator of a TV show: "There are eight million stories in the Naked City. *This* is one of them."

The doors open. We step back, get a last look at the man realigning his onions.

The station is sharp-smelling and scary: a urinal. We rush outside, toward the ferry terminal.

As soon as we enter the building, we hear the ferry's mournful horn. We jam our nickels into the slots, gallop up the ramp and onto the boat, breathless, filled with self-congratulations. We made it, wow, we did.

Not that we have a destination, really. We're just here for the ride.

We take our place on the prow. It's a bitter night, and Brad is a navy brat from warmer places: Honolulu, San Diego. He goes belowdecks to get warm. The frigid air blows through Dora. Pinpricks of icy water burn my cheeks. I am about to give up and join Brad when I see the lights from the Statue of Liberty.

I cannot bear to think of my parents; their voices, their faces, are like a knife in my chest. But I think with tenderness and ease of my grandfather, whom I never knew. His story is as remote as a fairy tale: wicked stepmother, horse-drawn cart. Protecting his wife, fleeing with her from Okno to Balta to Rotterdam, across the ocean to New York to see what I was seeing then.

Brad returns. I begin to tell him my grandfather's tale, when suddenly the shell of the story cracks open. Inside is a dead mother, a new name, a lost language, buried children, so many farewells. My chest feels heavy.

"My father *loved* children!" my mother always said. Loved to take them to the movies and to the circus. "Nothing made him happier than the sound of children laughing."

"My father would not let my mother cry," my mother said. "Crying was forbidden. Even at weddings and happy times. It was too European, he said. He did not allow it."

Didn't *allow* it? As if his sadness were something he could place in a box and bury on the distant shore. Maybe he believed that when he crossed the ocean, his sorrow became as useless as his mother language.

"I never cried, but you should," my mother said. "It's good for you. Tears cleanse the soul." She meant this, but something twisted inside her when she heard a child cry. Something made her mocking and mean. "Look at her with her big upside-down mouth; *oy*, the *shraying*." "Waaaah," she sang, her voice a siren. And my father bleated, "Maaaaah," until I was frantic and hysterical from shame. And when I cried harder, they laughed harder, pointing fingers and bleating.

It is dangerous to feel such strong emotions. Easier to mock, to hate, to turn away.

Easier to say, as I do of Brad: He's just a friend. When he asks if he can spend the night with me, it's okay, because we're friends. This is something you do for friends; they need a place to stay, you let them crash. And when he squeezes into bed beside me, that's cool, too; the floor is hard, the chill has followed us both inside. Brad is warm and smells good. "Love the one you're with," the song says. It's what you're supposed to do, unless you're uptight.

The sun floods the apartment in the morning. When I open my eyes and see him, I'm all churned up inside, my stomach full of burrs. His face is sweet: warm eyes and lank pale hair. You'd think I have a morning job, the way I rush out of bed. He reaches for me, but I slip free and stay out of reach. I'm good at this. I give just enough that people rarely know how carefully I keep my distance.

He comes up from behind. I'm like his cat, he says. Always watching, checking things out. But look, he says, trying to hold me. Soon as I am in his arms, I'm wiggling loose, ready to jump.

Well, he's leaving, isn't he?

Not exactly—he still has one more day, twenty-four hours to convince me to join him. "You might just—entertain the possibility," he says, laughing at his own language.

Because I know it's impossible, I allow myself to picture what he describes, the little rented house near the beach, the tolerant town with surfers and hippies. The blue skies and warm sun.

"Your skin is so pale," he says. "You need to blossom. Maybe I'll kidnap you; maybe *that's* how I'll get you to come with me."

The next morning I give him my backpack, on which I've written in laundry marker, *When you ain't got nothin' you got nothin' to lose*, lyrics from "Like a Rolling Stone." Then we take the subway uptown to catch the airport bus. When we arrive, there is already a long line of passengers. "Write me, okay?" I say, just as I had said to my sister's fiancé four years before.

I walk off, feeling wistful. Only when he's gone can I wish that I could have stayed with him. Only then can I hear the sound of his laughter, see him throw his head back, remember his saying, "Maybe I'll kidnap you."

· · ·

We wrote the whole time we were apart. Letters gave me distance and connection, just as they had with my parents. Brad mailed long letters, full of rambling tales about his housemates and his busboy job. He had been president of his Hawaiian high school class, the adventurous, "most likely to succeed" type of guy who'd chosen a college halfway across the world. Now, he wrote, he'd lost all motivation. He'd shelved his plans to go back to school, had no urge to sleep with the girls who wandered through the house he shared, including the occasional one who drifted into bed beside him.

I appreciated the bleak humor in Brad's letters, never sensing the despair that is so vivid to me now. In return, I revealed to him the details of my secret desires. I was so puffed up with plans. Not a husband or children, not a bottomless stash of recreational drugs, or money to buy pretty things. I wanted to be published.

Even forming the words sent a shiver of longing through my body. I wanted it so terribly I often wondered what bargain I would strike, what part of my body I would be willing to sacrifice—arm, leg, finger? Without question I was ready to give up a piece of flesh to attain my dream. Somehow, it had not yet occurred to me that I had to write to make the dream come true, and not just letters to Brad, in which I described my Epiphany: how one night, while sitting on a crosstown bus that was winding through Central Park, I had read that Carson McCullers had published her first novel, *The Heart Is a Lonely Hunter*, at twenty-three. When the bus stopped on York Avenue, I stepped outside. The moment my foot hit the pavement I knew it was my destiny to do the same, to publish *my* first novel by that age, too. That I had no notion what my novel would be about did not seem to be an impediment: in those days, I

believed that will was enough. I rushed through school, graduating in January 1971, a half year early. Then I borrowed my
mother's portable typewriter and started to type.

After a few months, I had several hundred pages. I decided
to consult my former journalism professor, who occasionally
took me to lunch, a soft-spoken, elderly man with a pink face
and hair combed flat across his head. He volunteered to read
my pages. A week after I gave him the manuscript, he suggested we meet at his favorite place, a Chinese restaurant on
East Eighth Street. He sat across the small table, fondling my
knee and lavishing great praise on my work. The praise continued unabated through lunch, until, over litchi nuts, sweet,
slimy, straight from the can, he told me that he would take the
book, providing I had a carbon copy of it, and act as my unoffi-
cial agent. He had many friends in publishing, he said, giving
my knee a squeeze.

Extremely ticklish, I peeped like a bird.

He studied me for a moment. "You don't seem very gloomy,"
he said. This observation seemed to trouble him. "The novelists I know are a very gloomy lot. Not journalists: they're often
cheerful. But with novelists it's different."

"Oh, I'm *sometimes* gloomy!" I said, flushing defensively.

"Well." He sighed, and paid the check.

I had a new boyfriend at the time, yet another member of the
"Fillmore Family." Alex was a tall, gangly guy who wore his
unruly curls in the kind of Jewish-boy Afro Leslie called an
Isro. He was passionate and intense, a wearer of berets, a lover
of Godard, Truffaut, Capra, and Hawks, a star of his film
school class and member of the light show that had residence

at the Fillmore. By the fall of my senior year, we had moved in together and were, in the parlance of our relatives, "serious." In fact, we were serious. We were also fierce and ambitious, ravenous in the way we read, listened to music, and went to the movies, two and three in a row, emerging into the light only long enough to find where the next two features were playing. We were molelike, Alex and I, our pleasures all in dark places.

The Fillmore closed in June 1971, and the light show, Alex included, was hired to help convert four palatial old movie theaters in London, each with a different theme, into seatless, featureless dance halls for rock concerts. Alex and I had talked about my joining him there, taking whatever paying jobs were available to those without a work permit, and continuing to write my second book. I was so gullible and full of hope that I called the journalism professor to ask what he thought about this move.

The professor thought my plan to live in London was grand. He didn't say as much, but I could hear what he was thinking over the line: if gloomy was a prerequisite I seemed to lack, maybe London, with its damp, gray climate, would increase my chances of success.

And so that fall I moved, far away from home, five years and thousands of miles from the scene of the crime, with my only-child name and a boyfriend as affable and quietly wounded as I was.

When I arrived in London, Alex was already living in a dingy flat in the northwest part of the city. The poverty was apparent in the sameness of the streets: four-story attached houses, row after row, for miles in every direction. I was more used to the poorer New York neighborhoods, with their shattered glass, spray-painted curses, cars on cement blocks, screaming children: here it was dead still. Our building faced the side of the theater where Alex worked, an alarming black wall with a fire escape that zigzagged across the façade. Alex got me a key to the theater so I could take a bath in a heated room, since in our building there was only one unheated bathroom for all the tenants, and one toilet.

Sometimes, after my bath, I would sit in the empty theater and write letters to Brad. I thought of Brad in the same way I thought of the *zeyde* I had never met, as someone who evoked deep feelings inside me but seemed so unreachable it was as if he were already dead. I never wrote about myself or Alex, but instead described everything around me with great care and great distance. I remember writing him about the theater's domed ceiling, with houselights arranged as constellations, the Moorish villages with palm trees and mosques on either side of the stage, the mosaic walls and fountains in the lobby, the goldfish pools, all the grandeur that would soon be demolished.

For a while Alex and I had a great time. It wasn't merely that his interests and sense of humor were similar to mine, or that he had grown up in the same county. We were both chameleon-like and knew how to fit in quietly. In London, we were restrained by day, quick to decipher the complex social code encrypted in familiar words. We kept our voices low and stood in queues, compliant, blending easily. But entering our flat was like unlocking the door to the theater. Inside our bed-sitter, we stripped off all that chafed and oppressed us. Alone, we had sex, drugs, and rock and roll. Alone we had "our kids."

"Our kids" were what we called the series of characters I had invented, each with a different voice. Stuffy, Fluffy, Muffy—

there were others I can no longer recall. Alex was the straight man for these routines, which we launched into at home or in the street. In my memory, we were riotous, always collapsing into walls or each other's arms, weak with laughter.

Perhaps it was the news from home, or lack of it, that led to things changing. Alex's friends from film school had begun to get work in L.A. The professor had stopped answering my letters. We never spoke of our fears, but I knew that his desire to be a famous film director had begun to feel out of reach, just as I knew that no one was going to publish my novel. Nothing had ever stopped us before, and though we were far from ready to quit, it became clear that we had nothing apart from our dreams for success, no contingency plans, no escape routes.

We went to more movies, losing ourselves for hours in darkness. We adopted new kids, moguls and harebrained starlets. We began to hurt each other. We didn't mean to do this. It was just that we were young and aching inside.

I grew ill that winter, wheezy and short of breath. At first I thought, what a grand adaptation! For when I stood on the platform to wait for the tube—I was by then a typist in a cigarette-lighter repair shop—it seemed as if I was surrounded by people with phlegmy coughs and tuneful breathing. I thought of myself as one of the crowd, until it got so bad that I could no longer climb straight up to our flat without pausing on each landing.

I wore clogs in those days. Each time I made my slow, noisy ascent, the door on the second floor would open. Four Irish girls named Mary lived in this flat. The red-haired Mary liked to lean out and ask, "Where's Alex?" She flirted so outrageously and publicly with him that at first I viewed her as good material for another "kid." But often when I came home from work I found Alex and the red-haired Mary sitting over a cup of tea or laughing on the stairs in a way that did not invite my company. And I would continue up alone, open the door to our bedroom, and feel as if my breath were being snatched from me.

I went to a doctor at last, a quiet man who wore a linty vest. He listened to my chest and tapped on my back and asked me who was looking after me. When I paused, he patted my hand and checked me into a hospital.

There, away from the moldy flat that had made me sick, I recuperated quickly from bronchitis and a dreadful-sounding disease called "glandular fever" (mono, I later found out). I read long Russian novels, wrote letters, and submitted several times a day to inhalation therapy, using a device with tubes and corks and a ceramic canister that was positively eighteenth-century.

Except for Alex's occasional, uncomfortable visits, I was alone for nearly two weeks. This gave me plenty of time to mull over issues in my life. I had turned twenty-three and was not published. Nor was publication around the bend. I was not angered by the professor's silence, merely embarrassed, since, during my hospital stay, I realized that what I had given him were indeed pages and not much more. There was something else I knew. Alex was cheating on me, if not with a Mary, then with someone else. I had no evidence. I simply knew. Perhaps I had known before, but I had been strong enough to elbow the evidence aside, and now, flat on my back, I wasn't.

I was released from the hospital, cured of what ailed me, but tormented by the suspicion of Alex's infidelities. I could not question him in a normal voice, but Fluffy could ask, in her whispery, hiccuppy, hesitant voice, batting her eyelashes.

Fluffy began to ask all the time. She might be phrasing a question about the Tory Party, full of malapropisms, when the question came out. She might be in the middle of an addled discourse on Mickey Mouse's sexual orientation—*What's with the little shorts!*—when she would ask.

Alex grabbed at his sides. He chortled and honked, fell off stools, his lanky arms and legs flailing. He was such a goose, we were both geese: awkward, mated for life.

Then one afternoon we were sitting in the neighborhood pub with Alex's old friend from Chicago. Perhaps Alex felt safe in this public place, because we were shooting the breeze, talking lightly about past loves, when a confession began to roll from him: an old girlfriend; a member of the light show; his room, our flat, her loft.

His friend shifted in his seat, face flushed from discomfort. I began to laugh, a little at first, and then wildly. And when the laughter ebbed, it was not I who spoke up, but the evil Pancho Bastardnak, Russian–Mexican spy novelist, saying, "Beware, gringo, I have revenge *een* my heart."

We got funnier after that, but I had no means to face the hurt, apart from what I had done the night of Laura's murder. A current of unspoken despair wafted through our days. It was so lonely now. With all the voices of all our "kids," still he had no language to speak of his frustrations, and I had no words for the ways I felt betrayed.

In the spring of 1973, we returned to the States. We had lost our apartment in New York, so we moved back to our childhood homes in New Jersey. Of course we would live together again, we said. We were just crashing with the parents until we found work.

Even now I cannot bring myself to remember the details of my stay, only that I slept in my old bedroom, next to the neatly made bed against the wall, mailed out cover letters and résumés to scores of jobs I did not want, and had screaming fights with my mother that left me so battered and disoriented that sometimes in the morning I could not tell if they had really happened or I had dreamed them. To my mother, Alex and I were luftmenschen, people who lived on air, dreamers, impractical souls who thought we could eat stardust and sleep in the clouds. Maybe she was right. I felt aloft and ungrounded, as if some living piece of myself had been left behind in my travels. Alex and I had history and things in common, but we had lost the key to that private room. I was numb and miserable, so distanced that when he said, "Do Stuffy," I looked at him as if he had asked me to dress in drag.

Still, I visited him often. He was living with his mother, a difficult woman, embittered by her divorce and her former husband's remarriage to a perky, much younger woman, a shiksa, and could not spare her son the continual grinding agony she experienced. I knew that I was supposed to favor his father, who was lively and ingratiating, but I found myself drawn to his mother nonetheless.

Of course I knew her history: She had grown up in Poland during the war. When the Nazis invaded, her family was able to obtain a passport for her that had once belonged to a woman of similar age and coloring who was in a mental institution. Mrs. A., with her fair skin and green eyes, was able to flee to France, where cousins took her in, but her sister had not survived.

One night, she asked if I had any sisters or brothers.

"No," I said.

"An only child!" she said. "Spoiled, I suppose."

"Not really," I said.

Alex looked up from his book and said, "Was, too."

I had seen a picture of Mrs. A.'s sister. She had the long, straight nose and delicate mouth that Alex and his mother had, but her eyes were dark and deep-set, the kind of eyes that children in concentration camps always seemed to have. Even after all her years in this country, even with her honey-colored hair, her swanlike neck and long, graceful figure; even in her newly renovated kitchen with the adjoining family room, Mrs. A. had the look of someone who had lost a lot.

I never told her about my sister because I didn't have a sister. Then one night, during a lively talk about family vacations, I said, "My sister and I . . ."

My sister. How shaken I was to hear these words, which I had not even known were inside me. My sister. I had never slipped, never thought or said "my sister," not since her murder. And yet what I wanted, sitting at that table, was for someone to say, "What sister?" and demand that I tell what had happened. I could not speak of my own accord. I needed someone to shake the truth out of me, to slap me, to demand I tell the story, to use any means to make me speak her name. But no one said a word.

By the summer, Alex and I had found jobs and a place to live, a sunny, rent-stabilized apartment in the West Village, patrolled by a super so vigilant she would prop herself on her broom and query visitors when she did not like their looks.

Alex began to drive a cab—a job he seemed not to mind. On the nights when he took the late shift, he prepared elaborate dinners that were ready for me when I returned home from work.

I know I urged Alex to move to L.A. He was wasting his talent by staying in New York. While he was begging for tips, his friends from film school had begun to accrue real credits. But I see now that I pushed him to leave, for the same reason I stared at strange men in bars. I needed to know what would happen next. This rash action would jump-start me, wake me up, I believed. I couldn't imagine what it would be like when he moved. But two things were clear: he needed to live where he could work, and I needed to find out whether I would survive without him.

I had taken a job as an assistant editor for a magazine called *Intimate Story,* the kind of quasi-lurid publication we'd called a confessions magazine as kids, though the preferred name in the industry was "romance" magazine. This name was rather a hoot, since the stories themselves, all of them told in first person, featured women haunted by the conviction that they were unnatural or immoral, telling tales of rape, illicit sexual desires, cheating men, and unwanted pregnancy, an emotional spectrum that ran from guilt and shame to remorse—markedly short on romance.

The office had a spooky lost-in-time quality, fat oak desks, manual typewriters, cubicles divided by frosted glass. It looked more like the set of a B detective movie from the thirties than the publishing arm of a large media conglomerate.

Frances, the woman who hired me, was an emaciated, damp-skinned physical wreck of a woman, wry and remote, a former beauty—I knew this because she kept a movie poster on her wall from her brief career as a starlet. She seemed to require it less as a reminder of how lovely she had been than as a measure of how decrepit she had become, for she was frequently castigating herself. "Ugly!" she would moan, and I would hop up from my seat, thinking she was calling me. "Fool!" she would mutter into the mirror she propped against the Thermos of spiked coffee she carried everywhere.

How did I end up here? My résumé was blank, my experience completely unrelated to this job—my employment thus far had been as an office worker in a cigarette-lighter repair shop, a veterinary assistant (where I learned to squeeze cats with blockages in their urethras), and a light show "artist" for a musical called *Rock Carmen*. I can only guess that Frances hired me for my steady hands, since she had too much of a tremor to measure proofs, or for the steady, forthright look in my eyes. To all the world, I was a steady girl.

Frances's state did not dampen her wit or loosen her professional standards. If she had any love left in her, it was for language. The copy she handed me was flawless: she knew her stuff. She also kept a list of favorite misspellings and passages culled from manuscripts in which writers described their characters as "ughly" or "ball headed." Roy "fired a shit" that killed an assailant; handsome Brett drove a Merce-Benzedes. Frances's life might have been short on joy, but many times her barking laugh would filter over the wall of my cubicle and I would find her with her head on the desk, pounding weakly with her fist, coughing, howling. I would edge closer until she could compose herself to read, "It's a two-way street in the sea of marriage." Or, "Whoever imagined I would fall in love with a goy like Ted?"

At lunch one day my friend in production said, "If you think Frances is interesting, wait until you meet Eleanor. She is so inspiring. She's had *such* an amazing life."

Eleanor lived in the same building as Frances, several blocks from mine. For many years, she had been the editor of *Intimate Story* and now, retired and too infirm to leave her apartment, she worked for us as a freelance proofreader. My friend encouraged me to take the opportunity to hand-deliver and pick up the proofs.

Eleanor's apartment was not much bigger than mine, but it had been inhabited for a lifetime and was jammed with haphazard stacks of books and paper, stuffed furniture, and threadbare Oriental rugs. On a chair, nearly immobile, was Eleanor. She seemed ancient to me, her body covered by a shawl, so that all I saw was the clawlike hand, and the glass of rye on the chair's flat arm. She was happy to tell me the stories that had thrilled my friend from work, stories I'm sure I could not have asked to hear, since I was too shy to do anything but stand in the doorway of the apartment until she waggled her hand and said in a voice of mocking despair, "Oh, just *move* something and *sit*."

I was too timid to excuse myself, to turn down the glass of rye she proffered, or the refill. I did not know how to fake or decline. I did not understand that we had entered an arrangement: she would keep talking as long as I drank with her. That was how I got to hear how she had grown up on the Main Line, the daughter of a Philadelphia scion, a banker or stockbroker; something like that. The young Eleanor in her middy blouse and skirt at Bryn Mawr, where she graduated with high honors. Eleanor pushed toward marriage to boys who did not interest her in the slightest, dull boys who led dull lives.

And then—jutting her chin forward, brushing back the strand of fuzzy gray hair—she had left home, a thing not done. Arrived all by herself at Pennsylvania Station, the *old* Penn Station, in her straw hat, carrying her gladstone. All by herself, walked down to the Village. Stayed in a residence for young ladies until she found a place to live. Took a lover in the days when nice women didn't.

I loved these stories. I downed the rye like medicine, loathing the taste, and listened, barely interjecting a word. I got so drunk I could see the woman who had shucked off her patrician family's expectations. I could see her standing with her straw hat in Penn Station in the 1920s, young and tall, nearly as pretty as Frances, with that upturned chin, and that wonderful diction, a woman of good breeding and education. I could see her orient herself with her chin held high.

I might leave Eleanor's apartment and find myself standing under the bright lights of the produce department at Sloan's, holding a grapefruit in my hand, not knowing exactly how I had gotten there. Or I might end up walking east to the apartment where I had lived three years before, instead of westward and home. And I would think that Eleanor was just like Dorothy Parker, and think it as the highest praise. At twenty-four I saw Eleanor as someone to emulate, brave and independent, clever enough to spar with men. I did not see the waste or loneliness. My friends at work were younger versions of Frances and Eleanor, clever women, smart women. I did not see how emblematic they were of a certain kind of woman of a certain age in a certain city, witty, brittle, remote, their wit like a grate above a yawning crater. But I was heading in that direction, walking with a determined gait, eager to catch up.

On a night in the fall of 1973, I stood with Alex on the corner of Bleecker and Seventh Avenue South, waiting for a cab that would take him to the airport. I wish I could time-travel. I wish I could go back, way back, not to the street corner, since by then it was too late, but to the pub in London, so I could shriek and wail and say, "How *could* you?" and all those weak, unoriginal, pathetic things we end up saying when we have been hurt to the core. And maybe then we could have worked things out. Maybe then, after enough tears and apologies and time, we would have been over it. Or, if not, at least we might have parted before we moved back to the States, before that evening on the street corner, and the months that followed, in which I did get back, tormenting him as I flailed about in my own confusion.

The sky was so clear. We stood in silence, looking at the bright stars, searching for clues around us. I'd known Alex long enough to be able to intuit his mood, knew by his stance and silence that he was scared. As for me, I was—what? Heart-broken? Selfless for urging him to get off his duff and take this trip?

For a while there was no cab in sight. I put my arm through Alex's and murmured, *Dog*, one of the many names I had for him. *The Way I Love My Man Is a Sin*, I said. It was a cover line for an upcoming issue.

His Lovemaking Keeps Me Begging for More, I said.

Alex dug into his back pocket, found his airline ticket, put it back.

The wait expanded. *I Will Die Without You*. I believed this. For a moment I tried out believing that I was being brave in the face of what was necessary, like a young woman tearlessly sending her guy overseas to fight in the Great War.

Night After Night I Learned to Satisfy My Own Sex Needs, I said.

Alex smiled wanly and said, "You better."

He pointed to Orion's belt, straight above.

What an imagination those constellation namers had, to see meaning in these vague arrangements, I said.

They needed meaning, he said. They were afraid of the forces of nature.

We were afraid, too; only we had no belief system, no language for our despair or fear, only jokes in assumed voices.

I did not see this then. I did not see that I had lost the language of deep feelings. I did not see that my job was a perfect fit, a place where I could use words to distance and push away anything of meaning. Everything deeply felt was a parody there, complete with exclamation points—love outlaws! sex freaks! over and over! up and down! in and out!

And so, when I see the two of us now, I know that at once I was terrified of Alex leaving and could barely wait for the cab to take him away. When at last it pulled to the curb, he threw his bags in the back, ducked low, and crawled in after them. The door slammed. The last thing I saw was Alex's high-top sneaker as he pulled in his foot. He had forgotten to turn back to me, to put up a hand or throw a kiss. The driver floored it, and the cab hurtled down the avenue, rattling the manhole covers on the way downtown.

After Alex left, I was busy, the way I'd been after my sister's murder. I was, by then, the editor of *Intimate Story*. The day Frances had told me she was leaving, I walked into a department store a few blocks uptown, bought myself a military-looking dress, khaki-colored, with epaulets. The next morning I attached a junior pilot's pin I had gotten from an airline above the breast pocket. I was so detached from my drives and anxieties that if someone had asked me about my plans, I might have said, "What plans?" But that afternoon I had stood in the publisher's office, with its walnut paneling, its duck-and-gun motif, as if it were a men's club, convincing my boss that I could safely pilot this craft. What could I possibly have said to get him to hand over the editorship of a magazine that turned a profit and had a circulation larger than that of *The New Yorker* to a young woman who, for previous experience, had squeezed cats and done light shows? Did he look at me in my military dress and think: This kid has leadership qualities? Did he see my steady hands and steady gaze and think: "Lifer"? Perhaps the khaki dress was a poor disguise and he knew that a radical lurked inside, eager to change the magazine and make sure that women no longer had to suffer for their sins. Or maybe he simply didn't give a shit.

My nights were as packed as my first weeks as editor. One evening I had a writing workshop—my first ever—where the thrill of showing my work publicly and being treated with respect was dampened considerably by the fact that nothing I wrote held together. When I turned in what I believed was the best thing I had ever written, the woman I most admired in our class said my story was like a beautiful chair. "An *ex*quisitely carved chair; a chair designed by a wonderful, *talented* craftsperson. A *museum*-quality chair, with burnished wood and marvelous grain, a gorgeous chair. But a chair that wobbles, dear. It has only three legs. It cannot stand up."

I also began to go out with men in a manic fashion, my attention span too short to sustain any relationship. "With men" does not capture where I was in relation to them, for I might find myself outside my body, a spectator. I thought of myself then as uninhibited, in absolute control, because I felt no jeopardy in anything I did with anyone. How could there be when I was not in my body but floating above it? I gave nothing of myself, because the self that had my emotions in it was no longer in my physical body. Nothing hurt! Nothing mattered. And anyhow, I was a writer, and it was all experience. I was looking down and watching, a spectator of my own life, a narrator, catching the nuance, watching the courtship. Nothing could touch me.

Sometimes, and these were the moments I neither watched nor recorded, I came home and united with my own body and found myself in such a state of panic that I could not leave my apartment or answer the phone. I needed to hide from the people I had liked a day or week before. How odd it seems now that, in times of true danger, I was without fear. But when I was locked in my apartment, the sound of footsteps in the hall filled me with a kind of panic that took my breath away. I could not budge, could not pick up the phone, could not answer the knocking on my door. I was sure that whoever was outside had come to do me harm.

I cannot say how I managed to emerge from hiding. Perhaps it was the responsibility I felt as editor of *Intimate Story*. Perhaps it was my fierce desire to do a perfect job, to increase sales, to change the lives of women from Cape Breton Island to West Nanticoke, PA, by passing on the word, the message I could not seem to absorb myself: There will be no more suffering for imagined sins.

Would I be a writer? Would I move to L.A. or stay in New York? Should I marry Alex? He was miserable in L.A. and pressing for me to make a decision. I went out with other men but talked with Alex about marriage. Did I love him? Didn't I?

The person I chose to help me solve these problems was a psychic who lived in the Ansonia, on the Upper West Side. A man who was brilliant, I was assured, who would tell me everything I needed to know. All I had to do was bring him something personal to hold during our meeting and a check made out to cash.

I expected the psychic not only to tell me whether to marry Alex but to reveal why my short stories were flawed. The notion that a psychic could address this problem was absurd, but in some way I expected him to intuit what I could not understand at the time, that language was something I used to obscure, a fancy dress, a lacy curtain, a way to dodge with charm, and that when I used this language to construct stories, they were quirky, ill-formed pieces.

Mo, my friend from work, had also booked an appointment. The two of us crept somberly into the old building when the day arrived. In the dingy corridor that smelled like pot roast, we were seized by such an attack of the willies that we grabbed each other's hands. You'd think we were going in for same-day brain surgery, we trembled so violently. Would I marry Alex? Would I be a writer? I needed answers badly. Something was wrong. I needed a little sense knocked into me, a little what-for, as if I were an appliance in my mother's kitchen, on the fritz until she smacked it.

The psychic was busting out of his short-sleeved plaid shirt. His poodle was asthmatic. He asked me to write my concerns on a piece of paper.

"My *concerns?* I asked.

"Things that worry you," he said.

"Things that *worry* me?" I repeated stupidly.

Should I marry Alex? Would I become a writer? If I kept the box shut, that was all there was. But if I opened the lid an inch, the rest sprang out: Would I die in a strange man's apartment, of a gas leak in my own, of botulism, or toxic shock? Would I be hit by a cab, get a weird neuromuscular disease, lose a limb, become a quadriplegic, go gray early? Would I move to California? Die in the big quake? If I let myself go, I would never stop.

If I had been slightly more centered, I might have been able to ask: What's wrong with me? Why don't I have any feelings anymore?

The psychic took the paper on which I wrote the most superficial of my worries, rolled it tightly, and slid it through the ring I had brought for him to hold. If he was a real psychic, he would have known by then that I was haunted by three ghosts.

But he was a fake, "a waste of good money," as we said in our family, his patter so dull that I watched his eyes roll back, watched his fingers work at the rolled piece of paper, listened to him say that all my dreams would come true, so fraudulent that all I could hear was the echo of my own desperation.

A shrink, I thought after that. What the hell. Everyone was seeing shrinks. "My shrink says" was the opening line to half the conversations I heard. Maybe a shrink was the answer. After all, I had a real problem, not just vague, free-floating feelings, but a *something*, an actual, concrete, verifiable problem that I could not seem to solve alone. The therapist cost more than I had, far too much money for something so intangible, but I could not get straight in my own head how I felt about either of these large decisions. Should I follow Alex to L.A. the way I had followed him to London? Should I marry him?

I wanted answers to my questions. I wanted a fortune-teller, only this time a good one.

The shrink had a dry, ironic voice, and long, thin, elegant legs, most often clad in close-fitting velvet pants. Her legs were so mesmerizing I thought of her as gorgeous, despite her homely face, and the ears that stuck out from her lank hair.

She was a no-nonsense, ask-me-no-questions style shrink, so I knew nothing about her, apart from the fact that her family was from a Baltic state, hence her odd name, and that she lived two blocks from the bank with old-fashioned bars on the tellers' windows, where Woody Allen had shot *Take the Money and Run*. If her style was classic therapist style, her room was classic therapist's room, all burnt-oranges and browns, more clocks than an antique dealer. Lots of boxes of hankies.

She wanted to know about my mother.

No mothers, I thought. You start with mothers, the next thing you knew it was penis envy.

She waited silently.

"There's nothing to tell. I'm from New Jersey."

She shifted, recrossed her long legs.

Nu? I thought, as if the least she could do was say "Har-de-har-har" like my mom.

Patience she had. So did I. I sat in silence until the room began to pulsate, and the clocks ticked money, money, waste of money.

"All right," I said. "I have a mother. And a father."

"And?"

It was out of sheer Yankee-style thrift that I said, "I had a sister."

"You had a sister."

"I had a sister."

"Do you want to tell me about your sister?"

I meant simply to say, "No." I meant to say, "I don't remember anything." I did not want to speak. I certainly did not want to tell her of my sister's affection for me and how undeserving I was of it. What good was it to recall that Laura's life had been hard, while I had been nothing but an obnoxious little goodnik, Mama's darling, dying to please? Why bother drumming up memories about the room we shared, or the fact that we had spent nearly all our time together the last summer of her life? What difference did it make that as soon as she arrived at school, she sent me a gift and a letter and that I hadn't responded right away. I had meant to, but I was lazy and self-centered and let it slide. It was meaningless to wonder if Laura had gotten my letter signed "love," to imagine that she had been stabbed to death without knowing how much I adored her.

I did not remember Laura, would not talk of her, but some wrenching awful sob came out of my mouth. I did not want to cry, could not risk it, pushed it back in, pushed and pushed so I would not die from it, too.

I kept coming back, though, and I kept talking. I tried out that word, "sister," and I made my first tentative steps to admitting that she had existed on earth, that she had slept in the bed beside mine for all of our childhood.

I wrote a lot.

I wrote at home, and at the office, when my work was done. I never wrote about Laura.

That winter, I showed my workshop a story about a woman who was not me who lived in a bleak, impoverished section of London, with a kind but emotionally distanced guy who was not Alex. A second guy, not Brad, shows up one day. He says:

I've come to take you back to the States. He is a sweet, skinny, sandy-haired guy from a navy family, last address Honolulu. She takes him all over the city, to flea markets and museums and Chinese restaurants, where they share huge pots of soup with two of everything inside, two gizzards, two won tons, two pieces of pork. She tells him stories about the other tenants in the building, four Irish girls named Mary. Her good cheer is relentless and disappoints him.

On his last night in London, she buys a duck to roast for him. They return to her flat early that evening. Your spirit, your energy is being dissipated in this bleak gray place, he says, as they hike up the steps to her attic flat. Stop living like this and admit that you love me.

She unwraps the duck and begins to wash the pimpled carcass. He reminds her of their secret weekend, of the time they stood together on the bow of the ferry, of the first time they made love.

Say you'll come, he says. If not that day, then sometime soon.

But love and despair are deep inside her, entwined like ancient roots. Reaching one means reaching the other. She will not leave. She takes the giblets out of the bird and lets the water run straight through the carcass. She tells him she's there with someone else. The duck's flesh looks human. He notices the way she averts her eyes, and speaks with growing anger of the risks she ought to take, never understanding the depth of the risk it would be merely to meet his troubled gaze.

She will not choose him, will not choose someone who asks for so much and so directly, who wants to touch the sensitive places where tears and heartache and love are twisted together.

The interloper goes back to the States alone. Then one night, not long after, on a road not far from Santa Cruz, he crashes his VW van and dies.

. . .

The class went wild when it was time to discuss this story.

"The guy *dies?*" the man beside me roared. "That's how the story ends—he *dies?*"

"Are you suggesting that it was suicide?"

"You can*not* have a story that ends in suicide. Ever again. It's overused."

"It's a device."

"Completely unmotivated. You've got all this conflict, and instead of resolving it dramatically, you give us this, pardon me for saying it, this cheesy cop-out deus ex machina."

It was the first time I had ever ventured so close to what wounded me, and no one was even wasting class time telling me that I had made a fine, beautiful chair, a work of art, if flawed.

I smiled and shrugged and said, "Hey, *thanks*, everyone." I told the class how great their comments were, how tremendously helpful the discussion, the whole time thinking: Die of the plague, each of you.

The class was right. The ending was ridiculous, a joke. It was so unacceptable that the night a mutual friend asked me to meet him at Ratners, intending to break the news of Brad's death, I took one look at his ashen face and refused to let him speak of it. I clowned around, made him order cherry cheesecake, and watched him choke it down, trying to push the words back into his face the way I had pushed back my tears over Laura. I did everything in my power to deflect him, as if his silence could bring Brad back to life.

As for the story—I ripped it up, turned my words into confetti and then into ash, careful to think neither of Brad nor of my flawed work about him. Then one day, a year or so later, I heard what sounded like his laugh. When I looked back, I saw a sandy-haired guy with a bouncy, back-on-the-heels way of walking. I stood foolishly in the middle of the sidewalk, frozen by the memory of Brad coming up beside me, how we had fallen into step and simply stayed together.

When I revised the story, he did not die late at night, stoned, depressed, or just unlucky. He left of his own accord, abandoning the not-me character. This revision completed the story in a fathomable way. She deserved to be left behind. She knew then, as I do decades later: when Brad died, we lost the purest, freest, most unfettered spirit I have ever met.

9

FIRST I HAD ADMITTED to myself that I had a sister. Then I spoke her name aloud. Laura, I said. It was as if I were calling out to her and she was answering me, for I began to dream about her all the time.

By then it was 1974, and eight years had passed since the murder.

The dreams were intensely real, nothing fractured or dreamlike about them. Most often we were children again. We play cards. We're on Crown Street in Brooklyn, chewing candy dots off paper, racing past the row of old women who sit on orange crates with their stockings rolled down. We're marching through Baba's apartment, holding her hand mirror up to the ceiling, so the arches become hills we must climb, and the cord from the ceiling fixture becomes a pendulum.

These dreams were so vivid that when I woke, the world was still upside down and the taste of paper and sugar filled my mouth. For a moment, I welcomed the ache; I was glad for it, needed it, the way I needed to feel my teeth pulled out so I would know what was real. But then I knew that Laura wasn't real—not anymore. She was dead. And I was so heavy with despair I could barely move from bed.

In dreams, as in life, she comes upon me primping in the mirror and says, "You have a cute figure, toots." And when I'm waiting for my date she takes me aside and whispers, "Be good, bubby. Don't do anything I wouldn't do."

Bubby, she called me. Bubby, Baby, Marfa, Toots.

In dreams she is alive and in love. My skinny contentious sister, now lithe and lovely, wrapping her arm through mine as we look at china and silver at the mall, then turning to ask, as she had in a letter, what I think of burgundy and teal as colors for her winter wedding. "You'll be my bridesmaid, naturally."

When I woke, I knew that I had made myself forget my sister's fierce love for me, not just her sisterly protectiveness, but her unabashed pride, the pleasure she took in my company. She loved me no matter what. I didn't have to be good or cheerful or neat; I did not have to earn her love. It was always there. When I shook off these dreams, I was left knowing that I would never again be loved so steadily, that even if I was deserving, it could never be mine.

Sometimes it was thrilling to have her back. But sometimes I woke from the dreams and felt that the burden of being alive was too great for me.

Then at night I hear her calling, "Bubby!" I feel her arm around me, as she takes me down the steps into the rec room, where her friends are listening to 45s. "This is Marfa—my baby sister."

Dreams turned into memories. The memories fell into that crack between pleasure and pain. The way we squeezed onto her bed together, two nearsighted sisters squinting at pictures in *Modern Bride*, and listening to records—Ray Charles, the

Butterfield Blues Band, Rahsaan Roland Kirk, Charlie Parker, Bob Dylan. How after dinner, when the weather was nice— and in my memory, all the evenings were balmy and fragrant that summer—she took me through the streets of our neighborhood on the back of her bike. I trusted my sister. My parents sat on the brick steps, having an after-dinner smoke, the dog and cat between them. Laura wheeled Louie from the garage and revved the engine. I straddled the seat behind her. I was not sad that this would be the last summer we would sleep together in the bedroom we chose to share. Marriage was on the other side. We believed, both of us, that marriage meant happily ever after.

We leaned into the first turn and waved to my parents. Then I wrapped my arms around my sister, the two of us fearless and innocent, as close as lovers.

After a few months, the dreams ended and Laura began to fade. But the process of remembering that I had a sister, had loved her and lost her, changed me for the better. Freed of the enormous job of obliterating my entire past, I was less brittle and guarded, less blindly destructive. I could feel this in myself and was proud to see that I was making decisions, rather than letting things happen to me. I was moving forward with clarity, putting myself back together, body and soul. I knew that I was not going to marry Alex or move to Los Angeles, that the damage we had done to each other was irreparable. I was going to stay at my job in New York and keep writing until I learned to do it well.

I began to get to my office early and work straight through lunch, so I would have time at the end of the day to write. Even my nights were productive: no more hanging out at Chumley's;

no more dates with weird, troublesome men. Instead, I saw the Baltic shrink, went to my writing workshop, and did calisthenics with a group of World War II veterans at the McBurney Y. I bought furniture and far too many plants and fixed up the tiny apartment Alex and I had shared. I clung to my schedule, could not easily manage any deviations from it. I knew I was rigid, but I thought I was staying on track, sticking to the direction I had chosen for myself.

One Sunday night, my best friend, Hinda, phoned. She, her boyfriend, and a man named Will, someone she had described in passing as "brilliant but crazy," had gone to a wedding reception at a downtown restaurant and were only a few blocks from my apartment. They wanted to know if they could stop by for a few minutes. I was in the midst of an intense game of Scrabble that night. If I lost I had to take my Scrabble partner to Umberto's Clam House, so that he could see where Joey Gallo had been gunned down some weeks before. When my friends arrived, I was cordial, but my attention was more on the game than on them. All I remember of the night, apart from the humidity and that I lost the game, was that the stranger with blue eyes and long silver hair lay on his back in my living room, absently stroking my carpet.

When Will phoned a week later and asked if we could meet for coffee, I was mildly surprised but accepted without much thought. It was only when I recalled my friend describing him as "brilliant but crazy" that I decided to break the date. Why would I want to make the acquaintance of someone who was crazy? Why now, when the pieces of my life were beginning to fit so neatly together? I meant to back out, but I could not find his phone number. Neither could Hinda or her boyfriend. It's only coffee, I thought, as I walked down to Barrow Street to meet him. Even if he is crazy, it won't kill me to sit with him in a public place for an hour.

He was not crazy. He was lively and offbeat and easy to talk to. What was odd, if extremely charming to me, was his wide-eyed awe of everything. It was as if he had no filter, no ability to designate something not worth his notice. The list of his interests seemed endless—fruit flies, dragonflies, horseshoe crabs, photography, movies, museums. Will sailed, skied, and co-owned a plane. He was a physicist, working in psychoacoustics at a large research lab, but taking coursework toward a Ph.D. in biology. His energy seemed boundless: he was so youthful in demeanor and looks that it stunned me to learn that he was forty.

At twenty-five, forty seemed a terrifying age to me, but it didn't faze him, he said. In his seventh-floor walk-up apartment, where mealworms grew in potatoes and plants sprouted from jars on shelves and floors, their long, straggly stems arching toward the windows, he had set up a tripod so he could snap daily Polaroid photos of himself each morning. He was recording his deterioration, he said. He was interested in what happened to "the system" with age.

Everything was interesting to Will; everything worth saying. I thought it funny how candid he was, how he did not inhibit any thought or awkward phrase or sign of pleasure. There was no waiting, no skittery, awkward, interpretive waltz on our first date. "I like you," he said while we sat over coffee. "I like you a lot," he said on the street. "You're really something," he said, on the stairs up to my apartment. "Let's neck."

"Neck" was actually the word he used, the only reminder that Will was fifteen years older than I, and had come of age in a different time and place.

I am tempted to lie, to list his finer qualities and say that they were the reasons I grew to love him. And it's true that I found Will's openness immensely appealing. But then I recall seeing him through the peephole of my door the next time we met, his huge blue eyes, his broad, smooth face and silky, silver, nearly shoulder-length hair. My hands shook when I turned the lock. I could hardly face him. I could hardly bear to turn away so he could follow me inside. And it seems more honest to say that I was drunk with love, nearly from the start.

We were always talking, always going places, always on the move. On weekends, we drove to a cafeteria on the Lower East Side that had murals depicting scenes from Ellis Island and a clientele made up of men in fedoras and overcoats, and women with crooked lipstick. We ate and talked, and when we got up, he left behind napkins covered with diagrams and flow charts that showed me that anything I wanted—medical school, a graduate program in writing—could be mine.

We often went from the cafeteria out to Long Island, to work on the old wooden sailboat he kept moored in the canal behind his aunt's house. I loved this world. His aunt looked like a story-book Grandma, with huge blue eyes like his, white hair pinned into waves, flowered dresses, and black lace-up shoes. While we picked caulking from the cabin roof, talking of places we'd sail when the boat was seaworthy, Will's cousin gamboled on the lawn with his girlfriend, his uncle watched the ball game from his rocker on the porch, and his aunt sewed clothing for dolls with bodies that were sand-filled dish-detergent bottles. For dinner she made cauldrons of spaghetti and meatballs.

Sometimes, in the evening, we sat on the glider, holding hands and listening to the springs squeak. Will liked to tease me, like an old-fashioned beau. Martha, he called me then. I would punch his arm and say, "Cut it out," but it was okay, really. Martha was just my old name, nothing more.

The first time he asked me to travel with him to the small Puerto Rican island he loved, a peaceful, untouristed place, I reached for my date book. "When?" I asked, flipping through the weeks to see what I could shift. "Tomorrow night," he said. "There's a red-eye that leaves at midnight."

My life was so structured, the pieces in such inflexible order, that it was hard for me to agree to a spur-of-the-moment dinner with friends. But his spontaneity loosened me, gave me access to the uninhibited part of myself that had been dormant for so long. "Yes," I said, letting go of my calendars, schedules, routine. "Yes," because I loved that he nudged the roots that I set down, tugged me outside, because it seemed in those days that the sheer sunniness of his nature brightened the sky. I loved the force of his presence, how I could not dodge him, avert my eyes, draw into myself. Meeting him full-face made me feel as if I had finally returned to life.

One winter night, four months after we met, we went to a party in Ho-Ho-Kus, New Jersey, where all the men were cops or lawyers named Bud or Jim—or so for years we claimed. Drunk on vodka and each other, we hid out in the powder room, laughing and kissing. Everything was charming then; that the week before, he had taken me to a dinner party on the wrong evening; that on the way to this gathering, he had picked up a second woman—a blind date, he realized, only when we saw the shocked expression on her face as she climbed into the back of the car. That night, squeezed into the cold powder room, he asked me to marry him.

"At least, I think he did," I told Hinda the next day. "But we had kind of a lot to drink, so I'm not positive."

"I proposed," he told Hinda's boyfriend. "But she was too drunk to remember."

We sorted it out before too long. He asked again if I would marry him, and I said yes without hesitation.

What did I know when I walked down the aisle at the Fifth Avenue Hotel, where we were married in July 1975?

Everything.

I knew that his beautiful old aunt's past was full of scandal and disgrace, and that the husband in the rocking chair had once been her brother-in-law. I knew that the tranquil Puerto Rican island we loved had been used for target practice by the U.S. Navy. I knew what hard work it was to live a life where nothing escapes your attention. And I knew that the man I loved could not inhibit his anger any more easily than his joy. But I was too drunk with love to see any danger.

I wore a long, white Mexican wedding dress. White wildflowers had been woven through my floppy hat and arranged in my bouquet. A woodwind quartet played the wedding march. I had no fears or reservations as I walked down the aisle. If I had been asked what problems we had, I might have said, "He's a saver; he's got all this *stuff*." Will might have said, "She's a worrier." We would have admitted our flaws, turned to each other, and laughed, because nothing mattered, not really.

No one asked. No one stood up during the ceremony and said, "Stop this wedding! Don't go through with it." And I can't imagine anyone wanting us to stop. That night, he took me from table to table, saying, "Aren't I lucky?" His startling eyes were luminous with tears. "Aren't I the luckiest man?"

I, too, felt lucky, beyond anything I deserved.

· · ·

I had been married for a year and was in graduate school when the Laura dreams began again.

In one dream, I find myself walking down a narrow flight of stairs in a steep room, rich with the brine and garlic smell of pickles. I'm in a screening room on the second floor of a big building on the Lower East Side where the *Forward* was once published. The carpeting is worn down to the horsehair mat. I'm concentrating on the steps when I see Howard.

Howard, that's what Laura called him. Never "Howie" but Howard, with her mouth around the "o" Chicago-style. Howard be thy name, I think as I slide in next to him. He's not wearing a wedding band. His hands are intensely familiar. I ask him about Laura, but he turns away.

"Howard," I say, and now I sound like Laura, I can hear the round "o" in my voice. "Please tell me where she is."

Laura had a baby, he says, then turns away, refusing to say more. My heart, the ticking clocks, my heart. "Let me see the baby, please." My shoulders and gut ache. "Please."

He will not turn back. I begin to beg until something breaks within me, and I am sobbing like a crazy person, utterly wild. Some small sane piece of me registers that there are people around, and that I have not since childhood disgraced myself by crying in front of people. And so nakedly, my face red as a squalling newborn's, and just as vulnerable. And now on my knees, sobbing, degraded; I am degrading myself, but I can't help it.

"It's okay, it's okay," someone says.

It's my husband, who's part of the real world, high up on our loft bed in our tiny Village apartment. He's holding me in his arms and crooning softly.

I struggle to place myself, ticking off all that I know of my life: Married, in graduate school. My sister is dead. "It's not okay," I tell him, before I can fully shake the dream.

All day the dream drags along with me, like a weight around my ankle. I cannot shake it.

I did not understand why I was dreaming about Laura again. I was deeply in love with Will, thrilled to be in graduate school, where I could read all day. I was writing a lot, too, but absolutely nothing about Laura or about myself, or so I was convinced.

The novel I had begun at the start of my first year in the program was about an entomologist, a tiny, introverted, dark-haired woman who studied ants. It seemed to take shape out of my desperation to submit something to my fiction class. True, it was filled with deaths, real and imagined, but that was the influence of a course I was taking, called "The Meaning of Death." The details of my protagonist's life in graduate school came from Will, who was working toward his doctorate in biology, and the details about entomology I had picked up in a class I took at the Museum of Natural History. As for her tendency to hide in her apartment when her unacknowledged losses crowded in, I couldn't say, exactly.

Meanwhile, I was dreaming, or remembering my dreams, in such a ferocious way that it was like being awake twenty-four hours a day. In dreams, Laura and I thumb-wrestled, polished the dog's nails red. We had kicking fights, like the real-life game we had devised in which we lay on the floor with the soles of our feet together and tried to capture each other's legs.

I decided that I was dreaming of Laura because the deep, knows-no-bounds kind of love I had for Will had made me suddenly, unbearably vulnerable. My love for him was so big it sometimes seemed apart from him, disconnected. His love for me, present, powerful, enveloping, unpredictable, brought me both pleasure and gut-wrenching fear. He was a gorgeous man, an eyeful; he adored me; his eyes filled up at the sight of me. I worried constantly about losing him. How would I survive if something happened? He could die on the turnpike on the way home from work. He could die driving eighty miles an hour with his knees on the steering wheel while he took off his coat. He did things like this frequently. My worrying grated on him; he could not wrench it from me with jokes. I worried so much about losing him.

And sometimes, I see now, I did lose him, for he was prone to rages that were like forces of nature. Sometimes I could see a storm building, but more often they materialized without warning. In a rage his face swelled and reddened, his lips got sucked in, his eyes bulged. In this monstrous transformation, he lost all sanity, all memory of tenderness. I fought back in the beginning though my head throbbed with guilty questions—what had I done; how had I caused this? But I saw that he could kill me if I fought. He was so much stronger; and he was, literally, "not himself." Anything could happen.

I could not think or speak about these incidents, could not so much as form the memory of them into words. I felt them instead, my fear like the boneless split-off self, something that was part of me, but not often of my own recognition. And so I tried to wipe each incident from my mind, determined to tough it out, the whole time feeling—"naked" was the word for it, as if he were my skin, my protection. *Without you, I'm nothing.* Those were the words to a song I had heard, a bad song, expressing the kind of helplessness I scorned when I was in my right mind, though when the rages happened, I was nothing.

Sometimes, when I woke in the morning and my body ached with a memory I could not articulate, I thought that the cost of being alive was to ache like this. Love, like life, was fragile, I told myself. To risk loving someone meant that I had to live with the knowledge that I was not enough. My work was all that counted, I decided. I could take my fears and sadness and shape them into someone else's story.

Sometimes, for long stretches of time, nothing bad happened. I would look at the man across the table from me, gentle and generous. Here was a man who respected my work and gave me space to write and think. We never had power struggles. We were of equal intellect, our careers of equal importance. We had the best relationship of anyone I knew. During these times, when the edge of a memory came back to me, I would tell myself it was a figment of my irrational fears.

Wasn't I the child who sat at the top of the stairs, listening? Hadn't I been afraid of the steam that came from the sidewalk grates in New York, evidence, I believed, of a great subterranean force below the street? Will was always chiding me about all my phobias, and he was right. Afraid of leprosy, afraid of my grandmother's kisses, afraid of the space between platform and subway train that might suck me into the dark world below? Fear, like laziness, was a flaw, something I had to work in excess to conquer. The bigger my fears, the harder I fought to conquer them. Secretly, I believed that life was full of danger. But I believed that to give over to this knowledge even the slightest bit would immobilize me completely.

I remember the day the building super stopped sweeping when I walked by and asked, "You sure you did the right thing marrying that man?"

"Of course I'm sure," I said.

She turned her back and continued to sweep. I started up the stairs. "The other one, he was nice," she said, her voice echoing in the corridor. "But this one has a violent temper."

"Not with me," I said, fully believing my own words.

"Doesn't sound that way when he's throwing things around."

I was on the top landing when she said, as if to herself. "You're a nice girl, so I can tell you this. I don't like him, uh-uh. Not at all. I wish you the best of luck, but not for him."

I opened the door and walked into our apartment. I saw for the first time a patch of dirt from a plant he'd flung. The night before rushed into my consciousness, so that I could not move or speak: the way he had pinned me to the closet door, huge and strong, his blue eyes immense with hatred, his face florid, spit flying from between his teeth. He was trembling, like a power lifter, squealing, grunting, exerting every ounce of control to keep from slaughtering me.

And if he walked in and asked, "What's wrong, sweetness?" what would I say? What's wrong was a picture, not words. Early on, I had tried, if tentatively, to push him about an incident of the night before. But he could not acknowledge these events either. If I persisted, he might say, "Last night was last night," or, "Today's a new day." Once the rage worked through him, it was over. A heavy door slammed; the incident was irretrievable. If I pushed hard, I could bring on another rage. Or I could let myself go with him into what was, indeed, a new day for him, one he greeted with great cheer.

These cycles began to repeat themselves. I could not give voice to my fears, nor could I totally forget what had happened, so the knowledge burrowed deep inside me. Now when he walked in the door, merely tense, I had no words: it was my body that remembered.

Sometimes, seemingly a propos of nothing, I provoked a quarrel. If he said, "What's that about?" I could no longer answer.

I was no longer "in touch" with my feelings about Will or myself. I was in love or in despair—emotional, unpredictable, riding on the great pendulum that swung from his elation to his rage. Sometimes I had the sensation of being without weight or will. I would look up, find myself somewhere—in the forepeak of a boat we had chartered, say, wrapped in the jib sheet—and wonder: What happened? It was as if I had not been fully present during our courtship, on our moving day, at our lovely wedding, as if I had dreamed walking up the aisle with Will, dreamed my father's feverish embrace, dreamed Will's arm around me, his saying, "Aren't I lucky?" It was as if I had dreamed the look on his face, so full of rage I understood that "scared to death" could be a literal thing.

Yes, I had dreamed it, I sometimes thought. I was neurotic, a worrier. There were no monsters. I was a married woman, grown up enough to understand that steam came out of the grates, not a creature from the underworld. I could switch on the lights the way my mother had when I wakened, screaming, from a nightmare. "See!" she would say. "You've made it up."

I tried out theories to explain my own surprise at the way my life was turning out. It was karma, I decided. *Beshert*, I thought, when I learned the Yiddish word to describe something that was meant to be. Another year I decided it was the fate of women. Men made decisions; women let themselves be blown about like leaves. I made theories of these airy, weightless feelings, told stories that explained things, that gave structure and sense to the situations that upset me.

I was married for a year when my sister's murderer began to take shape in my imagination, to become a creature of flesh and blood, not a force, not something that happened at night.

In a scene I imagined so clearly that it took on the shape of reality, the murderer served a few years and then got out of prison. The gate clanked behind him. He turned his face up to the sun and walked straight into the future. Married, got a good job in a factory. Bought a little house near where he'd grown up.

One night, in the summer of 1976, ten years after Laura's murder, I called Information. I spoke the murderer's name aloud to see if they had a listing. Will was in New York. I was alone in Maine. The dogs across the bay were howling, their plaintive voices echoing in the night air. My door was locked, but the window on one side of the house was so low anyone could climb in.

The disembodied voice on the other end of the line recited a phone number twice.

I said, "Thank you," wrote down the number, and waited for my heart to slow down.

I knew, then, that I would find this man's house, that one day I would park my car on his street, walk past the Big Wheels and trike, past the dusty, weedy excuse for a lawn, and knock on his door.

He has no face in my imagination. I have seen the newspaper photos; I can conjure up every detail in this scene, the flame decals on the Big Wheels, the weedy lawn, but I cannot see his face. Everything else is clear: his hair, shorn close in a military way, his workman's pants and shoes, the baby he holds easily on one hip. He is lean and well-built, stingy with words, even alone with his wife, but he has manners. He opens the door, comes out on the front step, waits for me to speak.

"My name is Jane Bernstein." Even in my imagination, that's all I can manage. My feelings of shame and guilt are so intense that even in a moment I have made up it's as if we have changed places, and I am the murderer.

He looks at me without concern or curiosity, just pats the baby absently and waits.

What's left inside me? Not rage, not even anger. I don't imagine pulling out a gun and shooting him. I don't want him dead, because then he could not tell me who he is and why he stabbed my sister. This is what I feel he owes me. Just this at whatever cost.

"I'm Laura Bernstein's sister," I say.

He jostles the baby, cocks his head. He has no idea who I am talking about. He has forgotten everything. My heart begins to pound. It doesn't make a difference what I feel or what I do. I can shriek at him, pound his chest, and fall to my knees. He'll just stand there. He has left it all behind. He can do that. It makes me realize that I am no one, and Laura is less than that, less even than the dust beneath his feet.

I was exploring tentatively, like a person on dark, unfamiliar turf, foot brushing against the ground to see if it is solid, or if there are treacherous holes. Then when one day I opened my sister's high school yearbook and saw the inscription on the inside cover. *Really, Laur, your the Best friend and sister i ever had.*

Peggy wrote that, my sister's best friend, her sidekick for years. I hadn't seen her since the summer of 1966—Laura's last summer. She was on welfare then and living in a trailer with her baby.

I knew it would be easy to find her. She still lived in the town where we had grown up. My mother ran into her once in a while and always gave me an update. Peggy had gotten her receding chin fixed and looked marvelous. She was getting her GED. She was working for Dr. W., everyone's favorite GP.

"People say he's leaving his wife for her, but you know how people love to talk."

One night I called Peggy and told her who I was, stuttering over my old name and my new one.

"You remember Artie, Laura's old boyfriend? He and I were just down to the cemetery the other day," she said. "We were really upset. It's like we're the only ones who ever tend her grave."

I asked if we could meet. I didn't have an agenda, didn't know what I wanted, so I was surprised when she said that she was anxious to talk.

Several nights later, I borrowed Will's car, an old Reliant that was missing a backrest and had holes in the floorboard covered with cardboard. I thought about Peggy as I drove over the George Washington Bridge into New Jersey. She was vivid in my memory—a skinny, gawky girl with bad teeth, her hair dyed honey-blond and teased into a bubble. She was Irish, Catholic, poor, at least to me, her father often unemployed because of seizures from all the head blows he'd taken as a boxer, years back. A bopper, I thought, as if it were the 1960s again, and my whole world was in this suburban town, all my judgments and prejudices there. In those days our high school was neatly divided into two camps—Boppers and Rah-rahs. Bopper girls wore tight skirts and eyeliner, teased their hair high, and, if they finished high school, went straight to work. Rah-rahs, the college-prep kids, wore mohair sweaters and loafers. No one crossed the line or socialized with people in the other group—no one except for Laura and Peggy.

"The doctor," like many of the practitioners in our town, had his practice in his home, on one of the main streets. It was a big plantation-style house, with columns flanking the front door. A rusted anchor was propped in gravel in the center of the lawn. I remembered Peggy from ten years before, hugely pregnant, sitting on the edge of Laura's bed. She had lifted her shirt and let me put my hand on her hard, round abdomen.

The Peggy who answered the door was cautious and matronly. Her hair was pulled into a loose knot, and she wore an orange sweater and orange-and-blue-plaid pants. She studied me for a moment and said, "You don't look like her, but you do," then escorted me, stiff-legged, through an empty foyer and a living room dominated by a spiral staircase. The room where we sat was bare except for three folding chairs, one for me, one for Peggy, and one for her leg, which I now saw was rigid in a plaster cast.

She lit up a cigarette and in a few minutes began to tell me stories about the way it had been back then, when she and Laura were together all the time, the two of them like Mutt and Jeff, the way Peggy towered over Laura. There were others in their group, Mouse, Rho, He/She, but she and Laura— Bern and J—were inseparable. If she and Laura made a friend, it was together. If they met a boy, one would go out with him, break up with him, and the other one would see him for a while.

"We were really cool," she said. "We were *such* rejects," she said a moment later.

Remember the blue '51, Tom Collins, Dasie-Fish, 50¢ worth of gas, Sam, and the sinners, she had written on the cover of Laura's yearbook.

Did I remember how my parents called her their honorary daughter? Peggy asked. If we were eating, she'd just pull up a chair. If she was hungry, she'd just kneel in front of the fridge and scrounge around looking for something to eat. "Your mother made dynamite chopped liver," Peggy said. "She and Laura—they were always going at it. I'd walk in and they wouldn't stop swinging. I was like part of the furnishings. Your mother said some really terrible things."

Peggy was quiet for a moment. "She was kind of a sad person, your sister. Real insecure about everything. Hated her nose. Hated tests. She was always really nervous about tests."

Peggy remembered mornings with Laura at her house. Her mother, happy to "push breakfast" into someone else's skinny daughter, would make some oatmeal for Laura—lumpy oatmeal. Laura loved lumps. As soon as Peggy's mother went back into the kitchen, Laura would take out her books and ring binder. She'd tear paper out of the binder into little squares and write answers on them. She'd hike her skirt up to her waist, unfasten her garters, and slide the papers—gyp sheets, they called them—down each stocking, to just above the knee. History on the left, math on the right. During a test, she could cross her legs, push up her skirt casually, for just a second. *Congress of Vienna, September 1814, Napoleon on Elba. A permutation of a set of* n *elements taken* r *at a time can be denoted* nPr.

One day Peggy's mother watched from the doorway. "This is who goes to college?" she asked Peggy that night. "I don't understand."

Peggy could not understand either, could not bear to think about Laura going away. She was a year behind Laura in school—who would she talk to when Laura left? Who would have lunch with her? How would she live? She did not believe that Laura would ever really leave her, even after Laura was admitted to school, even after a date for her to leave was set.

I remembered well the night before Laura left for college. I had walked past the bathroom and seen Peggy and Laura wrapped in each other's arms in the bathroom, heard Peggy cry, "How can you *do* this to me?" The medicine chest, vanity, and clothes hamper had been emptied onto the floor. Stockings hung from the shower rod. The dog, old by then, stood in the corner, trembling, rooted to one spot, his tan dot eyebrows shifting. Our mother was downstairs, screaming, *Always leaves things for the last minute. Let her take a bus! I don't give a good goddamn!* Her fury way in the background, while Peggy sobbed, "How can you leave me without a life!"

Don't let our friendship die, she had written in the yearbook.

Laura went away. She hardly wrote to Peggy.

"I was p.o.'d like you wouldn't believe," Peggy told me. "I'd write her letters, like: 'You bitch, don't write me, I know your arm is broken.' Or I'd start a letter smack in the middle of a juicy story and number the page 'two.' Then Laura would call—collect."

That winter, Peggy dropped out of high school. She spent what little money she had on gas and cruised around town all day. Sometimes she'd cross the Passaic River, which reeked from the brewery, and drive down Route 20 in memory of the Paterson boys she and Laura had shared. Imports, they called them.

By spring she had met a boy who had also dropped out of school. Neither of them had a job, so they drove around together. At the time it seemed like love. Eight months after Laura left for college, Peggy got married. "You could say I exchanged her for a dud," she told me, trying to edge a pinkie down her itchy cast. "It was a quickie."

Laura visited Peggy often when she came home from school, but they began to fight all the time. They had always argued, always called each other names, then hugged and made up, but this was different. Laura'd had her nose fixed, and she was engaged, and it was, like, "*Voilà!* the queen is home from college." And then there was the pot. At every visit, Laura kept talking up the pot.

Peggy couldn't get used to the new Laura. "It drove me absolutely bananas. I'd kid her about her new nose, tell her she looked like a pig, that it was better the old way. I'd really beat her down."

But then, when Laura left, she would wonder, "Once you were a part of me, and you thought like me, and we loved each other, and now it's all changed."

One night, Peggy got so tired listening to Laura talk up pot that she said, "'Look, I'll do you a favor. I'll sit here and I'll roll one and I'll smoke it, and you better goddamn well think that when I'm done I'll enjoy it, because if I don't I'm going to get off this chair and kill you.' So I smoked a joint and it didn't do a goddamn thing, and P.S. I got off that chair and I grabbed her and almost killed her. Then I took all her pot and flushed it down the toilet. And she was pissed. Like super-mad. And she's crying and screaming at me, 'What I did, all this money, you don't know, you don't understand.'

"Finally, she shut up and we had a real good talk. I was convinced she was going to get off the stuff."

For a while, Peggy was out of contact with Laura. She and her husband had lost the apartment and were living in a trailer.

Then one night Laura came over. Peggy didn't know she was coming. She just arrived. It was like a sneak visit.

Peggy asked what was up, and Laura said she needed money.

"Financially, I was—I had my trailer and my baby, and my husband didn't work. So I wasn't too fixed for money. 'Great,' I say. 'How much do you need?'

"Laura says: 'Two hundred. Now. Right away.'

"I was living on soup and formula, so I tell her: 'I don't have two cents. I can't even sell anything. There's nothing here to sell.'

"But she needed it real bad. And when I questioned why, she wouldn't tell me.

"'Go to your parents,' I told her. 'If it's that bad, ask your father. You know he'll give you money.'

"'No,' she says. 'I can't do that.'" And Laura stormed out. That was the last time they saw each other.

"When she said she couldn't ask your parents, I knew something was up. Then she left for Arizona. And I have the feeling that maybe she copped out without paying someone money, that she got into something a little bigger than she thought she was getting into, and then whoever it was didn't want it to go without making an example to the other kids. You know, 'You can't get away with this shit.' Because it was too close and she was really bent for money, really bad news. And maybe it's not legit to come out with this, but I couldn't convince myself that it was any other thing with Laura. I couldn't see any rhyme or reason to it. You know, all I got was the bit your father fed me and what was in the papers. That it was just a kook. I couldn't swallow that. I just couldn't believe it. Maybe because we were so close. I can't believe she was wasted for someone's kicks."

For a moment, neither of us spoke. Peggy hoisted her leg from the chair. How alone she must have felt at Laura's funeral, I thought. A high school dropout surrounded by Laura's college friends, the other girls with folksinger hairstyles, flat and straight, while her hair, dyed honey-blond, was still teased in a bubble. Standing by herself, had she thought, "I am her best friend, her other sister"?

Peggy limped to the door, complaining with every step, just as she had the last time we'd met. Then it had been the way her husband was always off hunting with his buddies, leaving her alone every night with the baby. Now it was the broken leg. She'd miss the start of the golf season on account of it. She wouldn't get to ski until the following year.

She was getting married to the doctor in six weeks and more than anything she wished that Laura could be there. "I always think about what things would be like if Laura was still around, what our relationship would be like. I think about it an awful lot because I see what I went through and how I'm finally—I'm going to make it. It hurts so bad to leave someone where she was. Would she have straightened up? I wouldn't have wanted to see her if the last visit home was any inkling of the Laura that would've matured."

I thanked Peggy and wished her the best. Then I walked down the path of the big house where Peggy now lived, into Will's old car. I did not yet realize how much Peggy's story shook me, only that I could not drive home. Instead of heading back to the highway and to New York, I turned down Radburn Road toward my parents' house. As I was passing my old elementary school, I thought, How could I have accepted that my sister had died for no reason? How could I have just swallowed that story? There is a reason for everything—isn't that what we learn? What goes up must come down?

I thought about what Will said when I tried to find words for the monster, the rage that erupted for reasons that often I did not understand. "You bring it on," he said.

There is a reason for everything.

God does not play dice with the universe.

"You push me to the edge," said Will. And I knew that sometimes, out of fear or sheer anxiety, I did.

I drove past my parents' house. The lights were on in the den, the room where my mother watched TV and where, ten years before, I had found the clippings. I had not told my parents I was meeting Peggy, just as I had never mentioned the dreams I'd had. So many years had passed without our ever speaking Laura's name that once my mother asked, "Do you ever think about your sister?" I wanted to say that for seven years I didn't and now I did, but all I could do was nod.

I turned the corner and parked the car, engine idling, down the block from my parents' house. I tried to settle myself by thinking about our neighborhood, that rambling, festive "we" of kids playing bombardment and kick ball on our street, and the adults playing mah-jongg and poker. "The neighbors," we called them, as in "The neighbors are coming over." But then I remembered the comments the neighbors—the Jewish neighbors—made about Laura's "Jewish nose," and even those memories soured.

I hated that Laura had her nose fixed in Chicago and mailed a dozen pictures home of herself in profile, writing, "This is me with my new nose," on the back of each. She was so proud when she came home that summer that she had gone from house to house to announce her engagement and show off her new nose. It was as if the old nose had been a criminal element, the cause of all her problems, and now that it was gone, she herself was better.

I killed the engine.

Peggy had not lied to me. I knew that.

I remembered the night that last summer when we borrowed our mother's car and drove down to the corner where I was now parked. Laura had pulled over to the curb and said, "I'm gonna turn you on, baby."

That night the chirping of crickets was so loud it seemed to envelop the car. Laura took a Baggie from her purse and pulled out a lopsided joint. She lit the joint, drew on it deeply, and in a smoke-strangled voice said, "Don't tell Mommy."

"Swear to God."

She passed the joint, watched me toke and cough, then laughed with great delight. "You don't *blow* it out. *In*hale it. Like this." She sucked up the smoke, swallowed it, said, "Now remember. No matter how p.o.'d you get, you don't tell."

Impatient: "I *promise*."

When we finished the joint, she started the car, and the two of us drove through town, Laura, narrating: how everything tasted so great you couldn't stop eating, how everything was funny. And me, not feeling anything.

Until we reached a stop sign that leaned at a diagonal. And it was so strange, the way it leaned. A sign, I thought. No longer a stop sign, but a sign for me to tell her what had happened. I had wanted to let this story out, to tell it and dare to laugh. And so I began, as she did: Don't tell. No matter what?

No matter what.

I told Laura how, the summer before, Kenny had borrowed his father's car, a brand-new Chevy with a flat-looking hood and trunk. And though I had never before driven, never even shown the slightest interest, I had a burning need to drive that car, at that moment, while we were cruising the neighborhood, "doing the rounds," he called it. "Which one's the brake?" I demanded. That's how little I knew. "Show me the gas pedal." Kenny stayed in the driver's seat, but let me take the wheel. We were laughing, the two of us: laughing till it hurt. Laughing as the Chevy veered steadily toward the edge of the road. The car was crawling, but still we could not stop. Up over the curb, the telephone pole looming straight ahead. We laughed uproariously until the moment of impact. It was so strange, the way we let it happen. The way, even a year later, knowing the trouble it had caused, the impulse was still toward laughter.

Laura had turned somber then, suddenly parental, clicking her tongue, turning back toward the house. "I've seen people like that," she'd said. "Completely out of control."

And now this—the meeting with Peggy, the story she had just told, was another secret, something else I could not tell my parents.

I started the car and drove home.

After that, when Laura's name came to mind, all I could think was: My parents must not know. Even alone, I did not want to think about her, since to think about her meant I had to indict her. Thirteen years would pass before I could reread the transcribed interview with Peggy and see it as a story, subject to interpretation, told by someone who was trying desperately to see the world as a steadier place, just as I was. I could not see clearly enough to say that even if Peggy's story proved true, no one deserved to die because of a two-hundred-dollar pot deal. No one deserved to die at all.

All I could do in 1976 was to stop thinking about Laura. It wasn't hard. I had already lived without her for so long.

My will was very strong: Never again would I see a girl on the street with long, straight hair and for a stunned moment think: *Laura*. I would not dream of her for thirteen more years.

10

NESTLED IN PINE TREES on Quahog Bay in Maine was a place where nothing bad ever happened. It was the little clapboard cottage Will and I bought in 1975, shortly after we were married. It had been built by a chicken farmer and his father on land that sloped down to the water's edge. The front room was high on stilts and had large windows and a wonderful view of the whole bay. We made this our bedroom. Will found four driftwood logs to use as bedposts, and made the bed high enough so that we could wake and, without even sitting up, look out onto the bay. What we saw was always changing, and always beautiful. In the morning, at low tide, a heron might be poised on the ledge outside the house; gulls wheeled overhead. Cormorants lined up on the small island farther out. Sometimes we brought our dinner into the bedroom so we could watch the sun set.

It was a holy place. Will was a lovely man here. It was not merely that our life here was free of pressures, though that was surely true, but that it was the place of dreams. The first dream was to design and build a multilevel dock, but Will began to plan a larger house, too, big enough for children and friends.

We canoed and sailed and visited cousins and friends in the area. We also spent a good deal of time visiting lumberyards and hardware stores, looking at kitchen displays, chain saws, wood-burning stoves, and compost toilets. Will was at his happiest pacing, dreaming, planning, sketching. And it was fun for me to say, as I did at first: This is your project, your dream. Where else in life could he have these liberties?

When we had rough times during the long winters, we would think of Maine, this holy place. When the ground thawed, we got what we called "Maine fever" and began to plan when we could be there again, because everything was fine when we were in Maine.

We always quarreled when we set out on the seven-hour drive, but they were the kinds of fights I imagined other people had, heated but not scary. The two of us deeply annoyed, two or three hours behind schedule. He would drive in silence uptown, and onto the Henry Hudson Parkway, where we would forget our sulkiness, break into excited conversation, and inevitably miss our turnoff in Westchester. And so we had to institute the "conquer Yonkers" rule that specified the point at which we were allowed to talk.

We had so many rules and traditions that governed our journey: how we went, where we stopped, what we ate. What we felt when we saw the WELCOME TO/BIENVENUE AU NEW HAMPSHIRE sign. That we reached for each other's hands when we got to Route 1, Coastal Route.

There was a rutted dirt road to travel down before we turned onto our driveway, and then a gap between the trees, where, after all the stress of the year, after the quarrel on the way up, we would see the bay sparkle. And we would stop and turn to each other and kiss spontaneously—until this too became a tradition. We designated a tree our kissing tree, and always stopped and kissed, always, no matter what. And then we went down to the water, stepping on pine needles and roots, to take in the fragrant smells—fish, salt, sap, evergreen.

There was a going-home ritual, too, a last chore. After antifreeze was put in the pipes and the blankets stored in trunks, we would roll down the bamboo shades one by one and say goodbye to the bay.

Once, on the last day of the summer, we were standing in our bedroom, letting down the shades, when he put his arm around me and said, "One day, only one of us will come back."

I squawked at him for wrecking the moment. But I never believed it would be true. This was our paradise. There was too much happiness here.

Will studied for his oral exams at a little desk he built facing a wall. I wrote the first story I would get published at my desk facing the bay.

I spent the summer of 1979 dreaming and swinging in the Yucatán hammock, so hugely pregnant that by August, when I wanted to get up, Will had to push from beneath to get me out. That was the summer we practiced the breathing we had learned in childbirth class, the summer the UPS man brought the first copies of my newly published book.

We designated the little room at the back of the cottage the baby's room. And together we dreamed about this baby, whose gender we did not know, whose face I could not conjure up any more easily than I could imagine what it would be like to be a mother. All we knew was that this would be the baby's house. This life, in this house, with the smell of pine needles and the bay, with homemade waffles and blueberry jam and canoe rides out to the little islands—this would be our baby's life, quiet and safe, full of laughter and pleasure.

Our first daughter was born on October 23, 1979, after a labor that was so long I watched the sun rise and set and nearly rise again. I was naïve enough to have thought that labor would be a breeze for a jock, a tough guy like me. And so I remember the agony, and Will's huge blue eyes, brimming with tears, and the moment the nurse put this child in my arms. I looked at my baby—red, wrinkled, and tiny—and thought: Don't take her away from me. Please don't make me live through it.

Will went home. I slept, then woke, wondering if it had been a dream. I got up and padded to the nursery to see if I really had a baby. I did. They wheeled her bassinette into my room, and, comforted now, I fell asleep. When I opened my eyes, there was a baby, and Will in a blue surgical gown, and fruit everywhere. I loved fruit, so he had bought not merely a pear and an orange but melons and Concord grapes, pints of raspberries and blue-berries, enough for a banquet. For hours we ate fruit and watched the baby, a girl who would not be named Laura. When the fruit was finished, we sat and held hands. Later we unswaddled our new baby—Charlotte, we named her—and stared at her, mesmerized.

In snapshots, in this hospital room, we are so young, and our baby is so parched and wrinkled. When friends come to visit, Will tells the story of "our" labor, his voice breaking.

"If I'd known it would be so hard, I would *never* have asked her to get pregnant!" he says.

He takes scores of photos: I'm dressing the baby for the first time, afraid to bend her arms and cartwheeling legs to get her into her clothing.

I'm outside the hospital entrance, looking as pregnant as I had been when I arrived three days before.

I'm in the street outside our building, so happy I'm afraid it will be taken from me.

I'm walking past our building's superintendent, who has stopped sweeping to peer inside the baby blanket.

Yes, my eyes say. Yes, I'm sure. I'm positive.

My parents visit the next day. Their complaints about the climb up to our fifth-floor walk-up apartment echo on each landing.

"You won't be able to do this with a baby!" says my mother when she walks in. She is winded and seems angry.

"Grandma!" says Will, pecking her on the cheek. "Grandma," not "Ruth," which is what he has called her until this moment.

He leads her to the sofa and instructs her to sit, then sets up the camera on the tripod, looks through the viewfinder, and it's: A little to the left, more, a little more.

When he has her in frame, he brings her our swaddled baby.

"No!" she says with great alarm.

"Come on," he coaxes. "Hold the baby."

He lowers the baby into my mother's arms. And then it's like a silent movie, the way he sets the timer and edges beside my mother, leans into her, beams.

The flash goes off.

The baby starts to cry.

The photo captures my mother's grim expression, the wooden look on her face.

But not what comes next—the room suddenly noisy with mewling cries, the baby in my arms. My breasts swollen with milk, everyone standing over me—nurse her, burp her, change her, leave her.

And during this time in which nothing works, thinking: Why can't I do anything right? Can't stop the baby from crying, don't live the life my mother has imagined for me. Even a grandchild cannot make her happy.

Years pass before I can look at the picture and think what it must have been like for my mother, how hard it must have been for her to hold this girl baby in her arms when she had never allowed herself to cry over her own lost baby. She had learned so well—dutiful daughter herself—never to fill up with emotion, for fear that it would overflow. But at the time the tension built up in my own body, and I took her grim face to be a reminder of all my failures, of all the ways I could not, would never be enough.

I can't say that I fell into motherhood quite the way I had heard that others did. When I was pregnant, new mothers were always whispering, "You wait, nothing else will matter." I was not instantly transformed, did not leave the hospital feeling as if everything I had wanted from life before the baby was irrelevant now. I was the same person, with the same fears, desires, and ambitions. The surprise, then, was how unguarded my love for this baby was, how uninhibited my delight.

My obstetrician encouraged mothers to bring their babies when it was time for their six-week checkup. I remember putting Charlotte down on the examining table, unswaddling her, waiting for the doctor to say, "I've been an obstetrician for twenty-five years and I've never seen a more beautiful baby than yours!" I expected him to say this. I really did.

I had become one of the neighbors, a typical Jewish mother. I thought my daughter was a little darling, a genius in the making, absolute perfection.

I dutifully recorded her milestones in a baby book my mother-in-law bought us. I saved her first curl, took thousands of pictures, jotted down her first words.

"Cheese," she said.

And "Bo" for boat, looking out the window of our cottage in Maine, and "Mommy juice" for breast milk.

And later—after we left New York, full of regrets, and bought a house in the New Jersey suburbs, six miles away from the lab where Will worked—she said adorable things like "breskit" for "breakfast" and "mewsmik" for "music."

She was still very young when she began to ask, "What's wrong, Mommy?" and "Are you sad?" She would climb on me and try to rearrange my mouth. "Smile, Mommy!" she would say.

And I saw that this child—with her father's luminous blue eyes, his flawless skin, his catlike grace, his restlessness, his energy, his blazing intelligence—had become a watcher, like I was. She saw things.

Will never touched her, but she saw how his moods darkened for no discernible reason, and how sometimes, over a period of days, his actions grew more threatening and irrational until he was transformed into someone who could mow us down. She saw the gentle, tender man who helped out at her preschool, the father her friends loved best, kick whatever was in his way, and the next day hurl a bowl of cereal across the room, and the day after, grab me by the shirt and shake me until the fabric ripped into shreds, then leave the house, slamming the door so hard that bits of plaster were shaken from beneath the moldings.

When he was gone, I stood very still for a moment. I was okay—cool, emptied out, but fine. Then I saw Charlotte weeping in the corner, and I made myself understand that it was *not* okay, that it must never be okay for her. That was the day I phoned Will at work and told him not to come home, that we would not live with him unless he got help.

He would not go alone, so we made an appointment with a therapist in New York, a soft-spoken woman whose dogs slept at her feet. She liked Will, laughed at his irreverence, let him feel her respect and understanding. Here in this safe room, he talked about the pressures that built up within him, work and money, people talking, talking, telling him what to do. He spoke of the "violent fantasies" he had, precursors to the rage. It might begin with a real incident: a man who had tried to take his parking space. But when the incident was done, his rage did not abate. He described in a chilling way how all day he would imagine bashing in the man's skull with a tire iron, how the dream filled his head, full of blood, gore, and dismemberment that day and the next, until he "lost it." The details of these fantasies were so vivid and violent they made me shiver and retreat.

The therapist listened to his gory imaginings respectfully, saying nothing. To help prevent the real incidents from happening, she suggested breathing exercises, the equivalent of counting to ten, so he could catch himself before he lost all reason. If he began to get agitated when we were together, she would say, "Breathe, Will," and he would stop, take a breath, cool down.

He began to tell me about these fantasies when we were home. They frightened me, but I thought perhaps he could discharge some pent-up rage this way. I believed, too, that there was value in knowing, that forewarned, I could keep my distance until the dangerous fury had died out.

I tried. At these times, when I heard the key turn in our front door lock, I stayed where I was instead of greeting him. I let him change his clothes, lose himself in the easy, sensual pleasure of playing with Charlotte, throwing her in the air and tickling her. I tried to ask no questions, mention no chores or dates or obligations. Sometimes, waiting was like listening to the ticking of a hidden bomb. When he was tense, I became fearful and vigilant. I knew that anything I said or did could set him off. I knew it would eventually happen, but I did not know how or when I would trip the switch. Often, after several nights like this, the wait became unbearable, and out of sheer anxiety, I sprang first and, just as he said, brought his rage on.

The first time the monster emerged in the safe room, the therapist leaned back, her eyes wide. *Cunt*, and *fucking bitch, I'll shove my fist down your throat*—standing over both of us, trembling, shaking his huge fist, face nearly purple, spit flying, dangerous, no longer himself.

He slammed out of the room. For a few moments, we sat in silence. I could practically hear her heart beating.

"I hate him," I said. And at that moment I could feel the hatred boil inside me.

"Is this what happens?"

"Yes," I said.

"Does he hit you?" she asked.

"Not anymore," I said. And then, "Not really." I could not bring myself to say that he spit in my face or pushed me against the wall, could not explain that it was not what he did but the fact that I had to go dead to survive, that I had to bleed myself of every drop of emotion, because if I lost my temper, he would kill me. I did not tell her this. I wanted to, but I couldn't. I knew it was important, but as I sat, searching for words, the doubt began to creep in. Where were the bruises and broken bones, where was the smallest mark to justify my fear? There were no marks, and so, though I was convinced that he could kill me, I believed, too, that I was exaggerating what I felt, making it up.

"Do you want to leave him?" she asked softly.

"Yes," I said.

I was ashamed that the therapist had glimpsed this secret part of my life. And yet I was relieved that someone on this earth knew that the monster really did exist, that there was someone who could remind me that I had not conjured it from air.

Something else was in play that for years I could not articulate. I wanted the therapist to keep liking Will. I did not see her obvious affection for him as getting in the way of the treatment. I saw it as validation. She was the only one who knew that the monster existed and who seemed to understand why I stayed.

Maybe that was why a moment after I said, "Yes," with such conviction, I said, "I don't know," and, "It's so hard."

"I can help you leave if you want. Or we can continue to work on his anger so you can stay. But if you choose to live with him, it will have to be on his terms. Don't expect that life will be fair."

I didn't ask what that meant. I did not wonder why she was so accepting of his violence. I nodded, and when our time was over, I took a deep breath and left.

Will was hunched over a magazine in the waiting room. I held tight to my hatred. I walked past him, out into the hall. He followed me to the elevator. When it came, we squeezed ourselves against opposite walls. And then we spilled out into the street and into our old neighborhood, past the dorm where I had lived with Leslie, the hotel where we'd been married, the stores where we bought fish and bread. I walked briskly, well ahead of him, as if I knew exactly where I was headed, or where I would go with my little daughter if I left. Just walking, calculating the money in my pocket, dividing the money in the bank, my options, my life in one year, in ten.

Of course I could live without him. I had skills; I was not without resources.

His footsteps closed in. "I got a spot on Eleventh Street," he said, as if the knowledge that he had gotten a perfect place to park would make me change my mind.

I walked past him, turning the corner quickly. Still he caught up. "We have child care," he said. "We might as well eat. We can go to that little place where we saw the guy with chicken feet."

A man in a business suit wearing rubber chicken feet, as big as flippers. I laughed at the memory, despite myself. Then I returned to my calculations: enough for train fare, could sleep on the trundle bed in my office that night and the next. I didn't want to let things slide. I wanted to remember what it felt like to live for days in fear. I was determined not to give in, but it was hard when the man at my side, beseeching me, was sweet and seductive, the monster ephemeral, a figment of my imagination. Who was I, anyhow, but the kid who was always crying over nothing. I walked faster, trying to hold on to my anger. The pieces of my life appeared: kids and family, our house, the fun we had. "I don't hit you anymore," he could say, and it was true. "We're here. I haven't broken a single appointment. We're working on things."

I hated myself when I was angry. It was in such opposition to my promise not to live in the house of my childhood, where the air was so often rancorous. It was tiresome to take such tight hold of an ugly feeling, easier to let it slip away. And there was something I had to tell him.

I was still thinking these things, still struggling with them, when we were sitting in the little place where we had seen the man with chicken feet, and I was telling him about Charlotte's teeth, about a picture she had drawn. And we were laughing. And it was over, after all.

Once, after another painful session in which Will had reddened and threatened and slammed out, the therapist saw us holding hands and laughing in the street. "You two," she said, when we next met, "you have this marvelous ability to just push everything aside."

And so it went: the unbearable days cast aside, the good parts nurtured. And there was always Maine, there was always the knowledge that we had a place where nothing bad would happen.

We believed enough or forgot enough to decide to expand our family.

In 1983, our second daughter was born.

Will was the one who worried about Rachel first, because at six weeks old, she did not seem to track moving objects with her eyes. We took her to a neuro-ophthalmologist in New York. During the drive, I kept imagining the doctor chuckling after he examined her and telling me what a worrier I was.

She was blind, he said. Maybe she'd have light and shadow; it was too early to say for sure.

The night I heard these words, I went home and knew that no matter what, I could not fall apart. I had to wake and dress. I needed to keep this family intact, to cook dinner, make costumes, wrap presents. I needed to show Charlotte the face of something beyond sorrow.

I sat on the edge of our bed and what I remembered was my mother sitting just that way, saying, "Our baby is dead." I remembered that when she saw me standing in the doorway, she said, "I'm sorry."

Now that I was mother and daughter both, I understood her apology. More than anything, I had wanted Charlotte's life to be normal and happy. I had wanted her to be unscathed. "Go forward," I wanted to tell her. "Don't cry." But I remembered, too, that nothing my parents did made me feel better after Laura's murder. When they tiptoed, it was the worst; when their voices were soft, it was the worst; when they said nothing and asked for nothing, it was the worst; when they wanted something, it was the worst. I had no comfort, no place to hide, no solutions for their problems, no salve for their wounds.

After Rachel was born, the storms rocked our fragile house with greater frequency. Who was right, who was wrong, what I felt or feared—all this was irrelevant now. What counted was survival. I needed to be strong, to withstand everything, or we would all go under, and I knew how to do it, because I was the steady one, "the designated normal person," I used to joke. I knew how to push through the chaos, push on with all my energy, no matter how much my chest hurt and how much my muscles ached.

It was okay. I knew that I could live through anything. But I fretted for Charlotte.

"Tell her they're like a weather system," the therapist told me, when I asked how to shelter Charlotte from her father's dark moods. "Tell her that sometimes storms build up, and that when she sees the skies darken, she should seek shelter. After all, he's not a bad man, not the kind of person who wants to put his boot in your face."

"A lovely guy," my friend called him.

Hot-tempered like his grandfather, said his mother.

A good man, my own mother often said. He loves you so.

Fighting words, for then I wondered: Did I deserve his wrath? Was I that bad?

Yes. I was that bad, I often thought.

After Rachel's birth, my mother called every day, there in ways she had never been before. And yet I was sullen and disagreeable, so argumentative I would hang up the phone and wonder: How could I be so awful as to break my mother's heart a second time?

And yet—turn the pages of the family albums, proof that my efforts worked. All the county fairs and ski trips, the dog show, the family parties. Sometimes, I watched Will and Charlotte at the water's edge in Maine, collecting sea creatures for a salt-water aquarium—tiny lobsters and eels and hermit crabs—and believed that the worst of our discord was in the past. I watched them tend the aquarium and, at season's end, return the animals to the sea, and it seemed that no one was a better father than Will, that no matter what I felt, I could never deprive my children of his love.

Then I would think that I would never have chosen these things to have happened, but they had. And we were going to get through them. I hated when people assumed that there was something educational or ennobling about hardship. But I was tough, and I knew it. I would not be knocked down. I would not be defeated, if not for my sake, then for Charlotte's.

"I love her too much," I found myself saying.

"What do you mean, 'too much'?" a friend asked. "You're supposed to love your kids."

I considered this. Why did my love for her feel over the edge? Was it that I loved her directly and fearlessly? It was true that I thought she was beautiful and said so, thought her smart and told her, daring to tempt the fates. It was so wonderful to love someone without fear or anxiety, all-out, no matter what, that I did not want to stop myself. When had I ever loved with such trust?

Never! I often thought.

I would do anything for this child, anything.

Eat fish food?

Yes!

And if she asked you to jump in the lake, you'd jump in the lake?

Yes!

Often, on late-summer afternoons in Maine, I swam alone in the icy water of Quahog Bay. Sometimes, I swam to keep from drowning.

But sometimes, effortlessly, I reached the place where pinpoints of light sparkled like diamonds. I would turn onto my back, bob and drift and feel the sun on my face. Immense happiness washed over me then. I knew that good fortune was mine, too, and I would think: No more, please, don't test me any longer. But I could get to that place. And it seemed worth everything to be able to swim out and away, to be able to strip off the grief and worry and let myself be washed in pleasure. Sometimes I believed I experienced pleasure more deeply than other people because I swam toward it like this, knew how to stop everything to have it.

When I thought this, I saw forgetting as a gift that allowed me to move away from what was ugly and unbearable and grab hold of what was good. I believed, then, that it was best to avoid what I could not change. I tried to look away from what threatened to blind me. And for a while it seemed to work.

The Case

11

ONE DAY IN THE SPRING of 1990, six months after
my first trip to Arizona, I was sitting in my attic
office, surrounded by transcribed interviews, police
reports, and legal documents relating to my sister's case. For
the moment I had set aside my compulsive but fruitless efforts
to compose "the scene." It wasn't that I had lost interest. I
remained frustrated over my inability to write about the night
of my sister's murder in such a way that I could feel myself a
part of it. Intuitively, I knew it was important, and that eventually I had to get it right. But the trip and its aftermath had provided volumes of information. My intention now was to keep
sorting through all of it until I could get it to fit together logi-
cally, to create a lasting, accurate account of my sister's murder.
I fully believed that once I did this, I would be able to close
the case.

I was doing just this, reading through interviews and news
accounts, preparing to put my sister back on her bike and send
her to her death again, when I found a *New York Daily News* feature story about Laura called SHE MAJORED AS MURDER VICTIM.

It was a long, floridly written piece, the details of the crime culled from the Arizona newspapers. I hadn't read it since I was seventeen, and when I unfolded the piece I saw a description of the night my parents got the call from the dean of women, informing them that their daughter had been stabbed to death. In this version, my mother and I are helpless and weeping ("the two had to be put under sedation"), while my father is "in tight control." I was floored when I read this. It was as if my childhood dream had come true, and we were at last the kind of family I used to see on TV. "Bernstein in tight control," it said, transforming my father into the stalwart captain of a crew of spineless ninnies; not *Mrs.* Bernstein in tight control, *Mrs.* Bernstein who called the doctor and family friends, who made all the funeral arrangements, while Mr. Bernstein wandered through the rooms, mute and lost. This stranger is inventing our lives! I thought with outrage. He's telling the story the way he's decided it ought to have been—*Father Knows Best*—and not the way it was.

I was furious that my life had been appropriated and misinterpreted by this man who had never met us, that this same evening that I had been struggling to recall had been homogenized and presented the way it was supposed to have happened, as if all tragedy has the same unbendable logic and order, the same neat arc of grief, vengeance, and swift resolution, like a Victorian novel, where the wedding bells at the end signaled that life, thereafter, was bliss.

I did not see the way I, too, had invented my own life for myself and others. Despite my introspection—an embarrassment, a compulsion, a part of my profession—despite my relentless self-analysis, I could not see the trap of my own stories. I studied the glorious times, the duck pond, the shoe-store balloons, the mundane family life I said was mine, exactly the way, years before, I had studied the photos of the vivacious, remarkable girl whose sister had been murdered. The photos had helped me to re-create myself in the wake of the murder, but I was still reshaping myself to fit a story that was tolerable. It was as if I would fall apart, literally crack into jagged slivers, if I admitted to anything else.

Yet I had called the police. As I sat there, getting ready to send Laura to her death, the thought of what I had done five days before jolted me, filling me with such shame that for a moment I forgot my sister's case. Will had so terrified me that I had called the police.

If someone had asked me what had happened, I could not have explained with any coherence. It was true that all week I had felt his rage building. And then on Saturday he had woken, kicked whatever was in his path, thrown things in the trash. I shouted at him to stop, and he came toward me, and kept coming until he was inches away. I felt the hatred build within me, and I lunged for him, grabbed the glasses off his face, then raced downstairs. I heard Charlotte wake, and Will, throwing things and stamping on them. I was on the phone by then, calling the police, afraid for my life, the life that was no longer merely mine but one I was handing down to my daughters.

The shame I felt was so deep and layered that I could not speak of it, not then, could not bear to recall the sound of my own voice in the receiver, my own pinched, naked cry of "Help." I could not stand to bring into memory the look on the cops' faces when they walked into my living room minutes after I hung up, the way they stood, awkwardly holding their clubs, the short one studying the furnishings, as ordered as a still life, the tall one looking at my unmarred, untouched face.

As soon as they asked, "Are you okay? You want to say what happened?" I felt another level of shame. Liar, faker, crying over nothing. Will had not even touched me. Then I heard Charlotte gasping for breath behind a locked door and remembered that I did have reason to be afraid. It was no consolation, though. I was ashamed in my child's eyes that I had called the police, and ashamed to be married to her father.

Will appeared in the living room then, his fury concealed just enough for him to tell them, "There won't be any trouble. Everything will be fine." And before they could question him further, he reached for his briefcase and left the house.

I stood there, listening to Charlotte crying softly, thinking of my parents, who were expected for lunch that afternoon, thinking, too, of the report of this "domestic disturbance" that surely would be published in the local newspaper. I was wondering what to say to my daughter, what was right to do, what the cops would put in the report. "Responded to call, found jewelry box in splinters, beads and pearls all over floor." I could not explain why I had been so afraid. It wasn't that the week of waiting for Will's rage to erupt had driven me mad. It wasn't because of the look in his eyes, his reddened face, the strength in his huge hands. I called because I was losing the ability to back off when he was in a black mood. Lately, when I felt the storm coming, I wanted to hit back more than I wanted to live. In my own anger, I had stopped caring about consequences. That morning, I was afraid of myself. Maybe that was why I had called for help.

I found my daughters, held them close—Charlotte, who saw and was afraid, and Rachel, who absorbed our sorrow and cried when we cried, without fully understanding why—and I said, "I'm sorry." Such paltry and inappropriate words. "I'm really sorry."

How could I teach them that respect was their birthright in this house, I thought, as I cleaned up and made the beds. There was a slight tremor in my hands, but only I could tell. My calmness seemed terribly wrong, but someone had to hold things together.

When my parents arrived, I told them Will had to work—an easy excuse, the words spoken without hesitation. But I was prickly and irritable during lunch, so unbearable to myself that, after coffee, I slipped down to the basement to fold laundry on the washer lid.

My mother followed me downstairs a few minutes later. I supposed she knew that something was wrong and that it had to do with Will, because she began to ask, "Does he always go to the lab on Saturday?" And when I said that yes, he often did, she said, "I thought when his dissertation was done he'd have weekends off. He works so hard."

"I work hard, too," I said, as petulant as a teenager.

My mother's eyes briefly met mine. She began to praise Will, as she often did when I was upset, speaking of how hard he worked, how loyal he was, how much he loved the children. My mother had seen the scary edge of Will's temper and so her praise seemed full of an unspoken command. Stay married no matter what. Divorce is such a tragedy, she often said.

I looked up blankly, unable to respond. I felt expendable when she said these things.

Does it matter that we parted for three nights? Does it matter that I called him at work and said, "No more." I had said it other times, too. Does it matter that when he was gone, I became a cool, disembodied spectator of my own life: watching myself buy groceries, thinking: Look at her, turning each strawberry slowly to check for bruises, holding the melon to her ear to hear if the seeds rattle inside. Look at the way she scrutinizes the fruit, accepting nothing less than perfection for the children, nothing but the best. Later I took Rachel swimming and, hearing our laughter echo in the pool, thought: Listen to the sounds of her happiness. I played gin with Charlotte, game after game. As if her fate is in these cards, I thought. And I read through the documents relating to Laura's murder, studying every word in them.

Does it matter that on the fourth day Will came home unannounced at dinnertime, and the children dashed up, and it was, "Daddy, Daddy," and he leaned over to embrace them, his eyes as full of tears as they were the night our first daughter was born, and it seemed foolish to deprive them when he was decent at heart, "not the kind of man who puts his boot in your face." Seeing him with the kids weakened and confused me. They loved him. I could not cut him out of their life. I had to make this work even if it killed me.

And so Will came home. We kept our distance for a few days. We tried to push the past aside. With all our might we pushed. For years we were good at this, both of us. But I was so tired. I could not push, or risk my anger, or leave. I could not see my own death, but I was beginning to see my sister's.

I put the *Daily News* piece back in the folder and transport myself to Arizona on the night of September 21, 1966. I'm listening to my sister ask Jinx if she can borrow her bicycle. Jinx agrees. Laura gathers some records and gets the bike.

It's twilight when my sister pedals down East Lemon Street and turns onto Mill Avenue. She rides for a half mile or so, until she reaches what used to be Tempe's downtown and is now a blighted area of pool halls and bars. She rides past Perry's, on Fifth Street, a bar that can hold seven hundred people, and a block away, the Asylum, a notorious biker bar and hangout for members of the Dirty Dozen, a motorcycle club with an active local chapter. She sees all their choppers lined up outside, the hairy bikers with guns, chains, knives, and dynamite caps hanging from them like Christmas ornaments, everything out in the open, because, in Arizona, territorial law is in effect, and state statute permits people to carry loaded weapons, as long as they are not concealed.

The Casa Loma, a seedy residence hotel, is on Mill and Fourth. It has the roughest bar on the street, with enough room for four hundred brawlers to cavort. For all its seediness, the street is safe, the arrests mostly for drunk and disorderly. The police have a cozy relationship with bar owners: they root out the most disruptive drunks, and shake down the high school kids for the switchblades they carry, a status symbol in those days. That it was illegal didn't matter. The kids emptied their pockets and the cops took the knives. At the end of the day, they threw them in a big box in the briefing room, and when the box got full, hauled it off to the property room. There were so many knives the cops used them for letter openers.

My sister is small and easily frightened, but perhaps Mill Avenue and the bearded bikers revving their hogs do not scare her. Nothing bad has happened to us. No one we know has been held up or raped; no houses on the block where we grew up have been burglarized, no children abducted. Crime for us is a lost wallet never returned. Or Rudy the Nudy, the name the kids in our neighborhood gave to the legendary flasher who in the summer of 1963 was said to lurk in our part of town, and whom we fervently wished to see, the way, when we were little, we had hoped to see the tooth fairy. Murder is something that happens on TV shows or in the mysteries my mother absorbs, several a week. Murder is committed by the obviously deranged, by weirdos who skulk in dark alleys, men who are evil to the core. You'd know one if you saw one by his crazy eyes and wild hair.

And when, in June of our last summer together, things began to change, we could read about the drifter named Richard Speck rampaging through a dorm where Filipino nurses slept and murdering all but one, shiver and put it from our minds. We could read, two months later, about Charles Whitman, the former Marine who climbed to the top of the University of Texas tower, gunned down fourteen people and wounded another thirty-one, and scoff, "Texas!" the way my mother had, for Texas, with its gunslinger reputation, bore the permanent stain of Kennedy's assassination. We didn't see these things as harbingers of violence to come.

And so when I imagine my sister riding her bicycle down Mill Avenue at twilight, I see her as unafraid. Howie loves her. Perhaps she believes, as I did, that love will protect her. She dismounts her bike and takes it around to the back of the Casa Loma Hotel. She is chaining it to the window grate when someone comes out of the shadows, stabs her four times in the body and twice in the head, and leaves her to die.

An hour later, a boy bursts into the Tempe police station, gasping for air, and tells the desk clerk that he's seen a girl he thinks is dead. The cops go to the crime scene. They secure it and light it, get her body chalked on concrete. The photos are taken.

Dale Douglas is one of the detectives who went to the crime scene that night. In my attic office, I imagined him circling Laura's body, careful not to touch anything, just circling, noting the facts. *Twenty-year-old white female*, with her address listed as Peoria, Illinois. Money still in her wallet. No sign of attempted rape.

Dale Douglas was the youngest of the three men assigned to the case, hardly older than Laura. With four years on the squad, he was still blond and baby-faced, pretty enough to be dressed in tight-fitting clothes and used as a decoy to trap the homosexuals who hung out at the Valley Art Theater—the crime he considered "really bad" in those days. He knew Mill Avenue well. He'd grown up in town, and had spent countless evenings tagging along beside his mother, a regular in the bars. His home life then had been "uncontrolled"; up through high school, he'd been "in and out of all sorts of things." But then there had been the army and police work, and by 1966 he was on the other side, patrolling, regulating, keeping order.

Dale Douglas loved being a detective, found his work "thrilling" and "fun." Years later, in a hesitant, almost tender way, he would describe my sister as "delicate," and imagine her, new in town, just looking for someone to "buddy up with." But at the time she was nothing more than the central clue, a puzzle piece. And so he circled and looked: long, straight hair, hoop earrings, jeans—these were the things that marked her as "trendy," like the kids who hung out at that new coffee shop called Euthanasia.

So he and another detective, Erich Schoenfeld, went to Euthanasia. They watched people swinging on the big rope that hung from the rafters, stoned out of their minds. A quarter of a century later he was still mulling over the sight, wondering: Where did all these people come from? What was going on in their heads? Sometimes he was repelled by the boys with their longish hair and the weird things they drew, but not always, no.

Sometimes he found that the scene fascinated him, too, enough to be aware that if there weren't so many controls on his own life now, he could drift that way, somehow get involved.

But Euthanasia yielded nothing, no leads, no motives, no connections to known drug dealers. Over the next two days they interviewed three hundred people. They interviewed Howie and his roommate, really worked over the girl Laura went to visit. They grilled every tenant in the Casa Loma Hotel and the apartment across the street. They learned absolutely nothing.

They kept going back to David Mumbaugh, the kid who had rushed into the station house to say he had found her body, because he had been there soon after it happened. "Butch" Mumbaugh had checked out: he had a job and his own automobile, and, in the chief's words, was "doing okay for hisself." Everything he'd said had been verified—that he'd worked late, the Dodge in the used car lot. The Dodge he'd been on his way to see was still in the Dana Brothers lot. He was a good kid, a local kid, who dressed in a familiar way and came from a crowd they understood. He was cooperative and patient when they called and asked him again and again to describe that night, their questions like the metal detectors that combed through the weedy lots. You had to do something. You had to keep going over the same ground, in case you missed something.

Samples of her hair, skin, fingernails, and blood were sent to the FBI, and teletypes were sent out to other agencies, describing the crime. They tried to find a link between Laura's murder and the murder of a young woman in New Jersey who had been stabbed to death with a very unusual knife. They tried to find a connection between Laura's murder and the murder of Valerie Percy, daughter of Charles Percy, soon to be an Illinois senator. The two were about the same age, their murders were four days apart, and Laura had once lived in Illinois. Nothing.

The contents of her purse were scrutinized. Wallet, tissues, doodads. A "vial of prescription medicine marked Tedral." A "black and white picture of a girl, possibly the victim's sister." "An envelope and letter addressed to Laura Bernstein from Martha Bernstein in Fair Lawn."

She had gotten my letter. All these years later, relief washed through me. She had gotten it, after all.

There was always a lot of mail when a sensational crime was committed. Letters from people who claimed to have clues, and people who claimed to have divine information. But the letters after Laura's murder shook up Dale Douglas, people writing to say that her murder was "retribution," that the devils were out there. A letter that just said, "chop chop chop hack hack hack," the pen pressed so hard it had nearly gone through the paper. Lots of stuff like that.

Eight days, nine days, still no leads. And plenty to contend with, people saying that the Tempe police were too backwater to solve the case, all this publicity bad for the university.

Late in the afternoon of September 29, four men stood in the back of the Casa Loma Hotel, scrutinizing the crime scene, discussing different scenarios, going over the same events, this time in daylight, hoping that just maybe they would see something they had missed all the other times. Tall, black-haired Erich Schoenfeld, Dale Douglas, the police chief, Bill Hill, David Mumbaugh. Mumbaugh, because he was there so soon after it happened, and because, as Douglas recalled, if there was anything they were going to find, it would be through him.

Mumbaugh was younger than the other men, only eighteen, but he was a local kid, almost one of them.

They were quiet, each of them, once again trying to summon up the night of the twenty-first. Douglas remembered that by the time he had arrived at the Casa Loma, it was so dark the police had to set up lights. And so he said, mostly to himself, "It must have been really dark in there."

Mumbaugh agreed. Yeah, it had been so dark he didn't see her at first; he kind of hit her with his foot as he was walking by.

The others turned and listened. Mumbaugh had told his story several times and never said anything about hitting her with his foot. He continued, this time with a long story about the big flashlight "setting" on the ground, how it had been off when he tripped on her, but reminded him of a flashlight he'd once had, how he'd run to get the guys across the street and when he returned it was gone.

And Dale Douglas noticed how Mumbaugh had broken out in "the damnedest sweat, how it just started pouring off him."

That night Erich Schoenfeld drove to the Mumbaughs' house, a neat, well-maintained ranch not far from the police station. The Mumbaughs were eating supper with their son. "Regular, decent, wholesome people," Schoenfeld would recall. "Television kind of parents," in Dale Douglas's memory. And David a boy who got a lot of attention, didn't want for anything.

"My wife thinks I'm hard," Erich Schoenfeld said, when we met, and he supposed it was true and maybe inevitable if you saw as much as a cop did. But he would never forget that night, how he'd stood with his head lowered and asked if David could get the shirt and shoes he had worn the night he found the girl. How the family, pausing over their supper, was much like his own. David, always agreeable, went into his room. Mrs. Mumbaugh, a small, thin woman, "mousy" was how people recalled her, asked, "Is my boy in trouble?"

Her boy, her only child.

David appeared with a white shirt and shoes. Schoenfeld said, "No, ma'am," and thought perhaps he was.

Meanwhile, the other detectives went over the original police report from the night Mumbaugh ran in breathless, knees skinned up, and said he found a girl he thought was dead.

One of them reread the interview with the young man from the apartment across from the Casa Loma. He was a graduate student Mumbaugh had never met before, not a "friend" as he had reported that night.

Someone circled the fact that Mumbaugh told the student, "A girl has been murdered," and not that he had found a girl he thought was dead.

In the original statement Mumbaugh said that he had been going *to* work, not returning from work.

Someone made note of the desk officer's initial report that David wore a plaid shirt, while the shirt he had retrieved at home was white.

And so a shift began from *one of us* to *one of them*. It was hard to free themselves from the perception of David Mumbaugh as a steady kid, "doing okay for hisself."

"You classify people to know how to evaluate them," Dale Douglas told me. "You size a guy up. You put one person in one category and another person in another one, because it saves a whole lot of trouble of having to develop an opinion about them. Experience tells you that it's not a good way to be, because you can miss a lot when you start doing that. But—that's what happens." Laura, with her long hair and hoop earrings, was a stranger, an outsider, a suspect. But David Mumbaugh was from the crowd they understood. He was one of them.

12

THEY ASKED MUMBAUGH TO DRIVE to the station that night, not because he was a suspect, the cops would later say, but to clear up some inconsistencies. As always he cooperated, seemed almost eager. He drove to the station of his own free will. At 8:09 he arrived. It was the old station house then, and their desks were set up pretty close, Hill, Schoenfeld, Douglas, with Mumbaugh sitting between them.

How much time did it take? How many yards away? The flashlight on or off? They had asked these same questions so many times that Mumbaugh wearied. Hey, he had this whole thing memorized and so did they, he said.

Yes, they agreed. They knew it pretty well. But there were some discrepancies they wanted to ask him about.

Going to or coming from the used-car lot? Flashlight shining, flashlight off? White shirt, colored shirt? And the shoes he handed to Schoenfeld the night the lieutenant had gone to the Mumbaugh house. They had had what appeared to be blood on them.

"How can you account for this?" Lt. Hill asked.

"I'll tell you the truth," Mumbaugh said. "I lied." His face and neck reddened. His jaw began to quiver. "I started to walk down the alley and I tripped over her. Honest. I didn't kill her."

The police stopped questioning him for a moment. It was 8:56 p.m. They gave him a piece of paper that said "Your Rights." *You have the right to remain silent. Anything you say can be used against you in court*, it said. *You have the right to talk to a lawyer for advice before we ask you any questions, and to have him with you during questioning. You have this right to the advice and presence of a lawyer even if you cannot afford to hire one. We have no way of giving you a lawyer, but one will be appointed for you, if you wish, if and when you go to court. If you wish to answer questions now without a lawyer present, you have the right to stop answering questions at any time. You also have the right to stop answering at any time until you talk to a lawyer.*

These rights are now such common knowledge that kids playing cop games on the playground know enough to say, "You have the right to remain silent . . . Anything you say can be held against you," before they begin their interrogation. But the Miranda rulings had only been passed in June, four months before Mumbaugh was in the police station.

According to the hand-recorded transcript, it was 8:57 p.m. when Bill Hill said, "Now, David, now is the time when you're going to have to stand on your own two feet and straighten up your problems. It's going to be up to you. Nobody is going to straighten them up for you."

Mumbaugh sat staring blankly, with his hand to his mouth, slowly shaking his head back and forth—*no*—but when the words came out he said, "Yes. I did it. I was going to Dana Brothers. She started to scream. I said what's the matter. She said get away. Then I hit her, and when she turned I stabbed her. Then I ran until I got my senses."

The police asked him to go over the details some more—which hand he used to hit her, how many times he stabbed her, where he got the knife, what he did with it after he murdered Laura.

The knife broke and closed, Mumbaugh said. He put it in his pocket and got back in his car. He started driving home, then changed his mind and pulled into a Richfield station. The blood on his shoes, well, he had kicked her once or twice to make sure she was dead, and now, in the gas station rest room, he stopped to wipe off the blood. Then he drove back. He returned to the Casa Loma and then ran to the police. The knife was still in his pocket when he went to the station.

"What did you do with the knife, David?" asked Lt. Hill.

On Dale Douglas's desk was a black-handled switchblade knife he'd gotten from the property room a couple of years before. In the silence after Hill's question, Mumbaugh saw the knife.

"You found it!" he said. "How did you do that? I threw it into the canal at Forty-eighth Street. I threw it over the top of the car, but I guess you found it."

Then, in a bragging way, he started to tell how he liked to throw things over the roof of his car while he drove, rocks or bottles, how he was so good he could throw a pop bottle over his roof and into the open window of another car at sixty miles per hour. He was driving forty miles an hour when he threw the knife into the canal at Forty-eighth Street that night and was sure it had gone in.

It had gone in. The next day, the canal was dredged with ropes and a powerful magnet, and Mumbaugh's knife, which was identical to Douglas's, was found.

That night, they asked him again why he killed my sister.

Mumbaugh said he didn't know. Then he said, "I wanted to see if I could get away with it. I wanted to see if I could fool you guys."

And afterwards how did he feel?

"Stupid," he said.

Did he feel it was wrong?

Yeah, but mostly what he felt was stupid. "I had that feeling again tonight of wanting to get hold of someone and beat the hell out of them."

Dale Douglas asked, "Do you think your parents know about this?"

Mumbaugh said, "I don't know. You call them."

Douglas said he'd have to do that himself. Mumbaugh walked to the phone and dialed his parents' number.

"Mom, let me talk to Dad," he said. "Just let me talk to Dad . . . I'm at the station. Will you come down? Just come down!"

Moments later, the Mumbaughs were there, Betty and David Sr. When Mumbaugh saw his mother, he said, "I did it."

"How?" she asked.

"With my switchblade."

"Honey, David!" cried Mrs. Mumbaugh.

"Ever since the eighth grade I've wanted to kill someone."

"Do you know what you're saying, son?"

"I'm not your son, Mother!"

"Yes, yes, you are!" cried Mrs. Mumbaugh.

And David Mumbaugh said, "Your son wouldn't do a thing like this!"

But he was their son, and he had just confessed to murder, and now they had to get him the best lawyer in town.

Easy to say, but imagine it further: A man and his wife are standing in a police station. Their son has just confessed to committing the crime that has been splashed across the front pages for the last nine days. My sister was a college student from out of town, not rich, famous, or beautiful. But in 1966 murder was not an everyday occurrence. Murder didn't happen in Tempe, not on Mill Avenue, never to a college student. The murder of someone's daughter was enough to make people shudder.

Their son, Butch, who would be described as quiet and polite, a boy who liked cars and collected rocks, got a "bang out of playing football" with "neighborhood youngsters" and never missed a day of work, their son looked up at them and said, "I did it."

The Mumbaughs, described to me as unsophisticated people, "lower-middle-class," had moved to Arizona from Youngstown, Ohio, six years before, seeking a better climate after Mrs. Mumbaugh's heart surgery. "Modest" is the word that kept cropping up. Of modest means. They had probably never met a lawyer, but I imagine them standing in the station, vowing to get the best lawyer in town. It's what you hear on TV and in the movies; it's what you're supposed to say if someone you love gets into trouble.

How do people who may never have met a lawyer, let alone the best one in town, go about finding one? The Mumbaughs have to think on their feet; they have to find a lawyer immediately. Mr. Mumbaugh is a salesman in the air-conditioning business; he's done work for a man who has a lawyer named Jay Dushoff. How does he know this? Perhaps the name came up casually, the way people say to each other at parties, "I have a *great* internist." Perhaps the man who bought air-conditioning from Mr. Mumbaugh said, in passing, "I've got this great attorney." So Mr. Mumbaugh got Dushoff's phone number and called him at home.

Dushoff, who was thirty-two in 1966, was a hot-shot graduate of Harvard Law who had moved to Phoenix in search of a society less stratified than in Philadelphia, where he had been raised. He had a general law practice, and no particular experience or interest in criminal law. In his eight years in Phoenix he had worked on fewer than ten criminal cases. But he had just taken on a new partner, Bob Corcoran, who had been a prosecutor and had the procedural experience Dushoff lacked. So the deal he struck with the Mumbaughs was this: he'd take their son's defense if Bob Corcoran could be part of the team, could be Dushoff's "comfort blanket."

I doubt that the Mumbaughs could have known how aggressive Dushoff and Corcoran were. It was a fluke that they had hired these gladiators, "bastards," one of the detectives said of them years later, "real pricks."

What Corcoran and Dushoff had when the sun rose the next day was a statement in which their client confessed to first-degree murder and named the weapon he used to kill Laura, a switchblade knife dredged up in the canal at Forty-eighth Street, exactly where he had said it would be.

Dushoff was no stranger to the old legal truism, "If you're strong on the facts, argue the facts. If you're strong on the law, argue the law. If you're weak on both, bang on the table and yell." The facts were that David Mumbaugh had confessed rather spectacularly to murdering Laura. But Dushoff and Corcoran didn't need to bang on the table, not yet. The Miranda decision was new. Police resented it. They were unused to the restraints it placed on them. To Dushoff, the police were "not exactly towers of integrity. Not rocket scientists." If the defense team could prove that the confession was illegally obtained, everything contained within it, every word, would be inadmissible in court. Even the knife would be inadmissible under the "fruit of the poisoned tree" doctrine. If the confession was invalid in a court of law, there was no case.

In Miranda, as it was set out in 1966, as soon as a person was in "custodial interrogation" he had to be given his rights. The *moment* he was a suspect. David Mumbaugh had walked into the station at 8:09 p.m., but did not sign the waiver until 8:56 p.m. What happened in those forty-seven minutes?

The police said that Mumbaugh was *not* a suspect, that the "custodial interrogation" did not begin until they questioned him about the discrepancies in his statement. He was free to come and go during those first forty-seven minutes. On other occasions before this evening, Mumbaugh had come to the station of his own accord, had shown great interest in the case, and left of his own accord. True, they had called him down on the night of September 29 to question him again, but he was not yet a suspect.

Laura's murder was no longer relevant; her death had no place in the legal maneuvers that filled the papers over the next months. Now it was a chess game, a contest between defense attorneys who saw themselves as a "brake on abusive governmental power" and prosecutors ("bloodthirsty zealots") determined to make the charges stick.

The arraignment date was set. Corcoran and Dushoff filed for a delay and received it, then filed a motion to seal the testimony, claiming that undue publicity would make a fair trial impossible.

"Undue publicity" because they pinned their hopes on proving that the confession, and all that it contained, would be ruled inadmissible. If that was the case, they didn't want it splashed all over the newspapers. The prejudice against Mumbaugh would be inevitable. "There's an old expression," Dushoff told me in an interview. "Even the judge reads the morning paper."

Their precedent was another sensational case, that of Dr. Samuel H. Sheppard, who had been convicted of second-degree murder in the killing of his pregnant wife. Sheppard's first appeal was unsuccessful, but he was released from prison on July 16, 1964, by the order of a federal district judge of Dayton, Ohio, who ordered a new trial on the grounds that "prejudicial publicity" and a "carnival atmosphere" at the first trial had tainted the conviction. Sheppard hired F. Lee Bailey as his defense attorney, and on November 16, 1966, was acquitted of all charges.

So, although Jay Dushoff would tell me that it was nearly impossible to win a case based on "undue publicity," without question this was a concern for the state in my sister's case. The newspapers printed enraged editorials about the inherent dangers of cutting off the flow of information. But the defense team won this round. The press and public were barred from the preliminary hearing, and the transcript of the proceedings was sealed. The newspapers ran the hearing as a lead story but were stuck running a piece which had so little new information that two paragraphs were spent naming the titles of the books witnesses had brought to court.

And where was I? What do I remember of this?

. . . creeping from my room one night, hearing my mother thunder, "I will not go!"

In my files was a letter Howie sent me. He had been subpoenaed to appear at the hearing. "Just having to see the boy was awful enough," he wrote. "They showed me some terrible pictures . . . and asked me questions I didn't like. Everyone is so concerned about his rights, but they don't think of Laura's or mine."

The case was tried on May 1, 1967. Mumbaugh pleaded not guilty.

His attorneys encouraged him to do this. "You don't want the prosecutor to see the case as an absolute slam dunk," Dushoff explained. "You want to be able to discuss plea bargaining."

The only hope the defense team had was to challenge the confession in an appeal. A not-guilty plea was needed for this reason as well.

They worked out a deal: The only evidence the prosecutors would bring into court would be the confession. Mumbaugh, in exchange, would waive his right to a jury trial.

In the courtroom, on the morning of May 1, Corcoran asked Mumbaugh if he understood that by waiving a right to a jury he was placing his fate in the judge's hands.

"Yes, sir," Mumbaugh said.

Did he realize that if the judge found him guilty of first-degree murder the judge could sentence him to death?

"Yes, sir," he said.

The trial lasted fifteen minutes, setting a record for brevity in a capital case.

Mumbaugh was found guilty and sentenced to life imprisonment.

Corcoran and Dushoff discussed their strategy for appeal with reporters.

"Freedom . . . is a distinct possibility," one news analyst wrote.

. . .

What did I feel? That afternoon in 1989, when I stood at the crime scene behind the Casa Loma Hotel, Erich Schoenfeld moved so close that I could feel him breathe. I shielded my eyes and looked around. The building now housed a restaurant called Mill Landing, an attractive, upscale place, done up Southwestern-style, with a pink floor and aqua and terra-cotta tile, a sandal shop, a bookstore, a yogurt shop, on a broad flat main drag of an overgrown college town.

Everyone seemed attractive and clean-cut. Lots of blondes with golden skin and guys in fraternity T-shirts, and racks full of dirt bikes and hybrids. ASU had nearly 40,000 students by 1989 and a championship football team that played in a stadium right off Mill Avenue. The transformation of the street had begun in 1972 with a million dollars in block grants from HUD, but the stadium and the thought that millions of Americans would be watching the Sun Devils on TV had been the real impetus for Mill Avenue's renewal.

What did I feel?

It was so sun-drenched.

Schoenfeld waited, eyes riveted to me. I knew I was a suspect, guilty of something. "You take someone to the crime scene, it usually opens them up," he had said. And he was watching me, waiting for me to speak.

"It's so benign," I said.

On the way back to the station, he asked about my family. I thought about the way we had squatted by the duck pond, on the day when the cherry blossoms were in bloom and the petals drifted in the water like little boats. Benign, ordinary.

"I have two girls," I said.

"I have daughters, too," he said.

"I've just sent a daughter off to college," Jay Dushoff had told me.

"I have a nineteen-year-old daughter," Bob Corcoran said.

I drove from the crime scene where I did not feel anything except the sun's daggers in my eyes, sat at dinner beside a man I loved and feared, and argued that rattlesnake was a vegetable. Then I flew home to see my daughters, two sisters, not a dead sister and a living one who could never be enough, but a whole one and a damaged one. Nothing I said or did could relieve Charlotte of the knowledge that she was the future, the only one who could go forward. Despite everything I had done, I had passed this to her, like a genetic disease.

13

WILL AND I HAD A MULBERRY TREE right outside the window of our house in New Jersey that
produced massive numbers of white berries. As
soon as the berries ripened, hundreds of birds descended on
the tree, so many that they made a wall of sound, lovely and
chilling both. On the night an advocate from the Maricopa
County Victim Witness Program called to tell me that David
Mumbaugh was petitioning to have his sentence commuted, I
was listening to this wall of sound. It was June 1990. Two
months had passed since I had called the police, eight months
since Will and I had flown to Arizona. I wasn't thinking about
my marriage or my sister's murder, but of the white berries,
and how in another week the uneaten ones would cover the
paths around the house with a fetid sloppy mess. No matter
how often I swept, squashed fruit could be tracked into every
room, and it would seem as if I spent all my spare time sweeping. I was thinking how tired I was, as if the physical effort of
sweeping had worn me out. I swept so much, even my dreams
were full of it. In one dream, the only clear space left in the

room was a tiny circle, and I swept as if on a turntable. When I woke, I remembered the super from my apartment building in the Village, leaning on her broom and saying, "Are you sure you did the right thing marrying that man?" I knew when I rose from bed that I could not answer that question, because I could no longer bear to think of it.

I knew that Mumbaugh was still in prison, but that night I learned that he had petitioned for his release from prison ten times, beginning in 1972, six years after Laura's murder. By 1990, under state statutes, someone convicted of first-degree murder in Arizona had to serve twenty-five calendar years flat-out before coming up for parole. But in 1967, the year Mumbaugh was convicted of first-degree murder, life sentences were "indeterminate" and had no set end date. Hearings for inmates who wanted release were conducted in two phases. First the inmate's petition went before the parole board. If it was found to have merit, it was sent to the governor, who could commute—set an end date—to the sentence.

I was surprised to realize how often Mumbaugh had come up for commutation. Where were we—Laura's family—during all this, I wondered. How was it possible for us not to know that Mumbaugh had been trying to get out? Why didn't we know that in 1980 his bid for freedom had been approved by the parole board, and that it was the governor who had turned it down? My parents had not wanted to know, but over the next few days I understood that they hadn't been meant to know, either. Although families of inmates had always been invited to write letters and appear at hearings, families on the other side were not allowed to be part of the process.

In the 1970s, things began to change, in part, some said, as an outgrowth of the women's movement, and because of well-publicized complaints from family members in highly visible murder cases. The mother of Sharon Tate, the pregnant actress who'd been murdered by Charles Manson, and the family of the Newport heiress Sunny Von Bulow were among the first to make public their demands for a say at parole hearings. In 1982, a presidential task force on victims of crime recommended that the Constitution be amended to afford victims constitutional rights. Although that recommendation was never put in place, a few states wrote victims'-rights statutes. Arizona was one of them. Sixteen years after Laura's murder, a law was passed requiring that "the attorney general, presiding judges, county attorneys, and victims be notified of parole board hearings." Even so, my family had never been informed of the hearing held for Mumbaugh that year, nor had they gotten notice about the hearing three years later.

Then, in 1989, Arizona Governor Evan Meecham was impeached, and his secretary of state, Rose Mofford, stepped into office. In May of that year, against the advice of her aides, Mofford approved the commutation of three lifers. Among them were James Hamm, who had gunned down a man during a drug deal, and Carl Kummerlowe. In 1969, Kummerlowe had butchered Harley Kimbro, his ex-girlfriend's husband, and placed the body parts in several ice chests. Kimbro's family had not been notified of the hearing as was stipulated under a 1982 law, and when they learned of Kummerlowe's commutation from the newspaper, they mounted a strenuous grassroots campaign to put a bill of rights for crime victims in the state constitution. Mofford tried to rescind the commutation of both Hamm and Kummerlowe, but there had been no improprieties in Hamm's case, and he was eventually released. Kummerlowe was sent back to prison.

Victims' rights stayed a heated issue, and a year later, in May 1990, a state constitutional amendment passed requiring that families not only be notified before a hearing but be given a chance to write a letter for the hearing and to make their opinions part of the public record. It was clear that the state could no longer afford to flout the law.

When the attorney with the major-felony unit got Mumbaugh's next petition, he asked an advocate from the Victim Witness Program to find my parents. The search was easy, since they had never moved.

Barbara Anderson, the advocate initially assigned the case, was a chatty young woman in the last weeks of pregnancy. In the midst of explaining why she phoned me, she cheerfully described her girth and her aching back.

Anderson had contacted my parents first. My father answered the phone. She asked if he would write an "impact statement" before the hearing, and he said he would. Before she hung up, she made sure he wrote down her name and address. "I made him take my phone number, too, in case he thought of questions later," she said.

An hour after that, my mother called Anderson to say there'd be no letter. She just didn't feel comfortable writing one.

"I tried to caution your mom that her silence might show an acceptance of a commutation. I told her that since the family had never been on record in any of the earlier hearings, a statement would help carry on for future hearings. I could respect her position. But I needed her to know the situation, and to know before she made her final decision, that this guy, Mumbaugh, wasn't going to give up."

The answer from my mother was still no.

Was there someone else who might want to write a statement, Anderson had asked my mother. A brother or sister—anyone? She tugged and prodded until, reluctantly, my mother gave her my number.

When Barbara Anderson told me this story, she was puzzled and disturbed by my mother's seeming lack of interest. She could not comprehend that when Laura was murdered, my parents got a phone call late at night, and in the morning flew to Phoenix. They went to the morgue, where my father identified Laura's body, then they came home, buried her, and tried to bury their sadness, as I had. There were no advocates in those days. Nor had there been a place for my parents. Everything that happened or did not happen regarding the circumstances of Laura's death went on 2,400 miles away, apart from them. To receive a phone call from a stranger twenty-four years later felt as random as a rock thrown through their window. It frightened my mother to think how easily this stranger had found their number.

I was sad that my mother had never been able to mourn Laura's loss, that she could not hold my newborn daughter in her arms, and, for a long time, could not allow herself to love another child—certainly not another girl. I was sad to see the way she drew away from those around her, people who did not know how to comfort her, in part because she would not let them try. I could see these things clearly because of the ways I was like her, and because it is easier to be wise about someone other than oneself. The night Barbara Anderson called, I thought of my father, too. I knew that, like me, he imagined seeing Laura on street corners, that he saw her in the small, slight dancer at the ballet, and that he saw an edge of resemblance in my daughter's face. But he was not allowed to speak of it. When I thought about my father, I knew that I needed to fly to Arizona for the hearing, that it wasn't enough for me to merely fax a statement to the parole board.

"Will David Mumbaugh be there?" I asked Barbara Anderson.

"I believe so," she said. "But this is all kind of new ground for me, so I couldn't swear to it."

"I'm going to fly in," I said.

I called my parents' house when I finished talking to the advocate and asked my mother why she would not write a statement.

"I feel sorry for the boy," she said.

The boy. It was as if we got old and tired but time stopped for him. I was a mother, too, and would not want to live through what had happened to her, but still I was furious and said: "It's irresponsible to look away."

"I didn't know you were so vengeful," she said.

Vengeful! If only I were capable of wrestling with such a large emotion. Instead, I swept, and the messes were getting bigger. I was so tired.

But privately, in my room, in that corner of my life detached from everything else, I began to wonder: Could you stab a stranger to death at nineteen, and after twenty-four years be well enough to walk the streets? And if the answer was yes, and Mumbaugh was sane, was I ready to say enough is enough?

In the few days before my trip to Arizona and the hearing, I did some more research. Commutation, parole, Arizona, victims' rights—more key words, more reprints, as many phone interviews as I could manage in the little time I had. It was as if I'd been locked in a kind of prison myself and was only now seeing all the ways the world had changed. I felt a sense of urgency unshared by anyone in Phoenix. Indeed, when I reached the county attorney assigned to the case, he would not talk to me: It was the end of the workday, and it was pizza night at his house. He would see me when I got to town.

I drove to my parents' house the day before the hearing. My kids would be staying there while I was in Arizona. They would sleep in my old room, Rachel in my bed and Charlotte in Laura's. At dinner, neither my mother nor my father mentioned the hearing. Nor did they drive me to the airport afterwards. Instead, they asked my cousin Roz.

Heavy rain was falling when we set out. Roz drove slowly. "Your mother has been very upset," she said after a while.

"I know," I said.

I meant to say more, but I fell silent, too. My memory of going home with her the morning after Laura's murder and waiting for her in the car when she stopped for milk was so vivid it was hard to believe how much time had passed between that drive and this one, how much had happened to both of us. It made me think, too, of David Mumbaugh, not married and with children as I had so often imagined, but confined to prison during this long stretch of time. And still my desire was the same. I wanted to see him. I wanted to ask him face-to-face why he murdered my sister.

A flash of lightning blazed in the night sky, lighting up the horizon. Roz pulled up outside the terminal and hugged me goodbye, saying nothing.

When I reached the gate, I learned that all flights had been canceled because of the storm. I bought magazines and checked at other airline counters, asking a dozen people what the chances were that a plane might depart that night. No one could predict. Hours passed this way. Anxiety rose within me. First I was afraid that I would never get to Arizona and that the hearing would go on without me. After that, I was afraid of everything.

Aloft in the plane that took off five hours later, I thought how fragile I was, mere flesh and bone, like my sister. I did not want my children to be left alone.

I was afraid of the cabdriver, who was so obese the steering wheel cut into his midsection.

I was afraid that at the hearing I would speak imprudently.

In some states, commutation hearings didn't really count—I had learned this much before my trip. Parole decisions were sometimes made ahead of time, the hearings themselves pro forma, the family members window dressing. But in Arizona, in 1990, my word counted for a lot. Governor Mofford had made a costly public error. She would not commute any more sentences without the consent of the victims' families. At the last parole hearing for Mumbaugh, there had been only one dissenting vote. I was afraid of this hearing because I knew that what I said had weight, that my opinion mattered.

My fluency made me uncomfortable. It gave me an edge, an unfair advantage I wasn't sure how to use. The sides in this debate were so polarized that ahead of time I could predict what people would say. On one side were those who believed in an eye for an eye—cops, prosecutors, wardens. "Remorseless" was the way a man in the criminal justice system described Mumbaugh to me. "Like a wolf on the prowl." You take a life, you don't deserve mercy, they said. "We're not like you," Erich Schoenfeld had told me, the day he took me to the crime scene. "You" meant liberals, bleeding hearts. "We don't believe criminals should have cable TV."

But neither could I find myself on the side of the "forgiveness community," alongside people who held midnight vigils and talked about the healing qualities of forgiveness. Often they seemed just as misguided. After twenty-four years, shouldn't the decision have to do with whether David Mumbaugh would kill again? Shouldn't it have to do with justice, and not with disembodied compassion or rage?

But no one wanted me to think about justice. Officially, commutations were based on whether it was felt that a prisoner had paid his debt to society. I stood for society. A murder was abstract when no one was around to speak of its effect. My presence made the crime concrete. My role, then, was to state the impact of the murder, to make it real to the parole board, to say whether the debt had been paid.

The system had no time or patience for ambiguity, no interest in fuzzy questions about justice or human nature. "The system has to operate. We have to keep it oiled," I was told by Michael Garvey of the parole board. "The system is like Old Man River; we just keep rolling along."

The system was like Will, who thundered, "Yes or no?" when I presented him with gray areas and doubts.

I checked into my hotel at 2 a.m. I turned the key in my lock and stood in the dark room, listening to footsteps and creaking floorboards. I could not take off my clothes. That night, or what was left of it, I slept fully dressed.

I had come to Arizona to say yes or no.

The office of the Maricopa County Victim Witness Program was around the corner from my hotel. I arrived there at 8:30 a.m. and waited in a room full of stuffed animals. My case had been reassigned to another advocate, Sylvia Conchos. She took me into an office that had portraits of Ninja Turtles on the walls, and drawings by children who had been raped, or whose parents had been murdered. I had always hated the label "victim," did not see myself as a victim, though the state called me that. But as I looked at the toys and drawings, "victims" was the word that came to mind.

We waited in a conference room for the county attorney to arrive. Conchos looked at her watch a few times, but professed no concern. When at last the attorney showed up, he tossed a bulging brown file on the table—Mumbaugh's file, I assumed—and sat heavily. "Nice table," he said. He had a boyish, sun-parched face, and was dressed in a short-sleeved shirt and blue-and-gray saddle shoes. The table seemed to mesmerize him. He grabbed hold of the edge and shook it. "This isn't exactly your government-issue piece of furniture," he said. "It would look good in my kitchen."

He opened the file and began to sort quickly through the top layer.

"Can I look through that when you're done?" I asked.

"You want to copy something?"

"Yes," I said.

"It's mostly boring stuff. Movements from unit to unit and from prison to prison, petty infractions—smoking marijuana, talking back. He's had a lot of furloughs, though. Thirty-six seventy-two-hour ones. Had a girlfriend. Been a statewide driver, a courier between prisons. Probably has skin cancer of the left arm."

I wanted that file. I knew that along with the boring stuff was the complete police report, depositions, legal motions, statements from Mumbaugh, and from his family and friends. I knew, too, that somewhere were thirteen crime-scene pictures—Barbara Anderson had mentioned this. The system had no interest in my struggle to speak justly. But the Freedom of Information Act guaranteed my access to Mumbaugh's files, to everything except his medical and psychiatric records.

"Will he be at the hearing?" I asked again.

"I don't know, I don't go to too many of these things."

He sorted through another layer of papers until he found the document he needed. Then, without looking up, he pushed the file toward me.

14

THE BUILDING where the commutation hearing was being held was only a few blocks from Sylvia Conchos's office. While she and the attorney debated whose car to take, I slid the papers out of David Mumbaugh's file and hurriedly sorted through them, looking for what Holden Caulfield would have called the "David Copperfield kind of crap"—Mumbaugh's early history.

Born in Ohio into an intact family on 2/14/48. An only child. With memories of pets and playmates, uncles and aunts, and many happy Christmases. His father, he told an interviewer, was "fantastic" and his mother "one step below fantastic."

The letters written by family and friends supported Mumbaugh's sunny remembrances. The elder Mumbaughs were "two of the finest people you'd ever want to meet." And their son, Butch, as he was known "to all of us who love him," was a "well-balanced, helpful individual, a frequent visitor to our home."

"He baby-sat for our children. He often helped in projects where physical strength was needed."

"If love and affection alone held the key to Butch's success on the 'outside' he would certainly begin at the top."

"Prior to the instant offense which led to his incarceration, Mumbaugh had no record of criminal arrest."

I was looking for the worm in all this. Looking to disbelieve it completely. Lies, I expected to say. All of it. The good stuff is a veneer that a skilled eye can penetrate. The good stuff is false. The neighbors and friends who had described him in such glowing terms—Butch Mumbaugh, all-American boy— they were just fools, understudies waiting in the wings to say exactly what was expected of them.

I was sorting through these letters with a critical eye when Will came to mind, and for a moment I imagined letters written in his defense. Loving father, they might say. Attentive spouse, serious, hardworking, compassionate, generous to a fault. These qualities were not false; he did not put them on for show. But he had hit me. Maybe Butch Mumbaugh had been a genuinely nice kid. Maybe it was true. But he had murdered my sister, a girl he had never before seen, and in his confession said that ever since the eighth grade he had wanted to beat the hell out of someone. So there had been something else, percolating beneath the surface.

Mumbaugh had a "slight speech impediment" when he was young. As a teenager he did not communicate well with his parents. They were disappointed by his poor grades in school. Hardly the kinds of details that predicted he would grow up to murder. What was the root of his violence, then? If I was to speak justly at the commutation hearing, I needed to find something that would make me feel that if he was released he would not murder again. I continued to leaf through the pages.

Where did the violence come from? Each time I asked that question of Mumbaugh, Will came to mind. I did not want to think about Will, not now, and so I went back to the file. But there was nothing else of Mumbaugh's past. The remaining pages—hundreds of them—were full of details from his years in prison. Even the briefest glance made it clear that his incarceration had been exemplary, though I had often been told that in prison it was hard to be bad. The reports acknowledged both these things. Yes, his behavior in prison was evidence that he had the "capacity to control his anger reasonably well." But "this also appeared to be the case before the instant offense."

Even after all these years, Mumbaugh had visitors twice a month. In the days when furloughs were still granted to first-degree murderers, he had gone home twenty-two times.

In a statement that asked his parents what plans they had made for his homecoming, his mother had written, "Nothing really . . . He is my son and we all feel good when he can come home."

And on another occasion, six years after the murder: "We are so in hopes that we will be able to have him even for a few days at Christmas. His grandmother, aged 83, is here with us from Ohio."

Give him a chance to return to his loving family, "with all of us who dearly love him," friends of the Mumbaughs wrote.

In the "much-prayed-for event of his commute," they promised him a place to live and a steady job.

"An immediate position" would be waiting for him with Mills Landscape Service, in McDonald, Ohio, if the state was good enough to free him.

He could work in refrigeration, if he preferred, or in home remodeling.

He was a trusted inmate, a good worker in prison.

A good man, said my mother of Will.

Again I tried to shake Will from my head. But I remembered how, after an incident, he always said, "I'm not a bad person."

And he would list his qualities then: loyal, loved his children, worked hard. Called when he was going to be late, helped around the house.

"I'm not the kind of man who goes to a bar instead of coming home. I never shirked my family."

"I have applied my energies in positive directions by learning to be an electrician and operate heavy equipment," David Mumbaugh wrote after twenty years in prison.

"I have remained law-abiding."

"The crime occurred as the result of my own emotional instability which I have since overcome," he wrote.

That was the extent of his comments about the murder. He did not look back. He did not even remember my sister's name. "All he currently recalls is that it was at night and a girl was riding her bicycle past him and she 'bumped' into him as she passed," it said in a report.

How could you know your own heart if you turned away so fast? I wondered as I read that. If you could not find the source of your anger or despair, what good were any promises that the future would be different from the past? How was it possible to know what you felt if you were foolish enough to believe that shutting your eyes would make something go away and never come back?

Mumbaugh did not remember my sister's name, and so her importance diminished. Laura was no one to Mumbaugh, or to his relatives and friends. The girl he stabbed to death long ago was as inconsequential as the chipmunk I once ran over. Best to forget the unfortunate incident, their letters suggested.

Best to forget. It was what Will always asked of me. It was what I had tried so hard to do.

To speak in favor of Mumbaugh's commutation, I had to believe in change, to be able to say that Mumbaugh wasn't the same person as when he murdered my sister.

When it was time to leave for the hearing, I put the papers back in the folder and followed Conchos and the attorney into the elevator and down to the garage, my mind racing. I was getting into the back seat of Conchos's car when I realized that my whole married life rested on the belief that someone could change. For fifteen years, I had put a frame around the times when Will was loving and generous and made myself believe that the past was the past, and that if only I could let it go, it might disappear.

Yet I had seen Will jump out of a car, brandishing a crowbar, because another driver had cut him off. I had seen him throw our dog across the room.

"Not the kind of man who puts his foot in your face," said the therapist in his defense.

I knew. I also knew that in a rage he could kill me.

"Do you hear what you're saying?" A friend had asked when I mentioned this in casual conversation.

Her outrage shamed me and I quickly changed the subject.

A good man, I thought, then remembered what Michael Garvey had said: "All this 'good boy' stuff is bullshit. You have to judge people on their overt behavior."

Will had not killed me—he had not killed anyone. Was it fair to judge a man for what he was capable of doing?

It's what I was trying to do when I pored over Mumbaugh's files. I was reading his history, judging it, trying to predict the future.

Mumbaugh had been in prison for so long. He was eighteen when he was incarcerated, twenty-seven in the earliest statements that were in his file. He was in prison when his grandmother died; when, several years later, his mother had heart surgery, and when, nine years after that, she died.

"I plan on becoming a productive member of my community," he wrote in a statement some time after his mother's death.

"I hope to build a future for myself."

Mumbaugh corresponded with a woman. He wanted to get married someday, he wrote. He wanted to get involved in the community.

His record showed no sign of working toward these goals; his words revealed no glimmer of self-understanding. It was only these same statements repeated over the years, his frustration palpable.

"A sentence of imprisonment for life is fitting for someone without any future outside prison. I am not such a person," he wrote at thirty-nine.

"I have did nothing but constantly improve!" he wrote three years later.

I am a good man, these statements said.

"Inmate Mumbaugh has the history since 1967 of non-violence, and it is on that basis alone that one would predict he would remain non-violent," a report said. And yet, in contradiction, it acknowledged that, "People with a history of violence are more apt to be violent in the future."

He will never change, I thought of Will.

. . .

One day, driven by my relentless curiosity and the shadow of a doubt, I found the Mumbaugh house. And when I did, I saw that the street was exactly as I had dreamed, with the kind of small ranch houses I had seen in Toms River, New Jersey, in Long Beach and San Jose, California, in Florida: "Modest," people would say. Neat, clean. Grass lawns, or pebbles and palms. An occasional cactus was all that suggested that this was the desert, that and the bright blue skies and dry air. Everywhere I looked, there were children on bikes and pairs of walkers, their elbows pumping.

I walked up to the door of the Mumbaugh house and rang the bell. A short, trim man in stocking feet appeared. "My name is Jane Bernstein," I said. "Laura Bernstein's sister."

It wasn't a dream. I was standing on the doorstep just as I had imagined. The only difference was that the son was in prison, and the man with the same name was his father. He had no idea who I was until I awkwardly explained. "Your son murdered my sister."

"Come on in," he said then, as if I were an expected guest.

The house had repeatedly been described to me as modest but clean, as if the cops believed the old dictum, "Cleanliness is next to godliness," and had difficulty accepting that a murderer had grown up in such a neat home.

It was a depressing place, though, small and spare, with a living room as long and narrow as a trailer, and lined up in a row, a recliner, an easy chair, an exercise bike. A Lands' End catalogue was on the hall table. It was so familiar it made me ache to be home with my children.

"Care for a drink?" Mumbaugh asked.

When I declined, he sat back on the recliner, where he'd been relaxing in his socks, sipping a Scotch on ice and eating chips.

I perched on the edge of the sofa. My dress suddenly seemed too short, and I tugged at it.

Mr. Mumbaugh seemed unmoved by my presence, as if he was neither more nor less comfortable with me than with anyone else. He made no move when I asked why he thought his son should go free. He did not even straighten in his chair. I waited. He ate a chip.

His son, he said at last, was a good worker. He had a good work record. He'd been a statewide driver, worked as an electrician. "He was a troubleshooter, out there at Fort Grant. When the power goes out, you know who they ask? They ask him," he said.

"As a child?" he echoed when I asked. "As a child, he was a liar. He used to lie. Built himself up. It really irked me." He wasn't too good a student. His mother had a bad heart from rheumatic fever. Maybe they paid too much attention to her instead of to David. But the thing he did was a one-time thing. "It came out of the blue. Completely out of the blue."

They had friends. He could get a job easy when he got out. If not here, then back in Ohio, where his mother's family lived. He was a good worker, had an excellent record.

"Do you think your son could murder again?" I asked.

Dave was steady, he said. Had a good work record. Had been a statewide driver, driving from prison to prison, three days on the road alone. That was how much they trusted him. And all the furloughs he had before the system changed five years back? He'd been home for twenty-two three-day furloughs and everything had been fine.

"And you didn't worry at all?"

"Never. Because, I swear, from this mouth to this hand, I'd kill him if he stepped out of line." He tapped the ice in his glass.

"It's a political thing, them keeping him in prison," he said. "It used to be they kept them five, six years and let them out."

And now?

He didn't understand what good it did to keep him there. Of course he wouldn't do it again, it was a one-time thing, out of the blue. His work record was excellent.

All of a sudden I was weary and wanted to extricate myself. "How much time do you think a murderer should serve?" I asked in desperation.

The question perked him up. "Either they should execute them right away or give them ten, twelve years," he said. His son, Dave, he'd do well to get out, find a girl and get married. Have a family. It was getting kind of late but it wasn't too late.

We talked about the weather, about the winters in Youngstown, where he and his wife had grown up, about how in the hot summer months in Arizona he used to take his camper up toward the Grand Canyon, where it was seven thousand feet above sea level, a lot cooler than Tempe. But he'd gotten lazy since he'd retired four years back. Didn't do much anymore. Worked in his wood shop some. Watched the idiot box. Lived on his Social Security and a few investments.

And then, "out of the blue" as he would say, Mr. Mumbaugh told me that his son had found Judaism in prison.

It seemed so bald, so desperate, the way he caught my eye, then looked away.

"How did that happen?" I asked.

"I have no idea. Certainly not from me," he said. "But he was very interested in Judaism."

And then, looking up slyly: "You won't find this in his record."

He was right, of course: there was nothing in the record about Mumbaugh's interest in Judaism, nothing about his finding Christ, no jailhouse conversion. His file was much the same as hundreds of others, packed with letters praising the prisoner and statements full of promises and remorse.

Outside the hearing room, I studied the half-dozen people milling about. Even though the most recent photo I had of Mumbaugh was from twenty-three years ago, I was certain that I would recognize him. He was not here.

Conchos joined me. Mumbaugh's family members had been invited to make statements or attend this hearing, just as I had been. But Mumbaugh himself was not permitted to attend at this stage, she had learned.

The large, dim hearing room was filled with rows of empty folding chairs. We took our places in the front row and waited for the parole board members to sit at the long conference table up front. I was shaky with disappointment and relief.

Conchos whispered: "Don't forget to tell them you're the only surviving sibling."

The county attorney opened his briefcase and took out the report he had slipped from Mumbaugh's files. Two words had been circled: "Insecticide." "Upper thigh." He held the paper flat on his lap so I could read the type.

"Inmate Mumbaugh has engaged in self-injurious behavior on two occasions since his placement in this facility," I read. "In November 1984, he ingested a quantity of insecticide. He was treated and subsequently transferred to ASP-Tucson for psychological evaluation and was returned to ASP-Fort Grant that same month. On September 26, 1989, inmate Mumbaugh inflicted wounds to his upper thigh with a pocket knife. He was treated for those injuries and was returned to ASP-Fort Grant . . . These incidents of self-injurious behavior appear to be somewhat related to his application for commutation of sentence and/or to institutional stresses associated with his prison work assignments . . ."

These incidents were not "the result of significant mental health disorders," the report went on to say.

"Both these incidents are best characterized as inmate Mumbaugh's need to call attention to his loneliness . . . rather than bona fide attempts to take his own life."

Maybe, I thought, as the parole board members began to discuss the case. But normal people didn't swallow insecticide. Mumbaugh had told an interviewer that he had only said he'd always wanted to kill someone because he was flustered and embarrassed and hadn't known what to say. Now those words resonated. I could see the boy who had always wanted to kill someone become the man who stabbed himself.

Mumbaugh had been incarcerated for a long time, a parole board member was saying. His record had been good. The board was eager to believe that Laura's murder was "a one-time incident." The last time he was up for a hearing, the board member who had cast a dissenting vote did so because of Mumbaugh's statement in the confession about wanting to fool the police.

They understood the young lady's sister was here. Did I have anything to say?

"Yes," I said.

I spoke then.

I said it was hard for me to convey in detail all the ways my family had been affected by the murder of my sister.

My voice sounded odd in the empty room.

I said that my sister was twenty years old when David Mumbaugh, in his own words, crept up like a cat and stabbed her twice in the head and four times in the body until she was dead. He was a stranger to her. Laura had been in Arizona for only ten days—she had traveled here to be close to her fiancé, Howard Trilling. They had intended to marry over Christmas vacation.

I miss my sister, I said.

I had never said this before.

All this time had passed, and I still missed her. I missed growing up with her. I missed seeing her marry Howard, have children, become an adult. I missed the fact of having a sister.

But for my parents, it was much worse. It was only when I became a parent myself that I came to understand the depth of their loss. They lost their baby. They lost a benevolent view of life.

It had been hard for them to love without reserve since my sister died, I said. When my oldest daughter was born, my mother could not take her in her arms. The last time my parents were in Arizona, it was to see Laura's body in the morgue. They could never have made this trip today. I was here in their stead—as their voice and as Laura's voice. I hoped I could also speak for the other young women in Maricopa County.

When David Mumbaugh killed my sister, he was eighteen years old. By all accounts, he was the all-American kid. I had looked for evidence to suggest that, if released, he would not commit the same kind of crime he committed in 1966. I was not a vindictive person. If he had been drunk, behind the wheel of a car that killed my sister, I would have been able to say, "Enough already." So I was not talking about my need to see him punished, but rather about our need—as citizens—to be safe from him. I had read David Mumbaugh's confession to the Tempe police in 1966. How he just felt like beating the hell out of someone. How he had wanted to kill someone ever since the eighth grade.

Time did not necessarily change or heal a person who was this sick, I said. David Mumbaugh had never seen a psychologist or psychiatrist in prison except, briefly, when he was preparing for a hearing. According to his own statement, evidence of his trustworthiness could be found in his good work record. A rapist who is trained in prison to be an electrician will come out of prison a rapist who can do electrical work. The job wasn't what mattered. An accountant who murdered a woman unknown to him might learn, in prison, how to file tax returns, but there was nothing to suggest that he would not murder again.

I said I thought that the parole board members understood this to be true. I assumed that they would agree that David Mumbaugh's ability to adapt to prison life said absolutely nothing about his ability to curb his murderous urges if he got out of prison. I did not believe that he had changed.

I understood that the prisons were crowded, but I asked the board members not to let economic considerations determine their decisions.

A moment later, the decision was made. Mumbaugh's appeal was denied.

I felt sad for Mumbaugh. Not sorry for him, but sad at the way this had turned out for all of us.

After the hearing, I followed the attorney back to his office.

"I'd like to see the crime scene photos," I said.

The attorney looked at me a moment. Then he motioned for me to sit at his desk.

It did not take him long to find the envelope. He handed it to me. Then he pushed a box of tissues my way.

After he left, I opened the envelope. I paused before I turned the photos over. I looked at the box of tissues. My heart was beating hard.

Thirteen 8-by-10 glossies were in the envelope. I took them out. I saw Laura's glasses, her scarf, her shiny hair. I saw my sister dead on the concrete. She looked as if she were sleeping. The knife wounds were so tiny. I was surprised by how small and benign they looked, little cuts, harmless, one would think. Her hair was rumpled, as if she were napping on the ground.

It was good to have her back. I knew it was odd to think that. I knew, too, that the words were inappropriate—good, glad, pleased. But that was what I thought. She was dead and I had looked. It was better to see her. I was glad that I had looked.

I flew home the day after the hearing. The next morning, I drove to Maine with the kids. Will planned to join us later in the month. Maine had always been a place where I could find peace, and I wanted more than ever for this summer to be a good one. I had a settled feeling about the events of the day before. I had looked at the crime scene pictures not so I might generate feeling but to acknowledge Laura's death, and I had spoken the words that for years I feared saying, and I had not died myself. And maybe for that reason, that I had looked and not died, the silent debate that had begun outside Sylvia Conchos's office continued to play in my head during the seven-hour ride to our cottage.

Where did the violence come from? I continued to wonder, and I did not push thoughts of Will from my mind. His parents were not wrathful people. I knew them well. I had not merely peered into their orderly house, my breath on the window-panes, but had sat at their table so many times I could say with certainty that they were decent people, principled, moral, devoted to their son and daughter and to each other. Married for sixty years, they held hands when they walked; my mother-in-law's eyes sparkled when she spoke of her husband. There were no secret molestations, no hidden mental illnesses. Will had been an adored boy, cherished and loved. His parents did not fill him with rage. Was it genetically determined that this darling baby would become an unmanageable child who was kicked out of Scouts for throwing a hatchet, and expelled from school for his violent behavior?

One day my mother-in-law saw Will's temper rise so quickly he knocked Charlotte's water glass across the table with a furi-ous sweep of his arm. He stormed from the room, then Charlotte did. My mother-in-law and I knelt and silently mopped up the shards of glass. When the floor was clean, my mother-in-law said, "Hot-tempered like his grandfather." I had wanted to ask her more, but to do that would break the rules. You did not ask. In her family, there were deep currents of emotion, but no digging, no discussion. If you were hurt, you turned away, no matter from whom or for how long.

"Least said, quickest mended," I heard her say. I remem-bered reading the *Little House on the Prairie* books to Charlotte, seeing those exact words, and thinking about the way these rules shaped so many people I knew. "Don't contradict, Laura," said Mrs. Ingalls, in these volumes. "Least said, quick-est mended."

Of everything, it hurt most that Mumbaugh did not remember my sister's name. *"All he currently recalls is that it was at night and a girl was riding her bicycle past him and she 'bumped' into him as she passed."*

And again I wondered how the future could be different if you could not acknowledge the past.

Our little cottage, once our holy place, was in shambles by then, with a boarded-up window, faucets that didn't work, and buckets to catch the leaks. Will had jacked up the water side of the house to have a foundation put beneath. Trees had been cut down, and a trench dug around the house for work that was begun but that I feared would never be finished. The fragrant bed of pine needles was gone.

Maybe I had suspected before this summer that the dream was what mattered to Will—the plans, the work in progress. Maybe for a long time it was clear that he did not mind the mess and disrepair, that, to the contrary, it seemed to give him a kind of comfort. That summer, I knew for sure that he did not want to finish the work, not really.

I would have sunk into mourning for the sweet old place and all that it represented, but one day early in July, Charlotte called me down to the bay, where she had been playing with her friends. The pristine water was murky. Worms had risen to the surface. The fish began to die next. First there were only a few, here and there. Then one morning, several days later, thousands washed up. They flapped around the shorelines, their gills still open and bloody. The following morning, thousands more washed up on the ones that had died at night.

Every July, the bluefish chased the pogies into the bay. In past years it had been beautiful to see the massive schools of pogies swimming past our window, a broad, silver streak of them, some jumping from the water as they fled. I called the Department of Marine Resources and was told that an unusually large number of pogies chased into the shallow waters had depleted the oxygen levels in the bay. That was why the fish and other sea life were dying. It wasn't a toxin or chemical spill. It was just nature, he said, as if nature were a benign mother.

"Forget the fish," I told the kids that night. "The tide will wash them back out."

I packed a picnic dinner and took the kids in the canoe, away from the fish and the house, out to the little islands we loved to explore. Nothing would stop me. This was what we had always done, and I was determined not to let some dead fish get in our way.

Every island was surrounded by dead and dying pogies. We paddled home in despair.

Another wave washed in the next morning. "This will be it," I announced. It had to be.

It wasn't. By then the fish had begun to rot, and there was no relief from the dizzying stench. Later, paint began to peel. The sulfuric acid from the dead fish had started to turn brass fittings black, I read in the newspaper. By then, the story had made the national press.

While I was folding up blankets, getting ready to leave, I thought of a story I would write about a newly married couple who buy a cottage, modest but perfect. The woman's love for her husband is so big she thinks it will hold her together. She cannot accept when things go bad. But the house, built on dreams instead of solid ground, begins to fall apart. In the summer of their worst year, the fish die.

I did not think: She stands on the dock, her heart breaking. I knew, though I could not bear to know, not fully, that the woman was me, and that the perfect house had once been mine.

15

IF I WERE A PROTAGONIST in a work of fiction, a character I had created instead of a living, breathing woman, I would have driven home after the fish kill and told my husband I wanted a divorce. After all, I had gone to the hearing, and though I didn't see the murderer, I had done my best to stare in his face, to confront the crime, eye to eye. I had looked at my sister lying dead on the cold concrete ground. I had spoken the words that had been locked inside me. And when I studied the prison files, searching only for clues about the murderer, I felt certain that Mumbaugh, despite his exemplary incarceration, could murder again, and that my husband, despite his goodness, would hit me again. If I were a character of my own invention, this sad understanding would have begun when I walked into our cottage, for this house that had represented the best of us, the place where bad things never happened, was in terrible disrepair. When the dead fish washed onto the shore, I would have felt this as an awful symbol of all that had gone wrong. And when I rowed with determination through the pogies and could not get around them, I would have felt in my gut the futility of trying to work my way past all that had gone wrong. On the drive back to New Jersey, I would have come to the realization that Will and I had been chasing the shadow of our love. I would have pulled into our driveway, paused to steady myself, then walked into our house and said, "It's over. We can't go on." If life were as neat and comprehensible as the art we try to make from it, I would have left Will. I knew everything. But it was as if the knowledge were a fascinating theory with no practical use, because I was completely unable to act on it.

Though I did not leave, I began what I now see as a long, slow process of separating myself from the life we had together. I took a job as a magazine editor in New York that offered predictable paychecks and health insurance. I began to look for a tenure-track position at a university. For years I had known that I would eventually do this, but now I widened my search to distant places. Each time I saw a position advertised, I wondered what life would be like in Memphis, in San Jose, in Pittsburgh. I looked up cities and states in almanacs and read about housing costs and per capita spending on education. I imagined living in these places, and when I did—when I walked down the streets of cities I had not yet seen—I was alone with the kids and it felt great.

Will and I rarely talked about my search, though I spent a good deal of time on the weekends composing cover letters and choosing writing samples to include with my vita. He did not take my job search seriously. Perhaps it's fairer to say he could not take it seriously, since only crisis moved him into action. In this case, the crisis came in the winter, when I made plans to fly to schools for on-campus interviews. These out-of-town trips forced him to see that the move was real, and he transformed himself from a man who had declared that he no longer loved me to someone who surprised me at the airport gate and made dinner for me when I arrived home, no longer in sullen opposition, but a helper, a spouse—a trailing spouse, he came to call himself, when he announced to friends that he was following me, with no clear plans of his own.

His enthusiasm was a relief. It was lovely to come home from New York at the end of a twelve-hour day and see my children happy and my husband cheerful. I did not let myself sink into the knowledge that he would not stay buoyant for long. I simply moved forward.

If this were a well-wrought novel, there would have to be a turning point, since, in fiction, things cannot simply happen for no obvious reason. Maybe it takes place on the night the protagonist carries out cartons of books. The man comes upon her. Because they believe this is a last conversation, they are unguarded and speak with candor about the ways they have been hurt. They listen to each other, without defensiveness or rancor. Love wins out. They drive west together.

Real life is so much less logical. I know it seems odd to say that I did not mean for Will to join us. But my desire for peace was so strong that I saw nothing else. This elusive thing I had chased for so long—happiness at any cost—was no longer in my thoughts. When it had looked as if I would move alone, I quietly made the arrangements by myself. When, without any discussion, Will began helping with decisions and thinking about work for himself in this distant city, I let that happen, too.

I was proud that I had narrowed my focus to a single goal, moving in a peaceful way. I didn't see the harm I was doing to myself and to Will. Capable, was how I thought of myself during that time. My daughters needed a stable household, especially now that I was taking them away from family, friends, and the home they had always known. That I would do anything to keep the peace felt like an act of great political skill. And peace was getting harder to attain, for now that Charlotte was reaching adolescence, she, too, was often in Will's way. When they fought, I saw myself as a member of a global peacekeeping force. I stepped calmly into the line of fire with my palms raised, saying, "Okay, you guys. Enough," just as I had done as a child, when my mother and Laura were at war. I spoke to each in private, interpreting his language for her and vice versa. Every day without an explosion was a small victory.

Late that summer, while packing up the contents of my office, I found the photos Howie had mailed me shortly after my sister's murder—Laura in the playground, Howie on the back of a burro. I found the jewelry still nestled in its cotton bed, and the letters that had meant so much to me. Over the years, I had thought a lot about Howie. Whenever I was working in the library, I would drift over to the collection of phone books, scan the bindings, and try to imagine where he might be living. Phoenix Metropolitan area, Manhattan, Metro Los Angeles? Invariably, I pulled down a few directories. His last name— Trilling—is uncommon, and most often there was no listing for that name, and I would put the books back. Six months would pass, maybe a year or even two, before I found myself standing in front of the phone books again, wondering— Boston, Tucson, New Orleans?—and pulling down a few.

Sitting on the floor in my stripped-down attic office, I reread Howie's letters, touched by how open and straightforward they were. Howie wrote that he would always love Laura, but was trying his best to forget what had happened to her by going out, no matter how he felt, by surrounding himself with friends, maybe even drinking a little too much, since that was the only way people knew how to have fun. "I hope that you are strong," he wrote in the last letter he would send. "Please be as you were—happy."

I folded up the letters and thought about the night my mother had asked me not to write to him anymore. Her discomfort was like an electric current that traveled through me, making me hot with shame. I thought about the inadvertent things I learned from my parents, and the inadvertent things I taught my daughters. It humbled and scared me, and made me hope that, despite everything, our new life would be different.

For a while, it seemed as if this was actually going to happen. We were in a different house, with new neighbors who quickly became friends, in a city far from our past strife and unhappiness. I loved my work, and eventually Will found a research position that seemed to steady him. This is not to say that our lives were free of stress. Rachel was completely dependent on us; Charlotte was pushing hard against our constraints; and Will's liver disease was beginning to affect his life. Often, he was tired; the sunniness that for years had offset his dark moods was seldom seen. Even so, those early months seemed a kind of rebirth, the days and weeks passing without overt domestic disturbance.

Then one night in February, during the start of a quarrel that should have been trivial, Will leapt forward and bit me, and the past months of peace vanished instantly. None of it mattered. Shaken and humiliated, I left the house, and, with no particular destination, began to drive. Snow was falling hard, the kind of thick, warm snow I had once loved most. I could not simply drive away. Charlotte was on a ski trip. At midnight, I had to pick her up in front of the middle school. What would I tell her when I carried her equipment onto the porch but would not go inside? I could not imagine saying, "Your father bit me." But to lie? She was a teenager now and interested in boys. I worried that she would feel the psychic pull of violence, be attracted by its familiarity, and that the cycle would repeat itself. It didn't matter that she was not home when her father bit me: she lived in our house and knew his temper well.

Each time I thought of telling her, my indignation began to ebb, and I would play down the incident, remind myself that the wound was trivial, that I could slap makeup on my face, pass it off as a scratch.

And then it was midnight. The buses had just pulled up outside her school, and the kids were beginning to climb out. Happy kids, full of laughter and conversation.

Will's friend was dying in the hospital. Will was sad, and frightened for himself. My fault, this whole thing. I'd been locked out in the snow. I hadn't known he was on the phone with the friend's wife when I had pounded angrily on the door. First incident in six months. She needed her father. I didn't want her to hate him, only what he had done. He's not a bad person, I thought. And heard, just then: *All this 'good boy' stuff is bullshit. You have to judge people on their overt behavior.*

I saw her clump heavily on her heels toward our van, the unmelted snow coating her long hair. I helped her put her equipment in the back of the van. The small talk came easily.

I drove from the school. I did not want to speak of it. And yet I had spent too much time looking squarely and honestly at painful things, truths long evaded, to lie to my daughter now.

And so I did tell her, and there was no pleasure in it, no satis-faction in hearing her cry, in knowing that what I said made her hate her father and me and everyone in the world. I could not even comfort myself by saying that it was good for her to know, only that, in the long run, it was worse for her if I kept lying.

If I had understood what I was looking for, I might have stopped my investigation after the commutation hearing, since by then I knew everything that could be known about the mur-der. Instead, I continued to search for people involved in the case, driven by the conviction that an essential something remained to be unearthed.

In the spring, I decided that maybe Howie would provide the answer, and that it was time to give more serious consider-ation to where he might live. It seemed to me that most people, even wanderers, ended up close to where they had been raised. Howie was from Skokie, so I pulled out the directory for the Chicago area. And there it was. Trilling, Howard, on Lake Shore Drive.

That evening, I locked myself in my office and called the number I had found. I had not really imagined how Howie's life might have turned out until a man picked up the phone and said, "Yes?" in a twangy Southwestern accent. In a rush, I wondered if Howie had married and to whom, and whether he was happy. What did I want from him, anyway? What might I ask? How did you pick yourself up after the murder of your wife-to-be? Yes, I supposed I wanted to know that. How did he start over?

My thoughts still rushing, I asked if I might speak to Howard Trilling.

The man who answered the phone said, "He's dead a couple of years."

Daid a coupla years. My heart pounded so hard it was as if he had been a close friend, a relative I had known well. Only what, forty-seven, and dead, like Laura. All I could do in my shock was croak, "He's *dead?*"

"Yep. Who are you?"

"I'm the sister of the woman he was supposed to marry," I said.

The man on Lake Shore Drive laughed. "You must be pretty old," he said. "Because this Howard Trilling, if he were alive, would be seventy-seven years old."

I eventually found the right Howard Trilling by calling the alumni office at the graduate school he had attended in Arizona, a school I eventually learned had been renamed the Thunderbird School and was located in Glendale, Arizona, not Phoenix proper. A secretary gave me his phone number and an address in Shawnee Mission, Kansas. Still on the line, I thought, Shawnee Mission, wow!—he's working on a reservation! In a rush, I remembered the night we had stayed up late eating fruit in my parents' kitchen and how passionately he'd talked about Vietnam, and the sit-in outside a segregated barbershop in Illinois that he and Laura had been part of. It was all so clear, the echo of the train rushing by, Howie's anger at the government, the intense pleasure I felt being with him. Shawnee Mission! I thought, awed and excited that his idealism had not died.

Shawnee Mission is not an Indian reservation, as I had thought, but a prosperous suburb on the Kansas side of Kansas City, and Howie was no longer an activist but a well-heeled businessman who had moved there five years before to head the marketing division of a men's sportswear manufacturer.

Whatever disappointment I felt vanished the moment I talked to him, for Howie not only spoke to me at length on the phone but agreed to spend time with me if I flew out to Kansas City. Although he admitted that Laura's death was still something he tried not to think about, he supposed it would be good for him to talk about her. If Howie was puzzled by my motives, he was respectful, and accepted my explanation that I was a digger, that it was my nature, or perhaps the way I had been shaped by circumstance. But he cautioned that I might be disappointed at how little he remembered.

And so I flew to Kansas City one Saturday in March, coolly curious until I was standing outside the baggage-claim area, waiting for him to pick me up. Then I began to panic. What if I didn't recognize this man who had played such a large part in my imagination, but whom I had seen only three times, twenty-five years before? What if we had said everything there was to say on the phone? What did I want from him? As soon as the large Japanese sedan with Kansas plates pulled up, I knew that Howie would step out. And there he was, just as I remembered him, except that his wavy black hair had gone silver.

That evening and the next day seemed, as I was experiencing them, very easy, deceptively easy, perhaps. Howie, with his calm demeanor, his wonderful hushed voice and its broad Chicago vowels, was very familiar, and his wife, Jo, welcomed me into their home. The moment I saw Jo I registered how similar she was to Laura, small and slender, as my sister had been, and like Laura, stylishly dressed—not so much that she wore expensive clothes, but that she had a way of putting things together that felt fresh. And their house, too: not rooms copied from a magazine layout, but timeless, interesting spaces marked by her own artistic decisions, a burgundy leather couch in an airy room with tall windows and varnished wood moldings, and art, everywhere, including bold oil paintings, many of them Jo's. Like Laura, Jo had studied art; like Laura, she had a tough, mince-no-words way about her.

The three of us had dinner that evening in a crowded Italian restaurant where the walls were lined with photos of Italian celebrities. We talked easily about the cities where we had recently moved, the places we were from, and places we might like to live. And we talked a lot about our children. Howie and Jo had three—a son just out of college, living in Israel, considering the rabbinate, much to their surprise; a wandering daughter, the middle child, always troubled, who had followed the Grateful Dead for years and was making earrings in Oregon; a second daughter still in high school. After dinner, they took me to their favorite bookstore, where we talked about books we loved, and I plucked beloved volumes from shelves and practically demanded that Jo buy them. It was as if my only reason to be here were social.

In the morning, I went for a run through the quiet city streets that surrounded my hotel. At eleven, Howie took me to brunch in a quirky little place downtown, where I ate a waffle, drank a lot of coffee, and talked with him about Laura. He was right to say that he didn't remember much. Not the month she had died, or the names of some of her friends, or what his own friends had done to support him in the early days after the murder. But he recalled my sister as "a person with a lot of spirit," and was proud of their involvement in politics and that they'd been "in the forefront" of their times. And when he described my sister as "emotional . . . the kind of person who didn't take no for an answer real fast," it was with admiration. He himself was an appeaser, a person without a lot of highs and lows. He knew how to defuse her anger and keep things on an even keel. They got along really well, he said.

Laura and Howie had lived twenty-five miles apart in Arizona, and on the nights they didn't see each other, they talked on the phone. He had been a little worried when he couldn't reach her on September 21, but there was no real reason to think she was in danger. He went to bed and slept soundly until 4 or 5 a.m., when the phone rang and a reporter on the other end started asking him questions about the murder. Howie remembered saying, "*What* are you talking about?" confused, disbelieving, "sort of freaking out," and that the reporter said, "I guess you don't know anything," and hung up. He went out for the paper then and, really, he had learned about the murder from reading the headlines. A couple of hours later, the police came to the apartment. He'd been at home with two friends on the night of the murder, so he'd never been a suspect, but they were looking for a motive, and they kept at the questioning, cold and businesslike, for hours.

That wasn't the worst part. What had been hardest for him was facing my parents at the funeral, because no matter what fights and struggles they'd had with Laura, they really cared about her and loved her dearly and wanted her to have the best, and this was such a terrible, terrible thing. Then after the funeral, which he had completely blocked from his memory, he had to go back to school, where suddenly he was known to people who had not known him before, and then there was the arraignment, where the police had made him look at photographs of Laura curled on the ground, dead.

But Howie discovered that he was resilient, after all. He made a conscious decision to "extricate" himself from whatever was painful, to live day by day, to let the past "slip away." Five months after Laura died, he finished the program he had begun in international trade and packed his bags, ready to leave everything behind, to create "a wall between me and that place." He moved from Arizona in 1967 and never returned. In Chicago—well, it seemed to him now that he had gone back to find someone else. And he did—Jo, who would become his wife eleven months after Laura's murder. He knew that "personality-wise, interest-wise" she and Laura had a lot in common. It didn't take Jo long to figure this out. She would meet many of Laura's friends, and from the start had to deal with this ghost from Howie's past who never aged or changed, whose memory grew dimmer but never soured.

At times Howie was still reminded of Laura. Her artwork had hung in their dining room until this most recent move to Kansas City. Howie's son was a digger too, he said, "also interested in past things," so he knew that his father had once been engaged to a woman who had been murdered. His daughters had never asked—before I arrived, he had to explain who I was to the daughter still at home. She had listened quietly and then said, "Well, gee, if you married her, I would never have been here."

Later that afternoon, we returned to Howie's house, and sat in the back yard. While Jo whittled at a tree stump, we continued talking until our conversation ran out.

And so it was nice, and they were nice, and I flew home, thinking nothing more than how pleasant our visit had been. I had just stepped into the foyer when Charlotte charged toward me, tugging and demanding to know what Howie was like, and what I had found. A veil of heat seemed to fall over me, and with a vehemence that surprised me, I said, "Leave me alone; I don't feel like talking about it." And then, even more startling, for I had not known that I had been feeling anything much, I said, "It should have been hers."

I glanced up at Charlotte, saw her surprise and meant to apologize for snapping, but I began to weep. Before I could catch myself, I was lost in it and could not stop. I sank onto the steps as if my bones had crumbled from the weight of all my pent-up sadness. The beautiful house, the handsome dark-haired children. They should have been Laura's, not Jo's. This lovely, temperate man should have been Laura's husband. He would have made her happy. I covered my face with both palms, but I could not push back the tears. I cried for Laura, for my own children, for Will, for the home I wanted but did not have, for the love curled like a knot inside me, for the way that everything had turned out, for the futility of my weeping. When I finally rose, all I could think was that I regretted this trip to Kansas City and my own compulsion to dig up things that most people have the sense to leave buried.

For the next few mornings, when I should have been at work, I wandered around the house, plucking dead leaves from plants and studying cracks in the plaster, unable to shake my sadness. I knew it wasn't Jo who made me sad. She and Howie had made a solid match—had raised children, shared dreams, planned a future, made a life together. They had built a marriage solid enough that Jo could hang Laura's paintings on their walls and graciously invite me to their home—solid enough that nothing from the past could nudge them.

I had deluded myself into thinking that the deepest purpose of this trip was for Howie to share a grand vision about how he had pulled through Laura's murder. Jo's existence, her generosity, forced me to see that I had expected Howie to hold on to Laura for me, to safeguard her memory. I had given him the job of remembering her. He was supposed to remain locked into the past, ready at my calling to unearth a cache of memories for me, to bring back the sound of her voice, the feel of her long, thin arms around me. He was supposed to free her memory so she would reappear for me, the way she had in the dreams of long ago. And though I couldn't say so for a long time, I had given him the job of returning comfort to me, now that I'd lost it, to return love that was permanent, to return safety, now that I felt unsafe.

But Howie was the same man who had thrown the ring Laura had given him into the grave. He had buried this symbol of their love, married a small, slender, feisty woman who loved art and minced words with no one. He had always wanted to marry well, have children, earn a good living, and he had built just this life, not on the shaky ground of forgetfulness, but by marrying a woman who was like Laura, but not her.

Howie had moved on. I was the one who had tried to put an ocean between my past and present. I was the one who had left on the distant shore my old name and all my history and now was stuck in this hazy place, rewriting the same scene over and over, as if just the right detail would make me feel what I had not allowed myself to feel when she was murdered. I was the one who dug up and logged in the tiniest, least significant details of the case, who watched Laura die again and again, unaware that I was searching for my heart, my feelings, myself.

Endings

16

DAVID MUMBAUGH'S next commutation hearing was set for March 1, 1993. I flew to Phoenix two days early. Everyone seemed consumed by two things: the freak rainstorms that had deluged the city and flooded the Gila River, ruining the lettuce crop, and the execution, set for March 3, of a man who had raped and murdered a young girl. It was to be the first death by lethal injection in the state of Arizona and was considered by many to be a positive step, a humane response to the last execution in the state, when the inmate, given a choice between gas or lethal injection, had chosen gas, then writhed and convulsed in front of witnesses for so long that a change of method was requested.

"The goal is not to punish them in death but to take their life," Michael Garvey told me. "You want it done clean. You don't want someone around half dead and brain-damaged."

There was something in this sentiment—do it cleanly, get it over with—that I heard repeatedly in 1993. People were angry about crime and frightened by the randomness of so much of it. They didn't want to hear about rehabilitation. They were galled by the notion that inmates had TVs and exercise facilities. They wanted prisoners locked in small cells or working on chain gangs, punished harshly, no matter what.

I believed in the possibility of rehabilitation, not because I thought it would heal me or because I needed to believe in it to justify my own life, but because sometimes people really did change. Even our harsh Puritan forebears knew that, when they built their penitentiaries, places where prisoners could be penitent, could show remorse and sorrow and atone for their misdeeds.

That was one of the reasons I had wanted to meet James Hamm, one of the men whose sentence of first-degree murder Rose Mofford had commuted in 1989. Hamm had been a drifter and drug dealer in 1971 when, in the midst of a deal gone bad, he shot a man through the head with a .38 caliber revolver. Shaken to the core by what he called the "absolute irrevocability" of the crime, he pleaded guilty to murder against the advice of his lawyer, and in prison began what he described as the long process of acknowledging his guilt and working toward redemption. Over the next eighteen years, he became involved in pilot work programs and enrolled in every self-improvement class offered. The son of an itinerant wheat-cutter, he took courses toward a college degree and ended up graduating summa cum laude with a 3.964 grade point average. Later, when he took the law boards, he scored in the top four percent, and was accepted into Arizona State University Law School, a decision that infuriated many.

Hamm winced when I referred to him as something of a celebrity, but his decision to attend a state law school and to argue publicly issues relating to punishment and redemption kept him in the news. He was right to say that the country was in a punitive mood, that many refused outright to accept people back into society after they had served their sentences. Hamm had murdered a man, and his crime was indeed irrevocable. But he had been a model prisoner, had proved that he could succeed on the outside, and had done everything possible to pay his debt to society. The family of the man Hamm murdered had not spoken against his commutation in 1989. If he had murdered my sister, I would not have spoken against it, either.

I did not see that I had changed when I walked into the parole room for Mumbaugh's hearing. It was the room, smaller and better lit, that seemed different. Sylvia Conchos was again the advocate assigned to the case, though this time there was no county attorney. Sitting in an empty row of seats was David Mumbaugh's father, the two of us the only ones left with any opinions about his son. We nodded to each other.

Seven parole board members sat at the long desk at the front of the room, five men and two women, all of them political appointees with a knowledge of the criminal justice system. They had been given Mumbaugh's file a week before the hearing, studied it at home, talked with each other unofficially before the hearing.

Stan Turley, a former member of the state senate, opened the hearing by mentioning that Mumbaugh had been approved for commutation in 1980. He reviewed the details of the case, asked about the number of furloughs Mumbaugh had been granted, and whether I was aware of his self-inflicted injuries.

"What do you think happened?" he asked Mumbaugh's father.

David had just graduated from high school, Mr. Mumbaugh said. He hadn't been a good student. He'd been "running under quite a bit of pressure" and something seemed to snap. But he'd had no problems prior to that. And he had a good work record.

"Do you keep in touch with your son?" Turley asked. "Over the years, have you detected changes in attitude?"

"He's settled down," said Mr. Mumbaugh. "He's pretty well aware of what's going on. For two years he's taken up studying a religion."

The parole board seemed eager to believe that Laura's murder was "a one-time incident."

Edward Leyva, once a deputy sheriff in Maricopa County, said he'd taken the file home over the weekend. "I want to believe that this was a one-time incident, but what concerns me is that in 1984 he took that insecticide in relation to stress, and then in 1989, in dealing with stress, he cuts himself. I look at the public safety here, that's my major concern."

The attempts were always after the commutation hearings had failed, Mumbaugh said. It was "a case of frustration."

"A lot of us are under a great deal of stress but the general public doesn't go round cutting themselves," said Leyva. "The world has changed a good deal since your son's incarceration. He'll have to come out here and deal with stress all the time."

"I like what I've heard," said board member Duane Belcher. "And I haven't made up my mind. But let's ask the young woman's sister. What do you want?"

What I wanted was to feel comfortable saying that David Mumbaugh should go free. It was a waste to keep a person in prison forever, a sentiment that put me at odds with nearly everyone I met. My sister was dead and would always be dead.

A whole lifetime had passed. It no longer seemed relevant what I felt about my sister's murder; other questions seemed more pressing. How come, in the twenty-seven years he had been in prison, the only counseling he'd had was to prepare for these hearings? The determination had been made that the inmate would not benefit from outpatient psychological counseling. Why not? He had murdered a girl, cut himself, swallowed insecticide. There was something shameful to me in knowing that the United States had a higher percentage of people in prison than any country other than South Africa and the former Soviet Union. Why couldn't he get psychiatric help?

The board had no time or inclination to discuss these issues. All they heard was my opposition to Mumbaugh's release. Robert Tucker, the former chairman of the Arizona Board of Pardons and Paroles, jumped in, saying that he, too, was concerned that Mumbaugh hadn't had any help. "The young lady he murdered didn't get any second chances . . ."

He trailed off. The discussion promptly ended. A moment later, the parole board unanimously voted against Mumbaugh's release.

The decision was so quick that I was stunned when Sylvia Conchos stood. I walked out beside her. Making small talk to dull the sadness I felt, I said, "This was kind of a small room, compared to last time."

She stopped for a moment. "It was exactly the same place."

Two months later, I got something from the Arizona Department of Corrections called a "Release Notification Letter."

I stood in my foyer in Pittsburgh, studying the letter. The words "release notification" seemed to slow my comprehension.

Released, I kept thinking, unable for a moment to move beyond that.

"Inmate—David Mumbaugh, ADC #27741," the letter said.

Under "victim" was my name, as if I had been the one killed.

Under Arizona State Law (A.R.S. 31-351), I had the right, as a victim, "to be informed of the status of the above-named inmate."

The status of the above-named inmate was dead.

I kept looking at the letter as if in time everything would be clear. Released, I thought. Yes, I suppose he had been released at last.

I thought of Mr. Mumbaugh, sitting in his reclining chair in his stocking feet, eating chips and reading the same letter, fooled for a moment, as I had been, by the words "release notification." I tried to feel sad for him because he was alone now, but I couldn't drum up much compassion.

That afternoon I called the prison. A military-sounding warden at Fort Grant would only confirm that Mumbaugh was dead. No, ma'am, he could not say exactly what happened: the incident was still being investigated. I asked the question several different ways, but the response remained a cool, flat, official "no comment."

The coroner's office had just as little to say. The cause of death had not been finalized. The autopsy was inconclusive. They would not speculate. They would only confirm that the inmate had been pronounced dead at 6:40 a.m. on May 12, 1993.

"Mumbaugh?" asked the Associated Press reporter I called later that afternoon. "He was found dead in his cell early in the morning with a sliver of glass in his heart. They thought at first that it was suicide. But that's a hard way to kill yourself."

Dale Douglas mailed me the tiny AP release that appeared in local papers two days later. It reported that the cause of Mumbaugh's death had not been determined, but that he "may have been slain."

The instrument of death was described as "a long slender piece of glass, from a picture frame found in his étagère."

I hoped it was homicide. It was ridiculous, but I did. "Live by the sword, die by the sword," I thought when I read the AP piece. If someone had killed David Mumbaugh, it would end a senseless story in a way that made sense.

Fort Grant prison, where David Mumbaugh had lived for the last seventeen years of his life, is a windy, dusty, remote facility in the southeast corner of the state. It's beautiful, if harsh, terrain, with scrubby foliage in gold and green. The nearest town is sixty miles away, and that town is a speck of a place, not much more than a gas station, a convenience store, and a couple of houses. On April 8, 1994, when I drove to the prison to interview the warden, the news of Kurt Cobain's suicide had just broken. During the long ride from Phoenix to Fort Grant, I listened to Nirvana and thought about Kurt Cobain. I thought about David Mumbaugh's many years at Fort Grant prison, about the statements I had read in his file before the second commutation hearing. His photo in the high school yearbook came back to mind, the faces that surrounded his, the fact that he belonged to no clubs and was remembered by no teachers. When my rental car grunted and bucked on the upgrades, I thought, too, about how isolated this place was. No other cars were on the road, and the only signs said things like, "Watch animals next 116 miles," and, "Do not pick up hitchhikers."

Charlotte loved Nirvana and identified with Kurt Cobain's alienation. I worried about how she would take the dreadful news of his sticking a gun in his mouth and blowing out his brains. At fourteen, she was beautiful and rebellious, with the kind of startling blue eyes that strangers noticed. Her long, thick chestnut hair was streaked with pink, and she wore giant pants that sagged so low at the waist you could see her bright, silky underwear. She was smart and lively, full of complex ambitions, and yet she hated school. Sometimes, in the midst of a quarrel about homework or cutting class, she would say, "I don't want to be like you!" and mean "someone who cares about school." What I wanted was for her to say, "I don't want to be like you!" and mean "a woman who takes abuse."

As I drove through the rugged country, thinking about Charlotte, I realized that I had come to love Arizona, and in an odd, unexpected way had begun to look forward to my trips here. These thoughts were not as separate as they seemed at first. My emotions had slowly begun to untangle. I was learning to speak the bitter truth and weep over what made me sad. I no longer believed that things had feelings and places did harm. At the end of my last trip to the state, I had driven to Sedona and gone running in the red sandstone mountains. When a friend, taken aback, said, "You ran in Arizona?" I thought, "These mountains did not hurt my sister." Not the mountains, the state, Tempe, Mill Avenue, or the Casa Loma Hotel.

Fort Grant prison looks like the army post it was more than a century ago. The inmates live in gray barracks-like houses, ten to twelve in the smaller units, and thirty to fifty in the larger ones. While I was reading about the fort's bloody history in a glass case in a brick administration building, a ponytailed young man in work shirt and jeans, an inmate, I realized, wandered around with a sprayer, attacking spots of dirt on the tile floor. Fort Grant was a cavalry post, and a "center of activities" in the major battles "necessary to subdue the great Apache Nation." The U.S. Cavalry regularly used Apache scouts to spy on their own people. "The mixed loyalty that resulted from using one Indian to find another sometimes resulted in tragedy," one of the captions read. In one infamous instance, three Indian scouts went on a rampage and killed several soldiers, and were in turn hanged by the neck until dead.

There were no arsonists at Fort Grant, no child molesters. Most of the seven hundred or so inmates were what Warden David Gonzalez called "lightweight" offenders, like narcotics violators, who had been transferred from maximum-level facilities and spent their last six to nine months here. The weather was cooler than in Phoenix, but the winds were so fierce you could feel the grit in your teeth. Some prisoners liked the farmwork and the horses, but the isolation drove the others crazy. Hardly anyone came to visit. On an average spring Sunday, thirty people might show up.

David Mumbaugh had been transferred to Fort Grant in 1976, when he was twenty-eight years old. He lived in the honor dorms with the other five lifers, including James Hamm and Carl Kummerlowe, the chemist who cut up his estranged girlfriend's husband and put his body parts into ice chests, and had seen his commutation rescinded.

Hamm had remembered Kummerlowe as a "serious, competent person who didn't laugh at the law." David Mumbaugh, thin, quiet, law-abiding, was harder to know. He was liked by the other inmates, though he kept mostly to himself. And he was trusted by the prison staff and known as a good worker, the kind of man who would do as much work as anyone asked. Everyone, including Hamm, used the word "meticulous" to describe the room where he kept an alarm clock, his books, a TV, and his yarmulkes. "It surprised me to learn he was Jewish," Hamm had said. The warden, too, had mentioned that when Mumbaugh wasn't at work, he spent hours "studying the Jewish religion."

This information, which I had to believe was true, puzzled and disturbed me. It was uncertain that Mumbaugh had ever met a Jew, and since he had no friends, it was safe to say he had no Jewish ones. I wondered whether his study of Judaism was an atonement, a way of acknowledging the young woman he had murdered. If so, how could he have understood its origins? Didn't remember the victim's name. Didn't remember the details of the crime. Didn't know his own heart or the root of his rage, and in this way was both tragic and familiar.

"Initially, it looked like natural causes," Warden David Gonzalez told me. "When I first saw him, it didn't look like there was anything wrong with him. There was no blood— nothing. Upon further examination, we found the hole in his chest. The hole wasn't big. It looked like a small scab or something. I'd seen a guy before that was stabbed by an ice-pick type of weapon, and it had a similar hole, so we played it safe and treated it like a homicide, which is our approach until you know otherwise. After the body was removed and we did a search, we found a long glass shard—real long, real skinny, stuck in his dresser drawer beneath some papers. His hands weren't cut. At one point, I thought maybe he had help. We thought maybe he had access to some painkiller, but they never found anything in his system. It's unimaginable that someone could take a shard of glass like that and stick it in his heart. You'd have to know where to place it."

In the official version, Mumbaugh took a long, slender piece of glass from a picture frame, stabbed himself in the heart, pulled out the glass, lay down, and waited to die. Eventually, the Medical Examiner in the state of Arizona ruled his death a suicide.

I discussed the autopsy report with a friend in Pittsburgh, a pediatric psychiatrist whose area of specialty is adolescent suicide. He suggested sending the report to Joshua Perper, coroner of Allegheny County.

Perper agreed that Mumbaugh's wounds were most consistent with suicide. But there were two unusual features. Petechiae—tiny bruises in the eye or arm—were reported. This suggested a struggle. Also unusual was the absence of cuts on Mumbaugh's hands. Prison was a violent place, he said. The psychiatric record suggested suicide, but the petechiae suggested the possibility of either homicide or assisted suicide.

How dangerous and how common it is to arrange the facts to promote the story we want to hear. I'd like to use Perper's opinion to make a case that Mumbaugh was murdered in prison. It's a far more acceptable end, full of irony. There's closure with this explanation: in a sad way, it makes sense. But I don't know for sure that it is true. Whatever the cause of death, I must confess to being haunted by this final image of a man who never knew why he killed my sister, didn't remember her name, but converted to Judaism and lay down to die in a room full of yarmulkes.

. . .

In the end, everyone had constructed a story, and every story was different.

In the end, Dale Douglas rose through the ranks until he made captain of the Tempe Police Department. The higher he got, the further away he was from the investigative work that he had found thrilling. After twenty years, he retired from the force and began to work as the director of security for a home-owner's association. He wore a shirt and tie and sat behind a desk in an office with no pictures or wall hangings, no plants, coffee mugs, magazines, or comfy shoes: only a photograph in a wood frame of two identical switchblade knives, and a memory of the case in which the kid who was one of them ended up being the murderer.

David Mumbaugh, the good son and trusted worker, wasn't the last person whose actions shocked him. Douglas had grown up in Tempe and knew a lot of people. Though he loved policing, "really thrived on it," he was disgusted by the things he uncovered. "You wouldn't believe the people I caught out in cars in lovers' lane," he told me. Teachers engaged in adulterous relationships; his favorite scoutmaster, a man so admired they named a school after the guy, had been caught in a homosexual relationship. It wasn't that he couldn't trust anyone, he said the day we met, but he'd become a loner. "I just kind of stay away from people," he said. In the years since Laura's murder, he had gotten divorced and moved to a small agricultural town south of Tempe. Like Mr. Mumbaugh, he worked in his wood shop, watched TV, and spent most of his time by himself.

My sister's best friend, Peggy, married the doctor, converted to Judaism, and became a *macher*—a big shot—in the synagogue whose rabbi had buried Laura. While I don't believe that she fabricated her memory of the evening in which Laura arrived at her door, being "really bent for money," nothing suggests that Laura was dealing drugs or had gotten into something bigger than she could handle. The police in Tempe found no evidence of this, and Howie, who knew Laura best, assured me that Laura's involvement with drugs was limited to "casual use of marijuana," though he reminded me that in 1966 many considered this a scandalous thing.

For certain, though, my sister was guilty of having left Peggy behind, with her baby and her "dud" of a husband. It was easier for Peggy to blame Laura. It was more acceptable, more comforting, to feel that Laura had been responsible for her own death, that her carelessness had brought it on, than to say that she had died for no reason.

And anyway, I had begun to agree with Peggy on this account. It *was* bullshit to say that Laura died for no reason. She was murdered because she moved to Arizona to be with her fiancé, because there had been a housing shortage, because she was, in Dale Douglas's words, "just kind of reaching out to anybody she could, to buddy up with somebody, to have a pal on campus." My sister was small and slight like David Mumbaugh's mother. Maybe when Mumbaugh saw her walking her bike across Fourth Street, his rage was triggered by their resemblance. Or maybe it was her long, straight hair that caught his attention. Often I think she died because she screamed when she was frightened.

Jay Dushoff, one of Mumbaugh's defense attorneys, would never say outright that he believed that Mumbaugh had killed my sister, even in the end. Each time we met, he reminded me that literature was "filled with incidents of thrill seekers who confess to murders they know nothing about," and that the police, under tremendous pressure to solve this sensational crime, might have decided to simply force a confession from this "mildly disturbed kid" who had reported the murder and showed such inordinate interest in the case. No matter what I reminded him of, that Mumbaugh had led police to the knife, for instance, Dushoff responded, "Isn't it possible that . . ." and put forth another scenario. Laura's murder had been a major news story for nine months; during that time Dushoff's friends and members of his synagogue constantly challenged him about his defense of the man who had confessed to it. And so I understood why, years later, he held on to his doubts and justifications.

Shortly after the trial that set a record for brevity, Dushoff gave up criminal law and focused instead on real estate. "I'm not a fearful person," he told me over lunch one afternoon in 1994. "I don't smoke, I'm practically a teetotaler, I exercise, I take care of myself. That's why cancer scares the piss out of me. I feel that way about mad-dog murderers. They frighten me. They're so fortuitous. There's nothing rational about their actions. They're scary the way colon cancer is scary."

Along with all the endings, my own story has a beginning, too, in a therapist's office in Pittsburgh, on a warm November day in 1994, a year and a half after Mumbaugh's death. When I sat on the wide, soft leather chair for the first time, I felt sure that my reason for being here had nothing to do with my sister. Laura's murder was like a rock thrown in a pond. I understood that even as my memories of her continued to dim, the ripples generated by her death kept expanding. It had taken me a long time to mourn her death fully, but I believed that after my visit to Howie, I had finally worked through it. I knew that I had lost not only Laura but her spirit, the pleasure of her companionship, the purest, steadiest love I would ever know.

I had made this appointment not because of Laura but because I had encouraged my husband to move, had nudged him out of the house, believing that my support was purely altruistic. And then I had stood on the driveway six weeks before and waved goodbye, wooden-faced, empty inside. And it spooked me to remember that twenty years before I had stood on the corner of Bleecker Street and Seventh Avenue South and waved goodbye to Alex exactly this way. When Will had left, I was just "keepin' on," going about things responsibly, with no visible signs of distress. But I was also on a quiet, frantic search. I tried on friends' responses to Will's departure, looking for one that fit. I danced wildly in my kitchen, as if to experience abandon. I fell in love with a stray dog, as if to drum up compassion. Only when I was asleep and unguarded did the sharp, unbearable ache of my despair rise to the surface, a kind of hopelessness I had never before experienced, not after Laura's death or Suzi's or Brad's, not even after Rachel's birth.

I didn't know what all this was about, only that I felt sure it wasn't about Laura. I felt certain, too, that nothing in my life could change, no piece could be tossed way. The therapist's job, as I saw it, was to remind me how to live. That was why I had set out the facts so plainly, why I had given him these guidelines and told him bluntly to skip the insights and hand over the recipe I seemed to have lost.

Instead of a recipe, there were insurance forms. At the start of our third session, the therapist set them on the table between us, showing me where to sign and pointing to a diagnosis he had entered in pencil. DX 309.81. Post-traumatic Stress Disorder.

He wanted to discuss it with me, to get my reaction. What did I think? he asked, settling back into his seat.

Total waste of time, I thought, clearly, visibly cranky. All this insurance stuff, this form-filling. Just choose a code and slot it in. I didn't care. He could call me whatever name or number he liked, as long as he helped me figure out what was wrong. My manners got the best of me and I said only that I didn't see how I was like an abducted child or a soldier returning from war, didn't think of myself as traumatized, merely worn out from a life that had become too complex, didn't see that I needed a diagnosis as much as a game plan.

But because I felt it only fair to understand what the therapist was thinking before I rejected everything, I asked for some definitions. He explained psychic trauma, and how it occurred after a sudden, overwhelmingly intense emotional incident. The diagnosis was a name for a pattern of behavior, a response to this kind of event. If I accepted it, I had to consider that the parts of myself I valued most might be aspects of a disorder, "maladaptive personality structures." I wasn't ready to do that. I wanted to defend what worked best for me. I didn't see myself as traumatized, but as tough and resilient. I wasn't a victim. I was a fighter, a survivor. *I ain't cryin'.*

In time I consented to read a book by Lenore Terr called *Too Scared to Cry* that tracked people ten and twenty years after traumatic incidents that had occurred in childhood. The children were different from me, as were their situations, but when I read about the symptoms they displayed in later life, I understood my own story for the first time. These children felt compelled in life and play to reenact the trauma they had experienced; they developed unexplained fears of mundane things; they numbed themselves psychically; they hid; they were hyperalert.

Most of these children grew up to be adults who could love and work, whose lives could be ordinary until something touched "the traumatic abscess." They did this by splitting themselves in two, as if cleaved by an ax. They maintained "the experience of perfect mental health" by splitting off the "rotten, helpless, ashamed self" from a self that had to be perfect. I barely had to read about the cost of maintaining that perfect self, where one had to "extrude all weakness, all helplessness . . . be totally strong . . . totally responsible . . . take complete responsibility for what was happening in the world at large."

Of course, I was not a child when Laura was murdered, and perhaps the abscess would have healed. But Suzi had died in a car crash and then Brad had been killed the same way. I had begun to accept these losses seven years after Laura's murder and, in the early stages of doing this, became unguarded enough to fall in love. I chose a man who loved me deeply but sometimes brought me into a state of terror, both awful and familiar. Then Rachel was born, and in my need to keep things together, I slipped further back to that place I had long ago known so well—hyperalert, benumbed, and scared. I knew how to survive, but at the cost of splitting off whole parts of myself, so many pieces that I had to say of myself, much as I had said of David Mumbaugh, that I didn't know my own heart or the root of my despair.

To confront all this history and the ways I had been mis-shapen, I had to dig deep, feel all the ways I had been wounded, muck about in the places I had never let myself go. I had to reclaim even the parts of myself I had hated so much I had refused to recognize them. When I began to do this, the story I had lived and the one that I had already written began to make sense. I knew why I had been stuck reenacting the night of the phone call, why for months without end I had written and rewritten the scene, unable to be in it or to experience it fully, unable to put it aside.

There was no moment when I could say that I had reclaimed all the split-off pieces, only a slow journey toward integration. But when I had acknowledged my past and my whole history, I had a kind of weight and balance that steadied me in the harshest of winds. I could see that while I was making Laura die, I was pushing away my fears and deepest feelings about Will.

Change is a slow, messy process. One day, instead of saying, "This is my life," I admitted aloud that I could not live in fear any longer. And on another day, many months later, I knew I would tell Will that I wanted a divorce. What fit inside these specific dates were stops, starts, separations, and reunions, all the messy stuff I had tried for years to keep at bay. I cried all the time, tears that I sometimes thought were made of acid instead of water, the way my "I ain't cryin" face broke up and dissolved in them.

One day I flew to Boston, sick with fear and sadness. Will took me out to dinner. I sat across from him in a restaurant and looked at him in such a way that he said, "You want out, don't you." And I said yes and flew home, foolishly thinking that we would extricate ourselves with grace and dignity from this marriage that no longer worked for either of us.

Years passed—more than two of them—before we were ready to finalize our divorce. Will had been determined to have no contact with me, no phone, nothing face-to-face, so all our negotiations had been through e-mail or a friend. Even his visits with the kids were carefully arranged so that we would not cross paths.

We had not seen each other for a year when he drove into town. During this time, our lives had changed radically. We had drifted back into habits and styles from before our marriage of twenty years. I sought an orderly life, with date books and schedules, dinner dates and travel plans carefully blocked out, while he was always on the move, driving spur of the moment from Boston to New York, from New York to Maine, dating two women in two different cities. Underlying his old habits was his disease, progressing forward; underlying mine was a sadness I could not seem to placate.

I did not know what it would be like to see Will. In our time apart, I had simply grown a skin, a hard rind over all my unresolved feelings for him. Yes, there had been the sheer relief of living in a stable, tranquil household no longer rocked by his moods. Still, I had never felt buoyant about our parting, had no impulse to blow up balloons and celebrate. Instead of the heady joy of liberation was something akin to what I had felt when I had looked at the crime scene photos of Laura. It was better this way. Not once did I doubt the truth of this. And yet I carried the guilt of having left a man who was not well. Whatever he had done to me could not soften this fact, nor did I want it softened for me.

And then the day came, and he was standing at the front door of the house we had shared, looking remarkably well. We greeted each other coolly. There was nothing awkward or emotional in our reunion. We started the work of separating our finances. For an hour or so, we were sober, businesslike, careful to keep our distance. Then, in the sheer ease of being together, we let slide our grudges and the nature of our business, and suddenly it seemed his mood had lightened, and he became funny and energetic. We went out for a bagel and, while waiting on line, ran into acquaintances who did not know that we were in the final throes of dissolving our marriage. There was something in our charade that was weirdly and bleakly humorous. As soon as they left, we shared a rueful laugh. From there, we drove to a notary public. While she was dutifully checking signatures and stamping documents, Will plunged his huge hand into the jar of candies on her desk, rattled around to pluck favorites, intent the whole time on learning why people needed a notary's service, how often they came, how rigorous the course for certification.

Next was the realtor, a handsome woman in her late forties. As soon as Will noticed that she wore no wedding ring, he asked her for a date. When she declined, he pressed her for names of friends, listing his assets in a charming, self-deprecating way.

There was more. There was the tripod in our dining room, bare by then, for our house was on the market. Will asked me to pose in a chair and hold up the notarized documents. Reluctantly I did. As I sat, trying to look cheerful, I thought of the series of Polaroids he had taken twenty-three years before to record his deterioration. Other documentary photos came to mind, other times when he wanted to catch the moment. Sitting at the kitchen table, surrounded by fruit the minute after my first book had been accepted for publication; standing in front of the hospital, face streaming with happy tears, newborn baby in my arms. Rachel, in a helmet, taking her first steps at two years old. The kids in the bathroom, trimming the mustache Will had vowed not to shave until he had successfully defended his Ph.D.

Posed in the empty room, alone, and then with Will, for he hurried over to sit beside me in his mock-rushing way, elbows pumping, I realized that I had been naïve not to anticipate how much would be destroyed when we parted. Not merely our

marriage, which had to end, but so much of what we had created. It wasn't just that we had smiled in these photos, but that
they caught and made immortal the parts of our life together
that had been genuinely good.

The next day we met at the empty house. In the morning
sun, the rooms looked dusty and forlorn. We sat at a makeshift
desk. Neither of us was happy having to deconstruct the legal
jargon on the divorce document. We were arguing over a pas-
sage when his rage flashed and he hit me hard across the face.

I left the house. My face and ear were throbbing. I didn't care
that he was sick or that he missed the kids. I despised him, and it
felt good. I walked down the block to catch my breath, considered getting in the car and driving off, and then thought better
of it. We had one more day of work. It was worthwhile swallow-
ing what I felt one last time. It would not blow me apart, would
not scatter the pieces I had worked so hard to assemble. I knew
that Will would not touch me when I went back inside, and that
when we were done, no one would ever touch me again.

I arranged for our last meeting to be in a coffee shop the
next day. We had no time to quarrel: a deadline of five o'clock
was pounding down on us. We worked without a moment's
pause, until the papers were at last amended, signed, and ready
to be delivered to the lawyer. This time we parted bitterly, no
best wishes, no flashes of intimacy or humor.

The sky was gray and threatening. I stood on the street corner and watched Will walk to his car. I had never felt so lost, so
uncertain of something as simple as which way I ought to turn.
After a while I walked down the block. Out of habit, perhaps, I
stopped at the supermarket. I chose a cart with four good
wheels and rolled it down the cold, bright aisles of boxes and
cans, swerving past abandoned carts. I moved slowly, looking

for something, for a single item to buy. Time refused to pass. I retraced my steps and focused hard on the job at hand, until, a half hour later, I had a box of crackers and three nectarines. The checkout lines were short. I paid for these things, then continued down the hill, until I reached the pharmacy.

As soon as I walked in, I saw Will waiting at the register at the front of the store. We smiled dryly at each other. Then I turned and started out. Thunder cracked, and the rain began to pour down heavily, sheets of fat warm summer rain. I stood beneath the overhang, waiting for the storm to pass, and thought how it really looked as if the heavens had opened. Then Will appeared and said, "My car is there," and pointed to the closest spot in the lot adjacent to the store. Without hesitation, we ran for his car together.

It seemed as if the rain would never stop. I buckled my seat belt as if we were going somewhere. It was dark in the car. The way the rain washed straight down the windshield made it look as if we were going through the car wash. I thought how the kids had loved going to the car wash when they were young, and how the dog would frantically scratch at the windows. I thought of Charlotte crying in the kitchen when she knew that Will would not return, "I *know* we were dysfunctional, but we had more fun than anyone." I took off my seat belt, and all the legendary bad novels that began on a dark and stormy night came to mind. And I said, "The worst part is that I could love someone who hits me."

Then we both began to cry. And I hated that I had loved him, hated that I was losing him, hated that I was leaving him now when he was sick. I hated that I had to ruin so much that had been good. And I hated what it was like to feel this much sorrow. Gales of sorrow. If this was what it meant to own all the pieces of myself, it did not feel worthwhile.

Endings

We held each other and cried, and the rain kept coming down. Then it stopped. The sky cleared, and a sliver of late-afternoon sun shone bright and low on the horizon. We moved slowly apart, touched each other's faces, and said goodbye.

And that was the end.

17

ONE SPRING, I taught a workshop in autobiography. It was early in the semester and the first submissions were about dogs, childhood dogs that died. Muffy of cancer, Snowflake hit by a car, Laddy drowned in the river. A few of these students had dreadful stories they wanted to tell and as the semester rolled on would write about greed and divorce, their deviant uncles and shattered families. But first they began with the deaths of their dogs.

These students were bright and sophisticated, but when they critiqued these early dog stories, their attention stayed focused on the dog itself. They wanted to know what Snowflake was *really* like, and why the narrator loved Laddy. I listened, reluctant to break up the discussion. After a time I could not hold back.

The dog is a metaphor, I said.

One of my students, a young woman with rosy cheeks and glossy black hair, looked at me, flushed with dismay and disappointment. "For some people a dog becomes a member of the family," she said.

Of course! I said. I *have* a dog. I love my dog. He is unique and important. Darling, I call him. Sweetheart. I let him kiss my face. I understand.

But the dog is a metaphor, I insisted.

Later, walking across campus to get my car, I thought about our dog, Buster.

The story of how we got our dog was a favorite one in our family. How one day my father just happened to pick up a copy of the *Journal-American* on a subway seat, "just happened" because it was a paper he never read, and opened to a feature piece about a local vet who had to amputate the tail of a lion at Palisades Amusement Park in Fort Lee, New Jersey, a town near where my parents had just bought a house. Once the King of Beasts, the lion was now limp with anesthesia, his tail hopelessly jammed in the bars of a cage.

My father on the subway: a trusting, outgoing man, everyone his friend. How easy it was to imagine him taking off his glasses to study the photo, then turning to either side, aching to nudge someone, even a stranger, and say, "That's Izzy!" because the vet in the news photo was my father's childhood friend, a man he had not seen in thirty years or more.

I can imagine my father coming home, snapping the newspaper onto the kitchen counter, where my mother is peeling potatoes onto waxed paper. My mother reading the caption and saying, "*Dr.* Berkowitz. You should ex*cuse* me!" This is what she says when she feels anyone has airs. "You should ex*cuse* me!" Or sometimes just "Fency!" from a longer expression her own mother used. *Zi is azoy fency zi pisht mit boiml.* She's so fancy she pees oil.

My parents got reacquainted with Izzy and his wife and we ended up with a discount dog; actually, a free dog, a stray that was hit by a car that Iz—"Berk" was his preferred nickname then—did not have the heart to put down. "A gentle animal," said Iz, a small, dour man. "Never showed his teeth, never even growled."

And so the dog, an odd mutt with a beagle's face and a small, thick, liver-colored body, arrived at our house. He had big paws and a cropped tail, like that lion, or like a pointer, though it was hard to imagine that someone actually thought this stubby dog, with his beagle face, might grow into a sleek, slender, long-legged hunting dog. Maybe they cropped the dog's tail and, seeing that he was not what they had intended, let him out on the road somewhere.

"Buster" was the name Iz gave him, and we kept it. But my father called him "Boy" and "Dog Boy," a name that suited him better, for he was most undoglike. He did not hump couch cushions or legs, did not bark much, but stayed unleashed on our patch of grass, watching children amble by, unmoved. A phlegmatic dog.

Laura's dog: his quiet devotion was to her. I feel slightly ashamed relaying all the tricks she taught him, which, given his nature, seem a little demeaning. He shook hands, rolled over, crawled long distances. He sang to the harmonica, played hide-and-seek, dunked for strawberries. He allowed us to polish his nails and dress him up in a babushka and underwear, making him look, with his round, expressive eyebrows, like an Eastern European bubby. When he got old, a certain restlessness took over, and he began to wander. But by then Laura was at college.

The night she was murdered, he was sleeping in my parents' room, dreaming whatever dogs dream when their legs move and they make their ticcy, muzzle-twitching, *mmmmmph*-y sounds. Perhaps he imagined things he never did in real life:

eating a bird, mounting a female dog, guarding the humans in the house, our strong-chested, powerful-looking dog. Perhaps he dreamed of Laura.

On the day of her funeral, when our house was packed with people, I went looking for him. He was downstairs in our recreation room, hiding beneath the couch, belly against the cool tile floor. I pulled him out gently, to brush his short fur. So much noise and confusion, all the people jamming our house, as if it were a party. I ran the brush over his sides and was listening to his old-man groan when his eyes rolled back and he stiffened.

Iz said to give him a little whiskey and bring him in the next day. It sounded like a stroke, he said. The dog was old; his time had come. Hadn't he been wandering for months, behaving in uncharacteristic ways? We could do nothing, but it would happen again. Or we could bring him in.

I don't know exactly how the decision was made, only that on Friday my father walked into a morgue in Phoenix to identify the body of his firstborn child and on Monday he carried our quaking dog to his friend's office. Dog Boy, that most distinguished name. Laura's dog, the family dog.

Crossing the campus that day, I could not bear to think that I let him do this alone, that I did not take the burden off him by saying, "Daddy, let me come." I let him drive the dog alone and return with only the leash and collar.

What did the dog stand for, then? That the bad news had not ended with Laura's death? That our family's life was really over?

In our desire to get a handle on things, we say, "Life goes on." And so it does, I suppose.

When shiva was over, I went back to school, where I would never again mention my sister but talked obsessively about my dog's death. I cornered people I hardly knew and told them about my dog and how he died. I took people home to show them the album I had with his photos, told them of my childhood dream that I would have him stuffed, like Roy Rogers did with Trigger.

My championship mutt, first-prize best-trick dog, second-prize dog with the shortest tail. My dog with eleven names.

Life went on. We laughed, quarreled, went to parties, groused about the weather, shopped. My father still woke early on weekend mornings, picked a few weeds from our lawn, then wandered down the block with a screwdriver or awl in his back pocket, to visit neighbors, pick their crabgrass with his pocket tools, play ball with the neighborhood kids. My mother, who could not turn to people so guilelessly, got a job. They began to travel. I went to graduate school, got married, had two daughters of my own, one disabled, both of whom I loved quite effortlessly. While our stacks of albums are packed with wedding photos, baby photos, pictures of the kids in costumes, blowing out candles, holding trophies, my parents' albums are full of travel photos: London, Paris, Oslo, Prague, Sarajevo.

Such a beautiful city, my mother often says of Sarajevo. "When I think of what they've done. We were *on* the Mostar Bridge."

Whole families, whole cities, whole ethnic groups. It reminds me of Laura, reminds me how trivial my loss, how utterly inconsequential her life, my struggle, this story.

And yet every time I read newspaper accounts and true crime stories about families left behind after a murder, it seems as if we are all flattened and pressed into the same mold, all of us readily identifiable characters: grieving mothers and vindictive fathers, our hearts full of justified rage. Even the words used to tell these different stories are the same—courage, grief, vengeance, forgiveness. Such cookie-cutter stories, including the ones written about us. Bernsteins not vindictive. Bernsteins "resigned to fate." Never anything about houses blown apart by the kinds of bombs you cannot see, people whose lives have been misshapen by mundane fears, or people who feel that punishment is their due for the crime of having survived.

After Will left, at a time when I had been experiencing the pleasure of an ordered existence, I met a man I liked. I had not been looking for anyone, and the surprise of finding that I could care for someone else was both heady and terrifying. Sometimes I felt that I had too much history, that my past was too high a mountain for anyone to climb. Sometimes I thought the whole notion of a new life was impossible. But it was true that I had always been able to love and work, and so I took more steps forward than back, and so did he. Then one year, during semester break, we agreed to look for a house we could share, a place with enough space for all our kids.

I found a big brick house on a busy street, full of old-house charm, but gutted and restored, with rooms that were pristine and empty. It wasn't that I fell for the clean walls and new furnace as much as the emptiness of the house, the fact that there were no fingerprints, no shadows on the walls where a stranger's pictures had been hung, no ghosts. When I walked through these rooms, I thought: We could leave the mountain behind. We could start out fresh, build our own history. It was the first time in a long while that I looked forward instead of back.

I loved this notion of the empty house, the place where something new could take shape. And I stayed true to it, so that when I moved from the house I had shared with Will, I was careful to winnow my possessions. It was my way to honor this idea of moving on.

Winnowing did not mean throwing out my past. It was here, in the new house, where I put out my photos of Laura. I propped up the old black-and-white of Laura perched on the hood of our parents' 1949 Hudson, and the photo of the five little girl cousins squeezed on Baba's couch in Brooklyn, Laura and I among them, with our lollipops and dolls. In my office, I put out a picture taken shortly before the murder. Howie, dressed in a flannel shirt, is seated in a chair, Laura behind him, her arms wrapped tightly around his chest, forever young, intense, and shiny-haired. Sometimes I turn from my desk, pause over this photo, and fill up with the kind of nameless, deep emotion that for years I worked to rein in. I don't rein myself in anymore. I look at the photo, feel it, and turn away.

There are rooms in this house for all the kids, five of them between us. Except for Rachel, the others, who are older, are in and out, not here enough, to my mind. As a young mother, I had struggled with domesticity, resisted and railed against it; later, in the sheer effort of holding my first family together, I was unable to see how much I loved to have a noisy kitchen. In this new house, in my new life, I know what I want, and this is part of it.

It's different now that time has passed and the kids are mostly grown. I write and teach and imagine all the seats at our table filled with family and friends. Sometimes they are. It's not that I'm lonely or bored. If anything, there's too much work, too many commitments, a calendar far too stuffed with penciled-in dates on the fringes of workdays. "Have coffee with . . . Run with . . . Bike with . . . Movie . . ."

All these plans are dependent on the kindness and reliability of the caregivers and behavior-management therapists who work with Rachel. She is a teenager and still cannot be left alone. When I am out of town, I think of her as little and gravitate toward children's departments. Then I walk in my front door and my tall, gawky daughter lumbers toward me, throwing her arms around me, nearly knocking me down. Rachel's abilities and interests are limited, but she has a love, like mine, for sport, a love, like mine, for talk, and a propensity, like other teenagers, for resisting chores, and for answering my demands by saying, "*What*ever." I think of her future often, and have begun to work slowly toward it on her behalf: in a home, near ours, with three or four other adults like her, a full-time caregiver, a job in a sheltered workshop, a life with the things she needs. My list would include safety, comfort, and love; hers: salad, basketball, music, and pizza.

When Charlotte is home, she leaves her shoes in every room, as if to mark her spot: running shoes in the kitchen; sandals in the living room, platforms on the clothes dryer. She has left her tumultuous high school years behind (if not her love of footwear) and is in college, pursuing her dream to be a filmmaker, and dealing, the way I never did, with her family's tangled history. Never whitewashing or repressing, but funny, bitter, and full of affection for things past. Her relationship with her father has evolved into one of love and respect. She knows him well, and sometimes says, with awe and sadness, "There's no one in the world like Daddy." And I nod, feeling the regret surface and subside.

So much time has passed. Our dog has been dead for over thirty years, like my sister. We almost never mention Laura, but several times each year, especially when someone new is around, my mother says, "Buster was a remarkable dog, wasn't he?" as if for the first time. "He was an unusual animal." And she asks me to tell the visitor about all he could do, how he sang to the harmonica and played hide-and-seek. My story is as stylized as his performance. How he sat and waited for silence before he would howl. How we walked him into the den when we played hide-and-seek, and Laura would sneak off, and I would stand at the door and say, "Stay! Don't you move. St-a-a-a-y." And then when my sister was hidden, we would say, "Go find Laura!"

Go find Laura.

Once my mother said, "I think he knew. Somehow he understood that she was dead."

If so, he was quicker than I.

Acknowledgments

I am grateful to Carnegie Mellon University, where I was given institutional and personal support during the writing of this book. The grants I received from the Faculty Development Fund and the Maurice and Laura Falk Foundation enabled me to travel and do the research necessary to finish it.

Thanks also to the Virginia Center for the Creative Arts and the Mary Anderson Center for the Arts for providing me with time and a room of my own.

I interviewed many people while working on this story. Some knew my sister or worked to solve her murder; others were strangers to me. I thank them all for their great openness and have used their names in the book as a way of acknowledging their generosity. Thanks also to Brian Skea, whose name does not appear, and to Marianne Merola.

I am grateful to my agent, Gail Hochman, and my editor, Rebecca Saletan, for caring so deeply about books, and for their unstinting efforts with this one.

And to my family and friends—thanks cannot possibly suffice.